SEX, ART, and SALOME

Historical Photographs of a Princess, Dancer, Stripper, and Feminist Inspiration

Bill LeFurgy

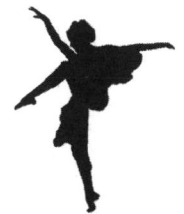

Copyright

Front cover image: Poster for the film *Salome*, 1918, Wikimedia Commons (Detail), retrieved 03/07/2022.

Back cover image: *Gertrude Hoffmann, Salome Dance No. 7*, 1908, Frank C. Bangs Photographer, Jerome Robbins Dance Division, New York Public Library (retrieved 09/29/2022).

ISBN (eBook): 978-1-7345678-8-5

ISBN (Paperback): 978-1-7345678-6-1

ISBN (Hardcover): 978-1-7345678-7-8

LCCN: 2022909676

First edition: October 5, 2022

High Kicker Books

Takoma Park, MD

www.billlefurgy.com

Also by Bill LeFurgy

PREFACE

I spent many years working with historical documents at the Library of Congress and other cultural heritage institutions. Historical documents, also known as primary sources, provide firsthand evidence about people, events, and ideas from the past. Primary sources can reveal great stories about what has—and hasn't—changed over time.

I drew upon the storytelling allure of source documents to write a series of historical mysteries set in 1908 Baltimore, Maryland. While researching, I found many archival photographs of barefoot women (and some men) performing on stage wearing jewel-encrusted bras and not much else. The performers portray Salome, the young woman credited with a famous dance in the Bible.

Odd and unexpected, these pictures. The women are depicted as sensual and seductive, as well as powerful and dangerous—in other words, completely at odds with prevailing notions about respectable femininity at the time. In 1908, women could not vote and were generally regarded as weak and subservient to men. A common myth held that women had no sexual feelings; for them, sex was often seen as a marital duty and nothing more.

I explore the changing roles and experiences of early-twentieth-century women in my fiction. My main character, Dr. Sarah Kennecott, struggles in a male-dominated world with little use for an assertive professional woman. Sarah is at the forefront of change happening slowly but inexorably across society.

Looking into the Salome phenomenon, I found a goldmine of evidence about the period. I came across so much information—and so many pictures—that I decided to put together this book.

Ancient texts briefly mention Salome. The Bible (Mark 6:21—29 and Matthew 14:6—11) and the Roman historian Flavius Josephus describe Salome as a Jewish princess, daughter of Herodias and step-daughter of King Herod. She danced before the king and, at her mother's insistence, demanded the severed head of John the Baptist on a silver platter as a reward. Salome's original character was that of a dutiful daughter with little personal agency.

After two thousand years, Salome had a breakout moment.

Salome circa 1900 was very different from the character in the Bible. The new portrayal—Salome 2.0—was a dangerous, sexualized figure who simultaneously shocked standards of good taste and helped usher in fresh ideas about art, personal freedom, and gender roles.

Early in the twentieth century, arbiters of morality encouraged the public to seek "uplifting" experiences and worked to suppress the lewd and unseemly. Women were literally kept under wraps: their bodies remained tightly corseted and covered from head to toe in multiple layers of clothing.

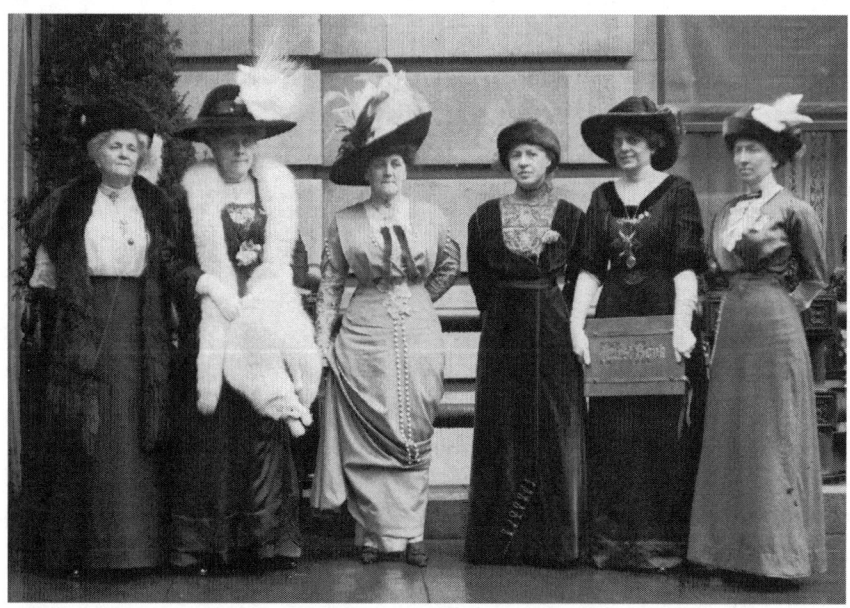

Image 1: *Mrs. J.S. Crosby, Mrs. Cullop, Mrs. S. Ayers, Mrs. Linthicum, Mrs. R.L. Henry, and Miss Hopkins*, Bain News Service, ca. 1912, Library of Congress.

Technological and social change were upending society in ways large and small. Young people flocked to cities to work, have fun, and escape parental control. The growing numbers of independent, educated women led to much talk about the New Woman and how she was charting a different course than her forebears. Artists asserted themselves against traditional forms and drew upon personal perspectives. A new appetite arose for challenging bourgeois standards and sentiments. Information and ideas spread fast in the media, and the shock of the new gained favor over the comfort of the old.

Audiences found pleasure at amusement parks, penny arcades, vaudeville shows, moving pictures, and other forms of mass entertainment. Belly dancing shows were among the edgiest of performance spectacles. First introduced to America during the 1893 Chicago World's Fair, belly dances involved women—supposedly of Egyptian or other foreign extraction—performing exotic "abdominal gyrations" with bare midriffs.

Western popular culture at the time avidly embraced a fictional notion of "the Orient," representing the cultures of North Africa, the Middle East, Turkey, India, and other nations of East Asia. These were supposedly places of sensuality, decadence, mystery, and romantic spectacle— perceptions that entertainment venues mined for box office gold. People were eager to see scantily clad young women perform a wiggly, if inauthentic, Oriental dance.

While such dances were controversial from the first, some performers— including several pioneers of modern dance—claimed a higher purpose. According to them, the goal was to express truth and beauty, not mere titillation. This blend of artistic refinement and sexy spectacle provided the perfect environment for reinventing the story of Salome. With the help of a scandalous writer and an opera composer searching for his first major success, Salome performances flooded the Western world and launched a craze known as Salomania.

Paradox accompanied fascination with Salome. On stage, the Jewish princess flaunted her unclothed body to seduce—but for the purpose of revenge and murder, not romance. Her passion was alluring but also terrifyingly out of control. She was powerful and commanded total attention but was doomed for madness and death.

Salome performances boosted the sexual objectification of women. Would-be Salomes were a favorite subject of racy postcards, the soft-core porn of the day. Yet the performances also encouraged women to break free of old constraints and become independent social actors. Susan Glenn writes, "Salome was not simply an erotic spectacle for men's voyeurism. She was also an important resource for women performers and audiences, a vehicle for female self-expression and sexualized assertiveness."

Salome was a particularly powerful influence among suffragettes in pre-World War I London. Judith Walkowitz describes how a group of London actresses staged a private performance of Oscar Wilde's play *Salome* in 1911. "Feminist [actresses] were drawn to Salome's dance because women could embrace it as their own cultural form and use it to claim possession of their own erotic gaze, albeit a hostile and aggressive one."

Salome stage acts also blurred the lines between "high" and "popular" culture; the character was a transformational artistic force in serious theater, music, and dance and wildly popular on vaudeville stages. Some interpreters were talented and original, while many others were not. But, for a time, Salome performers from opera halls to dime museums all profited from the energy and excitement that flowed from the character's newly found celebrity.

Salomania helped transform the performing arts during the first three decades of the twentieth century. The crowds paying to see Salome proved that people wanted to see a new kind of female character that was dramatically at odds with prevailing cultural notions about women as asexual and subservient.

Audiences could not get enough of this underdressed bad girl. Artists produced scores of paintings. Photographers snapped countless pictures. Publishers cranked out innumerable posters, postcards, advertisements, and magazine illustrations. The images were surprising, even shocking; some still are, even in our modern age of excess. Never before had so many people seen pictures of a semi-nude woman displaying desire, even lust. And never before had so many seen images of a woman as a monster, much less a monster driven to necrophilia with a severed head.

Preface

This book includes over 130 photographs and other images documenting Salomania from 1900 to 1926, around when the craze waned. While this is the largest compilation of Salome images to date, it is not comprehensive. I've only tracked down a fraction of the performers and pictures; many more are surely extant.

I have organized the book according to the entwined art forms drawing on the Salome story through the 1920s. The organization follows a chronological progression from studio art, to stage drama, to opera, to different dance forms, and finally to motion pictures. The parameters here are admittedly porous.

The boundary between Salome and other staged characters is also permeable. Some performers associated themselves with various Eastern interpretations, including the religions and myths of the Orient and the ancient world. Nearly all the pictures included here are of people explicitly billed as Salome, but some—those of Mata Hari, for example—are not. Still, Salome was so well-known that anyone dancing in an exotic, revealing costume was, in the public mind at the time, often lumped in with her, by accident or design.

Most of the images presented here were originally in black and white; I have converted a few to black and white from sepia or full color. Some images are cropped. Each image caption provides a citation to the original.

Oscar Wilde first wrote his play *Salomé* in French. The work became *Salome* in the English translation and I have used this form except in cases where quotes from sources used the French or another language version. The original play also referred to Salome's love interest as "Iokanaan," which became "Jokanaan" in the English version. Both names refer to John the Baptist, the form I have used except as noted above.

Bill LeFurgy
Takoma Park, MD

The mystery of love is greater than the mystery of death.

—Oscar Wilde

Contents

CHAPTER 1 - STUDIO ART: GUSTAV MOREAU AND THE ILLUSTRATORS

Artists depicted Salome over the centuries as the cold instrument of her mother's murderous intent. The head of John the Baptist, detailed with bloody grotesqueness on a silver platter, is the usual focus.

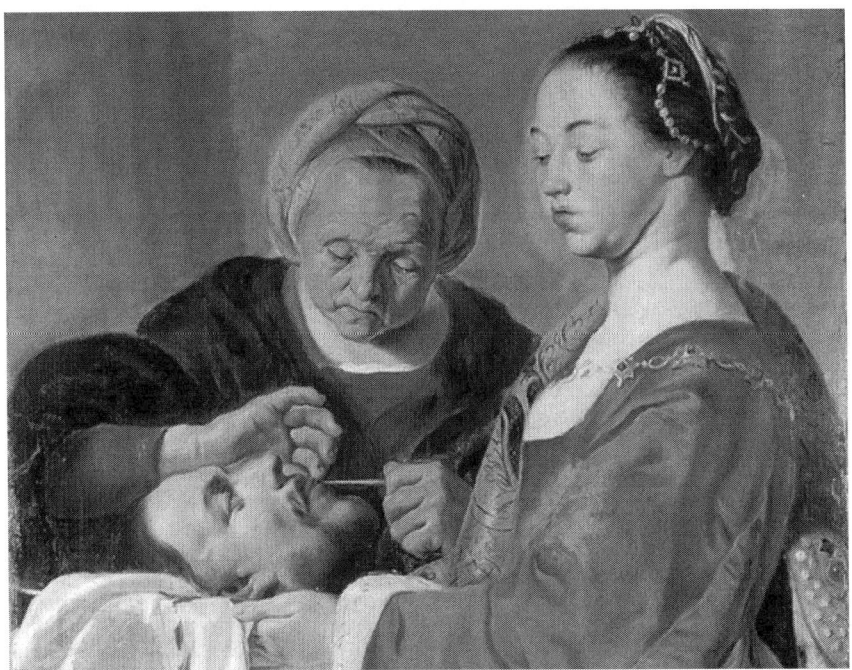

Image 2: *Herodias Mutilating St. John the Baptist's Head,* by Pieter Fransz de Grebber, ca. 1640-1649, Wellcome Collection, Europeana.

During the middle years of the 1800s, a group of European artists developed an interest in what was then known as the Orient (North Africa, the Middle East, Turkey, India, and other nations of East Asia). Fictionalized notions of harem concubines as sexual objects were especially inspiring. The artists of this so-called Orientalist school (men, almost exclusively) churned out paintings featuring exotic women in foreign settings, nude or nearly so, and seemingly comfortable with sex.

Artists also strived to evoke powerful emotions by exploring the thrill—and danger—of unconventional sexual visions. Women were frequently represented as carnal provocateurs, drawing men into exciting but perilous entanglements.

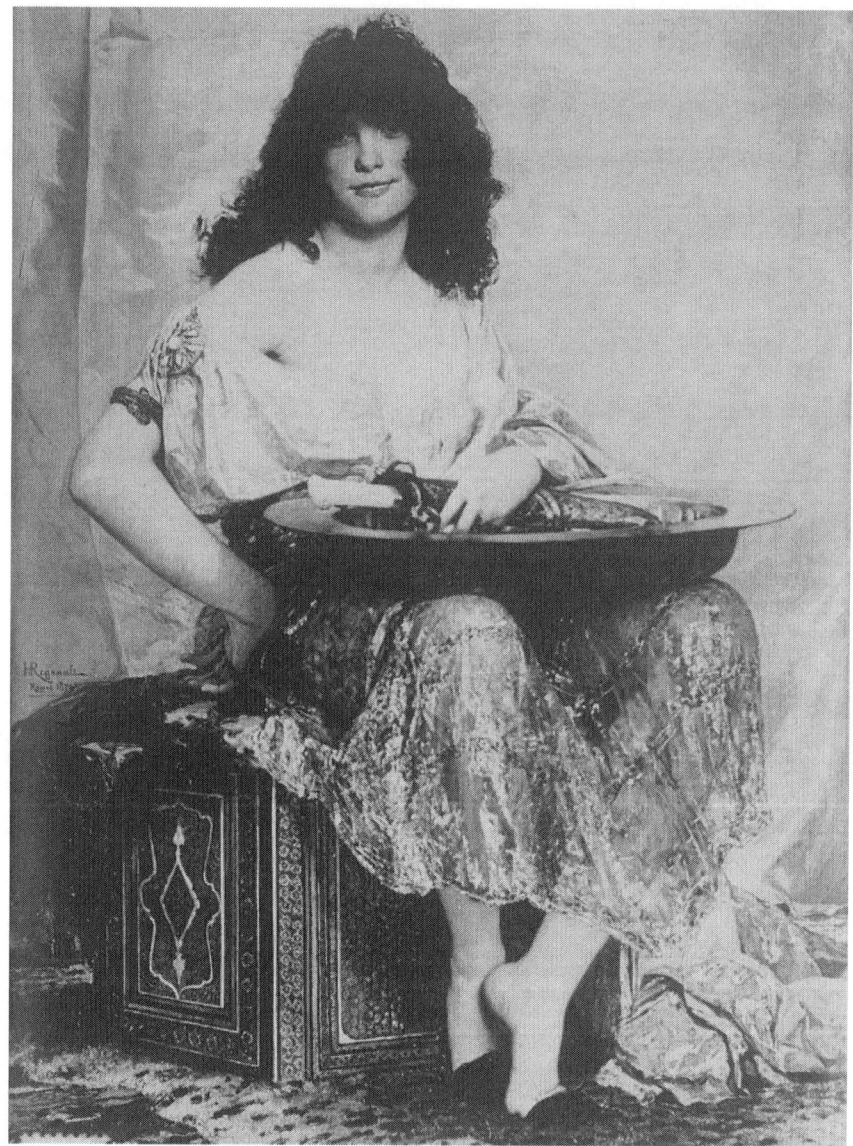

Image 3: *Regnault's Salomé*, between 1915-1920, Bain News Service, Library of Congress.

This was the perfect time for a Salome makeover. In 1870, Henri Regnault unveiled his painting *Salomé*, showing a bold, sensual princess of the Orient with wild hair and disheveled clothing. She exudes a sexual lethality, holding a knife and platter at the ready to claim her reward.

Around the same time, Gustave Moreau became obsessed with Salome and painted many pictures of her as a mysterious femme fatale fixated on John's disembodied head.

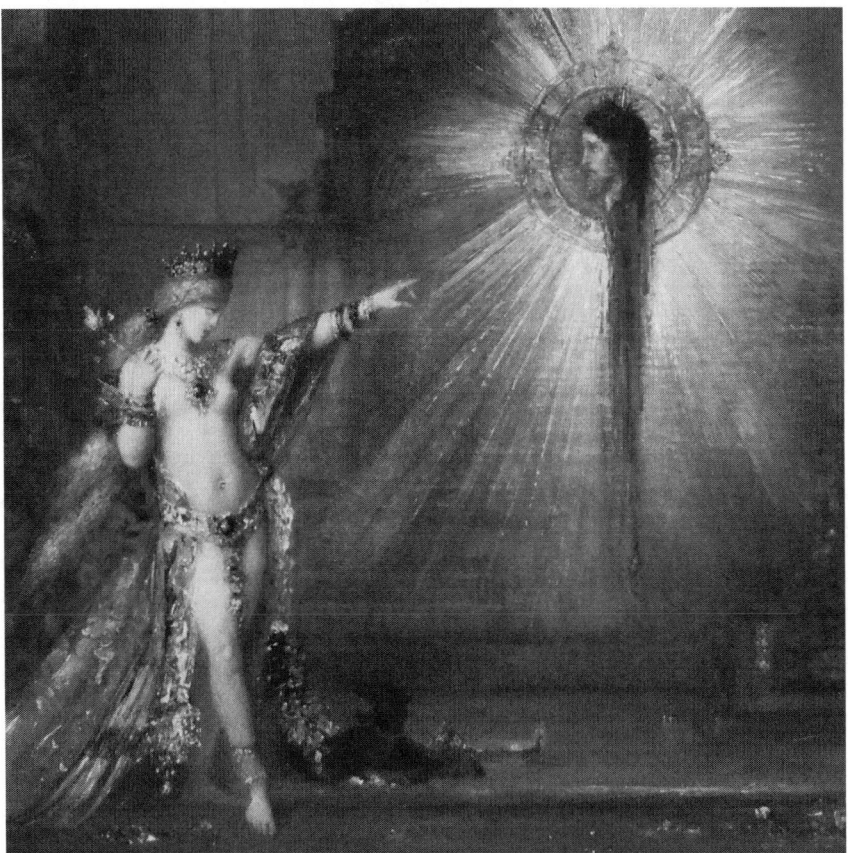

Image 4: *The Apparition,* by Gustave Moreau, 1876-1877, Wikimedia Commons.

Moreau's paintings caused a sensation. This Salome, according to the contemporary novel *À Rebours* by Joris-Karl Huysmans, was:

> The goddess of immortal Hysteria . . . A true harlot, obedient to her
> passionate and cruel female temperament; here she came to life, more
> refined yet more savage, more hateful yet more exquisite than before;

3

here she roused the sleeping senses of the male more powerfully, subjugated his will more surely with her charms—the charms of a great venereal flower, grown in a bed of sacrilege, reared in a hothouse of impiety.

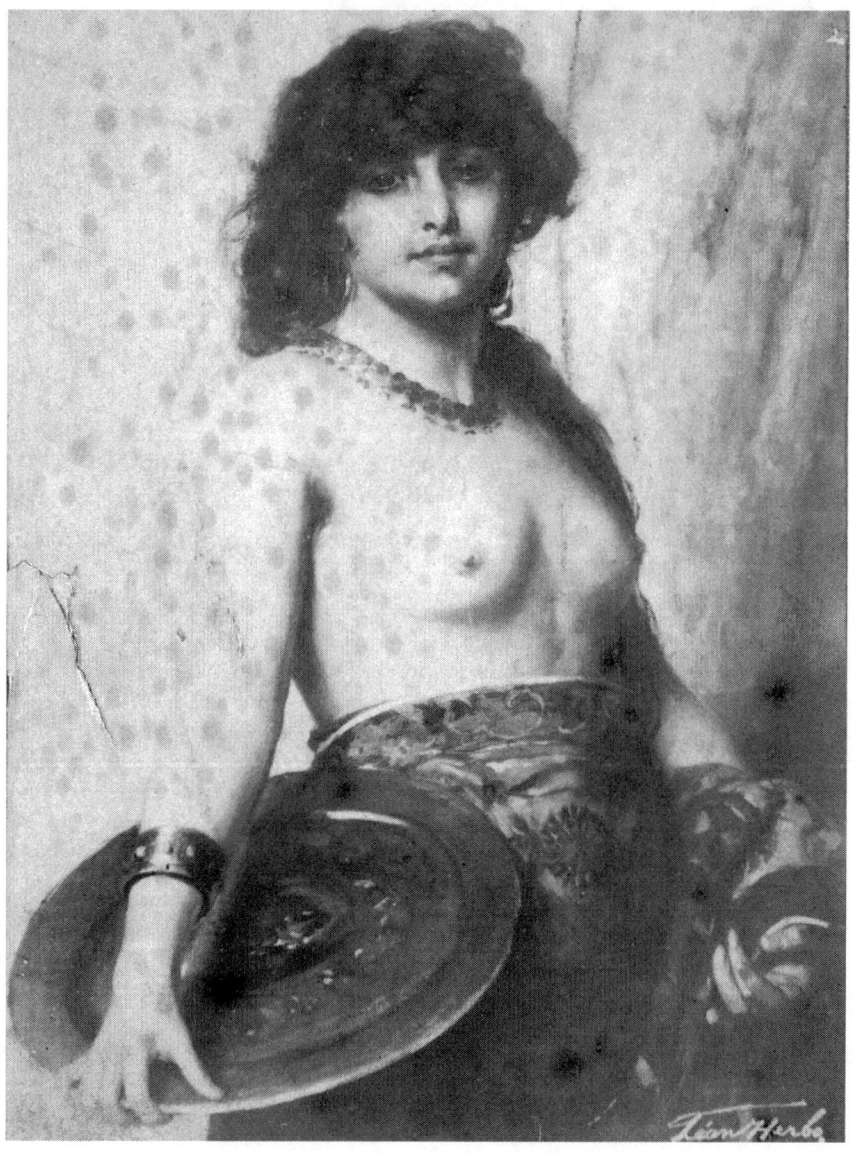

Image 5: *Fotoreproductie van een schilderij met Salomé,* after painting by Léon Herbo, ca. 1884, Rijksmuseum.

Other artists took up the subject, typically displaying Salome as a nubile but menacing temptress with complete confidence in her sexual power. Leon Herbo painted her topless, brazenly staring back at the viewer. Aubrey Beardsley drew her as a strange hypnotic creature whose roses and peacock feathers belie her lethality.

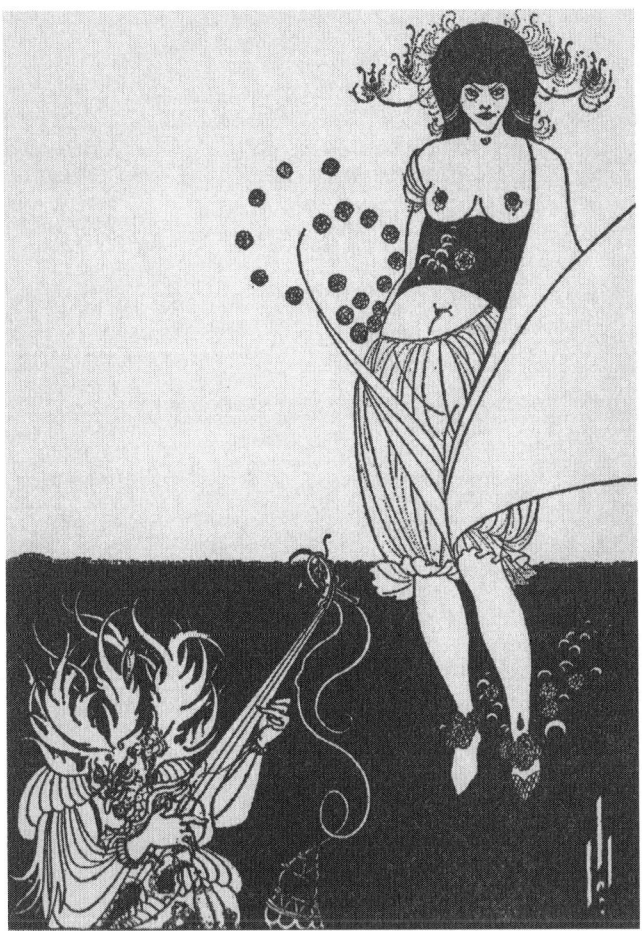

Image 6: *The Stomach Dance*, by Aubrey Beardsley, ca. 1896, Wikimedia Commons.

A revised look for Salome crystalized. She appeared as a passionate but poisonous beauty, flaunting her nearly naked body with ill intent. She is exotic and mysterious, dressed in opulent jewels and sheer veils, hair kinky and untamed.

This Salome is well outside the bounds of respectable Victorian morality. Painters, perhaps drawing on an enhanced sense of misogyny as well as artistic inspiration, represented her as an "unrestrained female" divorced from reason, a creature of wild emotion and sexual manipulation.

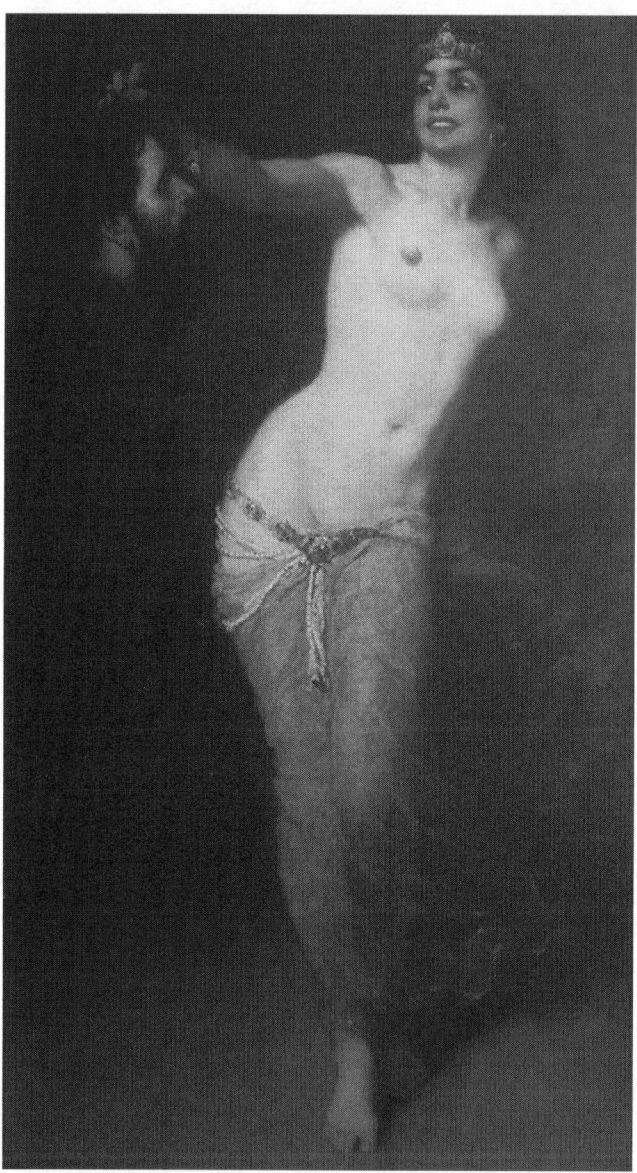

Image 7: *Salome with Head of John the Baptist,* by Gyula Éder, ca. 1907, Wikimedia Commons.

Two paintings illustrate this extreme version of Salome: Gyula Éder's *Salome with the Head of John the Baptist* and Franz von Stuck's *Salome*.

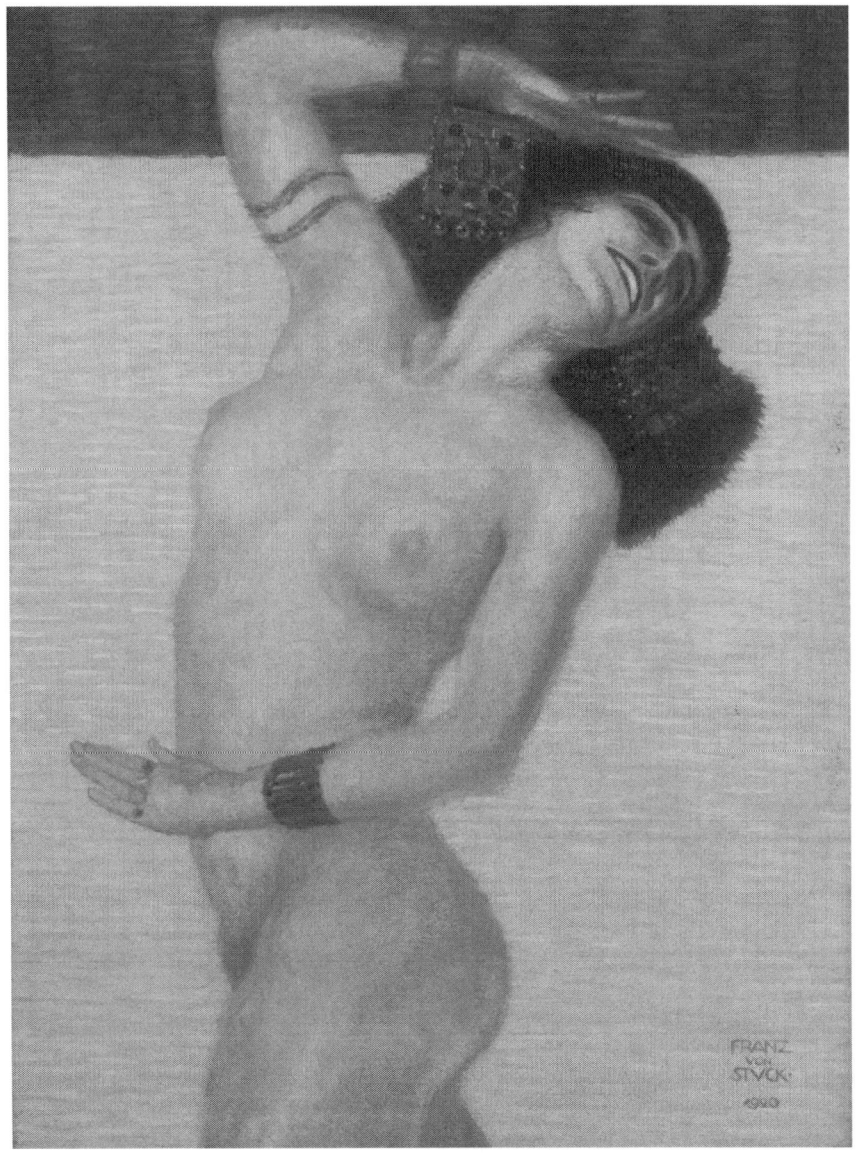

Image 8: *Salome*, by Franz von Stuck, ca. 1920, Wikimedia Commons.

Other interpretations were less erotic but equally dramatic, such as Edvard Munch's drawing *Salome*.

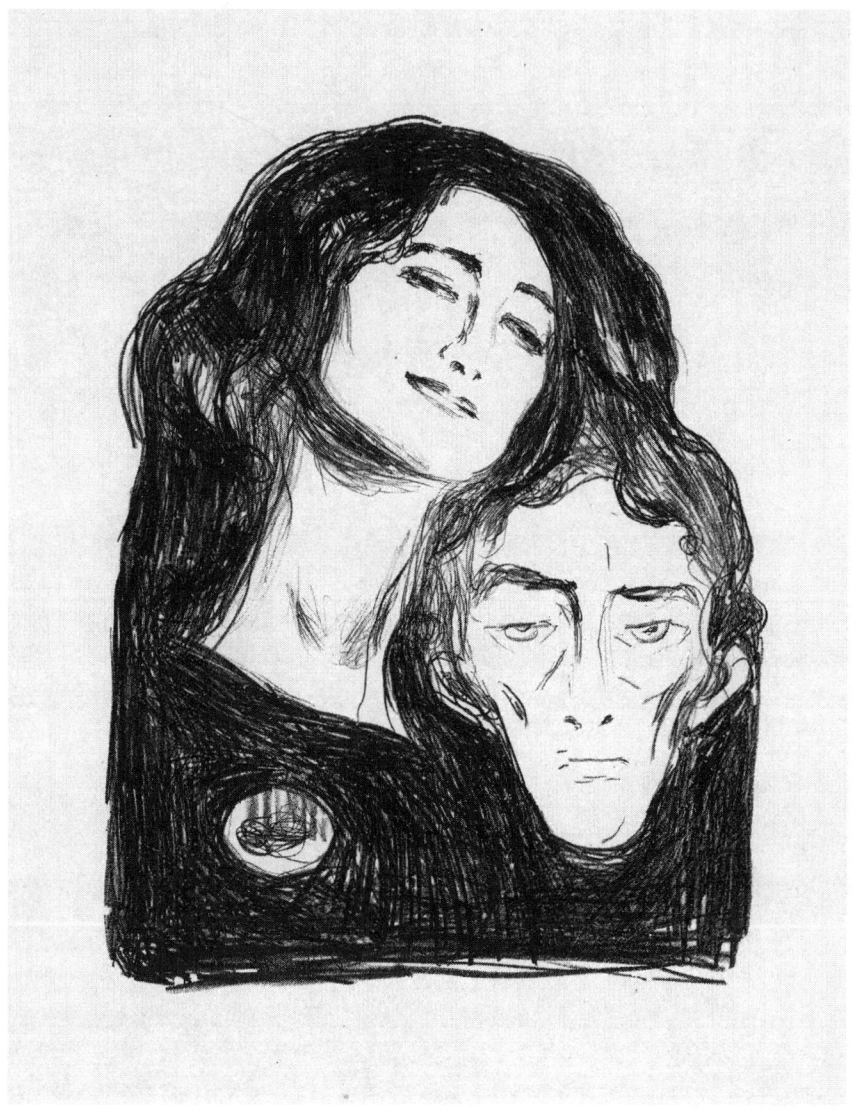

Image 9: *Salome,* by Edvard Munch, 1903, Wikimedia Commons.

Tamer Salome images crossed over into advertising copy. "Salome has nothing to do with clothing," teased an ad for menswear featuring a writhing (but suitably dressed) woman.

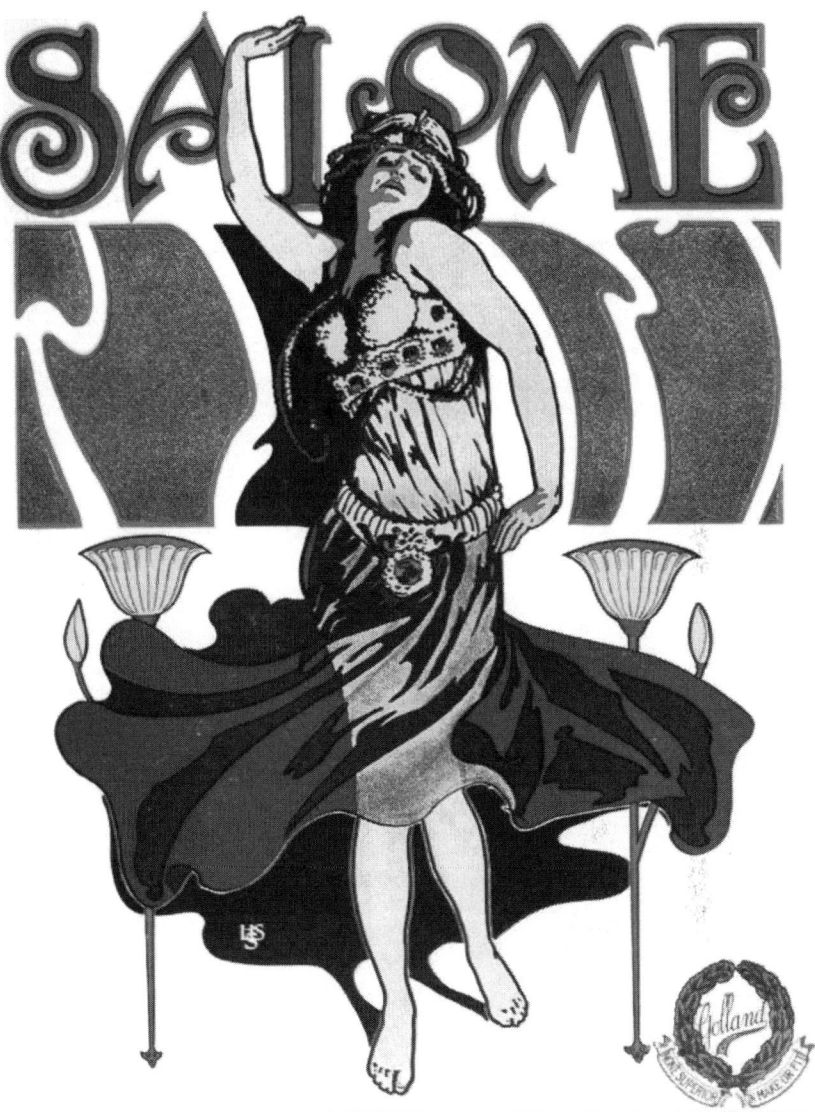

SALOME *"has nothing to do with Clothing"*

Now that the Election is over and the weather is more Seasonable you are probably in need of goods for immediate use.

But You Have

Image 10: Advertisement, *The Clothier and Furnisher*, 1908, Wikimedia Commons.

Some businesses explicitly branded their products with Salome, as with "Salome Perfumed Cigarettes."

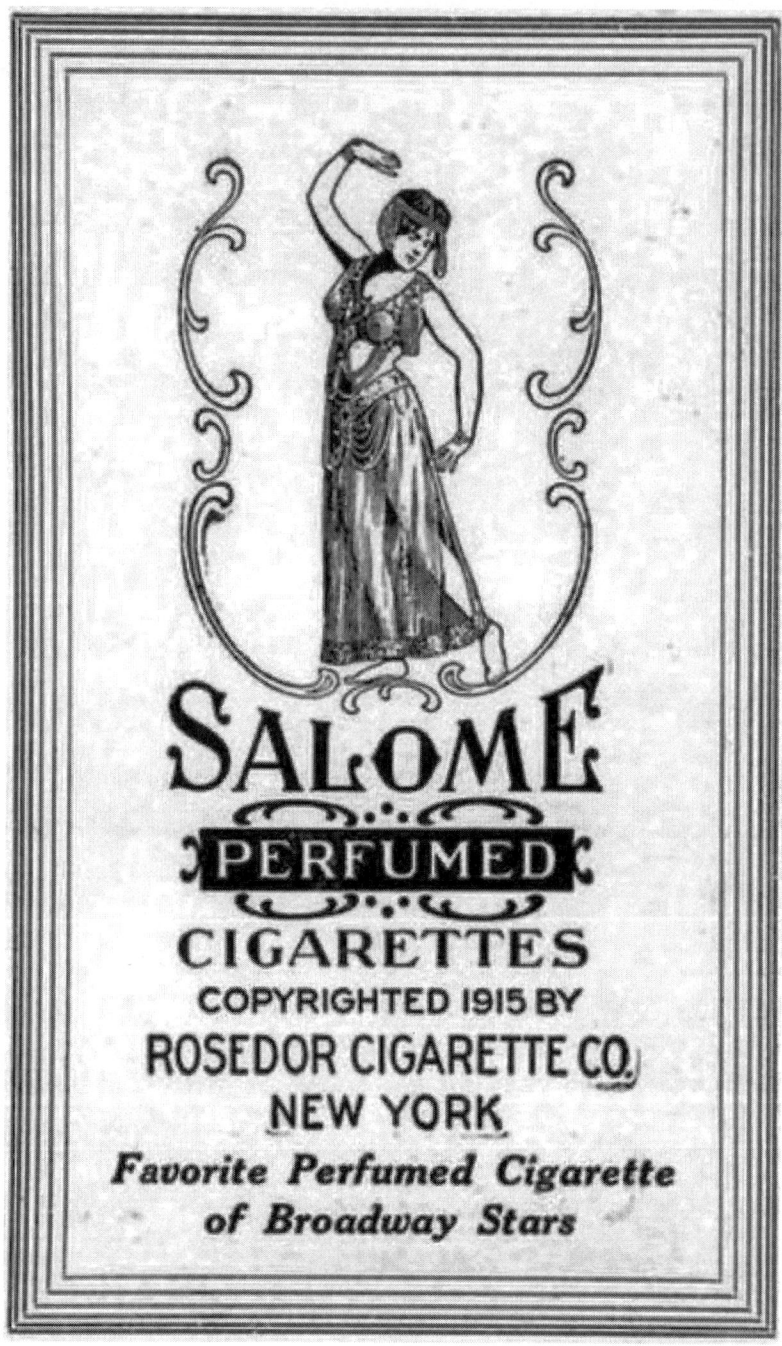

Image 11: *Salome Perfumed Cigarettes*, Rosedor Cigarette Company, ca. 1921, Wikimedia Commons.

The American Tobacco Company used a Salome-like character to promote cigarettes around the turn of the century.

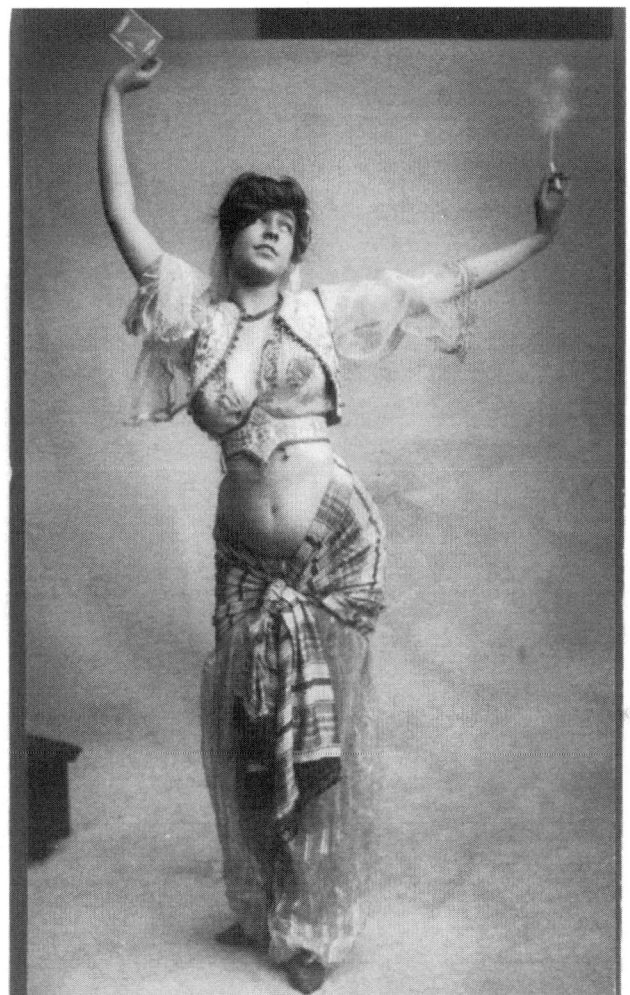

Image 12: *Woman in Belly-dancing Costume Smoking and Holding Package of Cigarettes*, Miscellaneous Items in High Demand, ca. 1900, Library of Congress.

Such advertisements specifically targeted women, whom tobacco manufacturers regarded as an untapped market for their products. Victorian morality strongly discouraged women from smoking, but post-1900 social and commercial forces were eroding that gender taboo, along with others.

Gustave Moreau and others inspired Oscar Wilde to extend the story of Salome into a darker, more sexually complicated realm. Wilde believed "Her lust must . . . be infinite, and her perversity without limits."

His play, *Salome: A Tragedy in One Act,* drew great interest—positive and negative—after its publication in the mid-1890s.

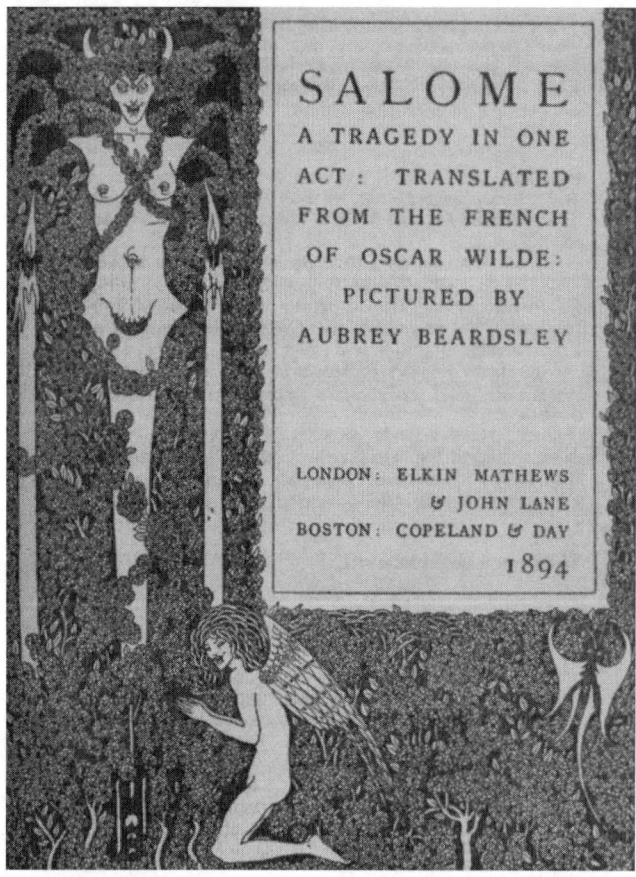

Image 13: *Salome Cover [Title Page],* drawing by Aubrey Beardsley, 1894, Wikimedia Commons

The play begins with King Herod at a banquet, conforming with the biblical account. But Wilde quickly alters the story: this Herod openly lusts after his lovely young stepdaughter and asks her to dance. She refuses, compelling the lecherous Herod to promise to give her whatever she wants—if she dances.

Salome agrees and performs what Wilde called the Dance of the Seven Veils. She finishes the dance disrobed, and when the aroused Herod asks what she wants as a reward, she demands the head of John the Baptist.

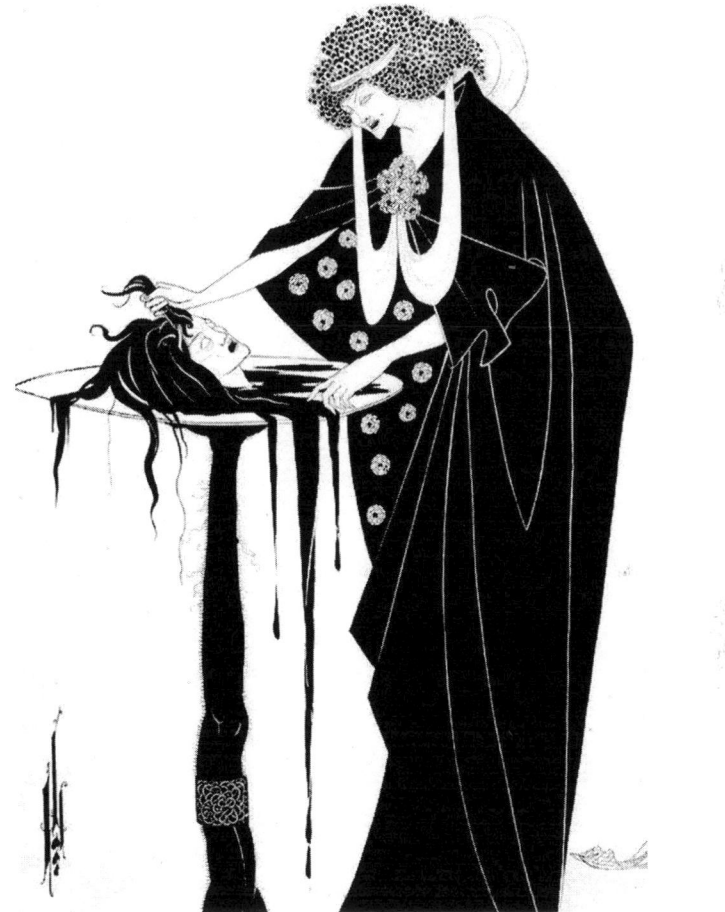

Image 14: *The Dancer's Reward*, by Aubrey Beardsley, ca. 1894, Wikimedia Commons.

Why? Wilde explains that Salome recently asked to visit John, whom her uncle has imprisoned. Upon seeing the holy man, intense physical desire inflames the virginal teen. She declares, "Let me touch your body!" and then, "I will kiss your mouth." But John denounces her as wicked and returns to his cell. His rejection twists Salome's passion into a perverse desire for consummation and revenge.

Salome's demand for the head horrifies Herod, who desperately offers her rare and valuable items instead. But she is adamant, and John's head is duly presented on a silver platter.

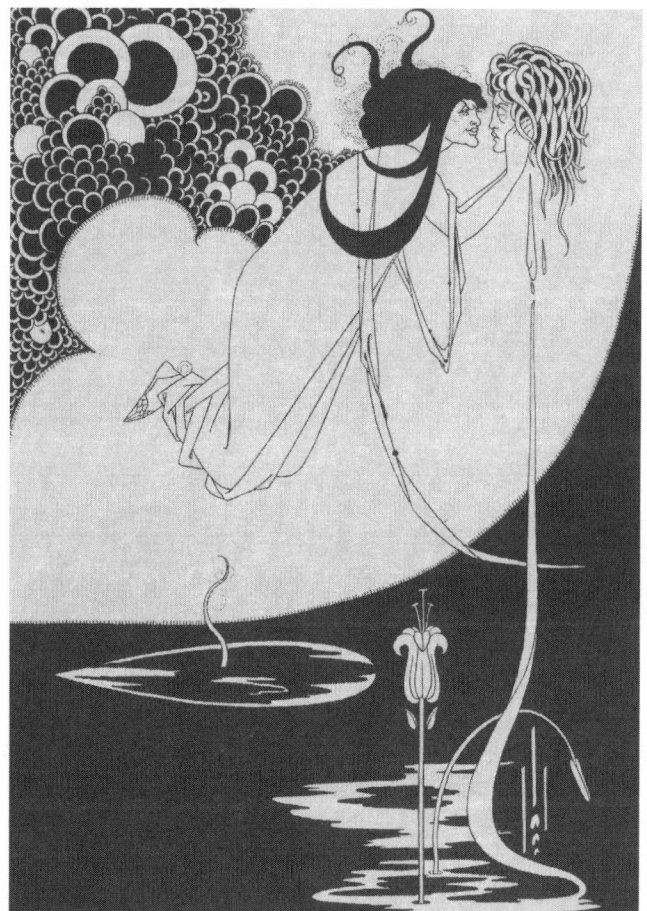

Image 15: *Climax*, by Aubrey Beardsley, ca. 1894, Wikimedia Commons.

Unhinged, Salome kisses John's bloody lips with orgasmic passion, revolting Herod. He orders Salome killed.

In the public mind, the play closely associated with its author's sexual orientation and legal troubles. In 1895, a British court convicted Wilde of "gross indecency" in connection with his sexual relationship with Lord Alfred Douglas. In the eyes of many at the time, the conviction branded Wilde as an immoral outcast.

Wilde's decadent reputation further heightened the cultural impact of *Salome*, which was shocking enough in its own right. Moral guardians tried to suppress the play immediately upon its publication.

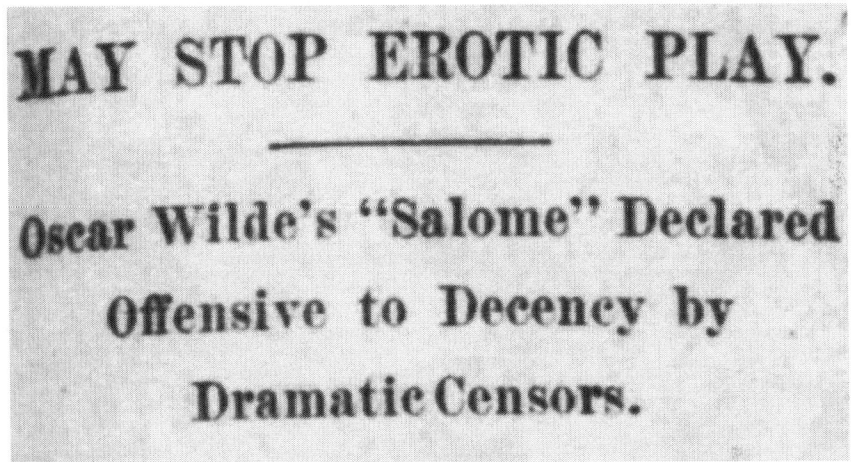

MAY STOP EROTIC PLAY.

Oscar Wilde's "Salome" Declared Offensive to Decency by Dramatic Censors.

Image 16: Headline, *Chicago Tribune*, 7 Nov. 1905, Newspapers.com.

Wilde nevertheless managed to enlist Sarah Bernhardt—"the divine Sarah," the world's most famous actress—to originate the role in 1892 London. Bernhardt was a top-tier celebrity, one of the most photographed women in history to that point. As Sharon Marcus notes, Bernhardt used "her scandalously uncorseted form" on stage to give "many the impression that she could reach across the footlights to touch, even attack, the audience."

Bernhardt was a potential bonanza for Wilde and his play, but British censors banned the show before it could open.

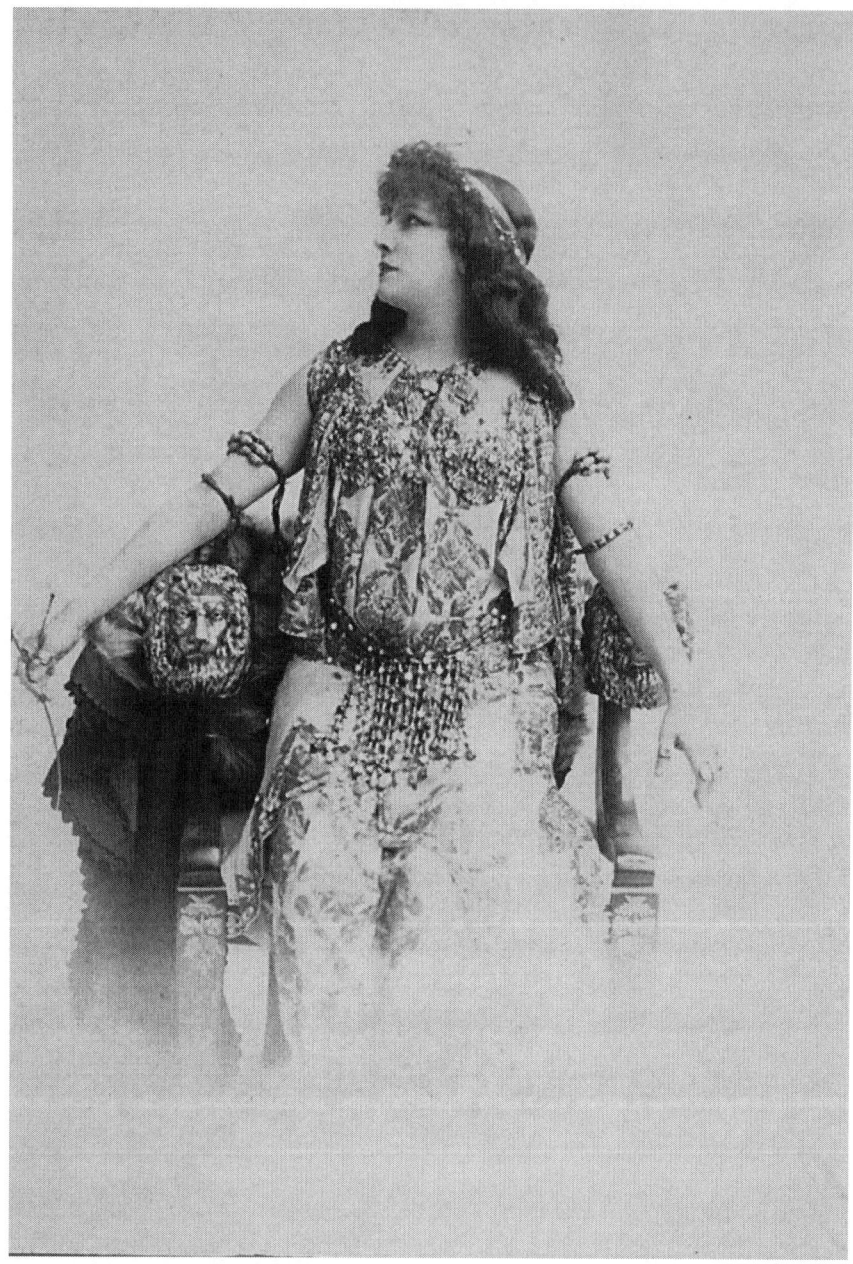

Image 17: *Rollenporträt: Sarah Bernhardt*, Sarony & Co. - New York, 1891, TheaterMuseum (used with permission).

In 1896, Lina Munte debuted the role of Salome during the play's world premiere at the Théâtre de l'Oeuvre in Paris. Staging the play was an act of courage, as there were threats of legal action. Critics gave the show mixed reviews, although the French were self-congratulatory for staging Wilde's play while the English vilified him.

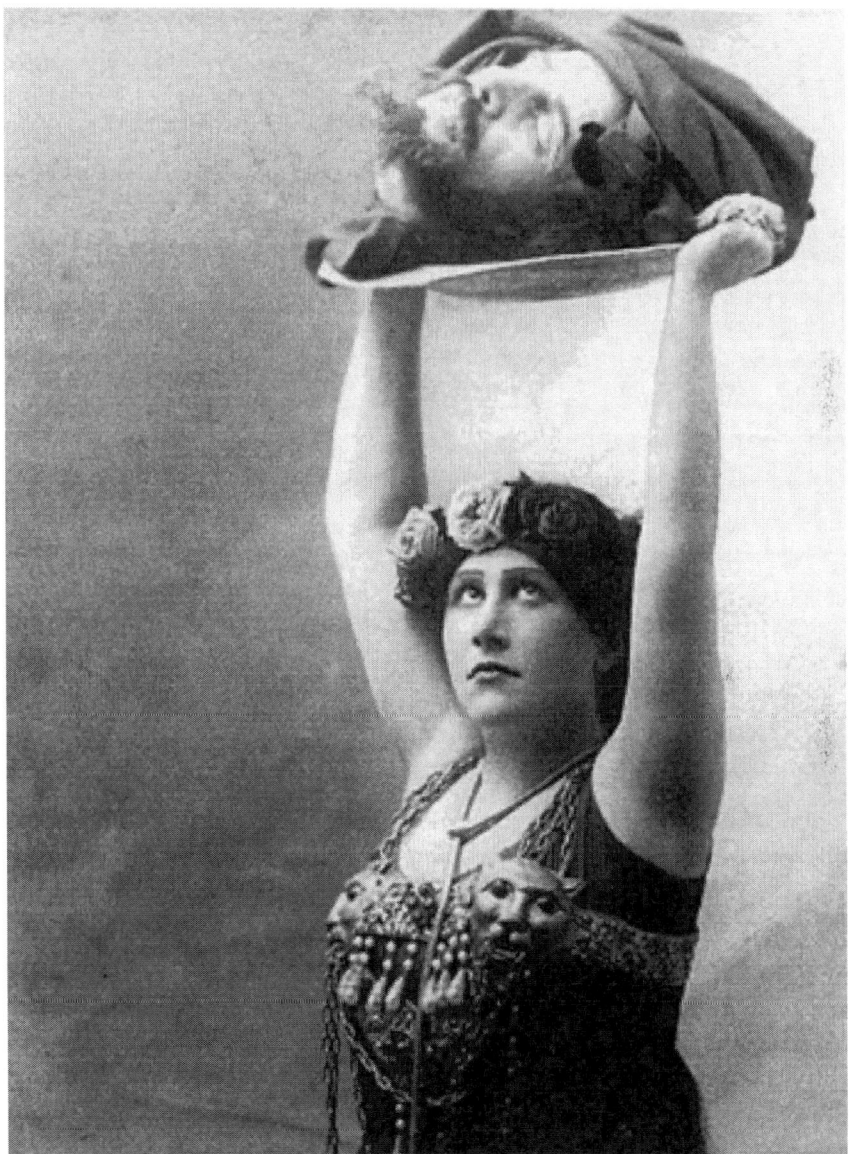

Image 18: *Munte-Salome-head [Lina Munte as Oscar Wilde's Salome]*, ca. 1896, Wikimedia Commons.

Many arbiters of taste regarded the work as too perverse for the public and it was widely banned. But some avant-garde theaters—particularly in Germany—presented the play to much acclaim.

The innovative director Max Reinhardt rose to fame after staging *Salome* in 1902 Berlin with Gertrude Eysoldt in the title role.

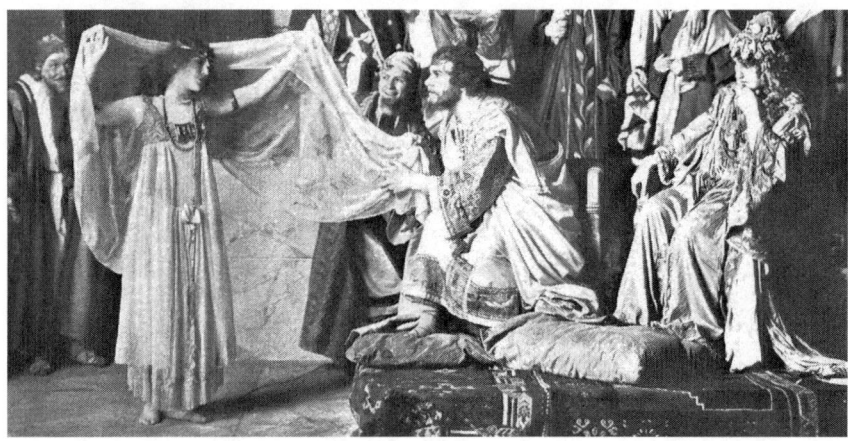

Image 19: *"Salome," Tragödie in einem Akt von Oskar Wilde [with Gertrud Eysoldt as Salome], Bühne und Welt*, 1903, HathiTrust.

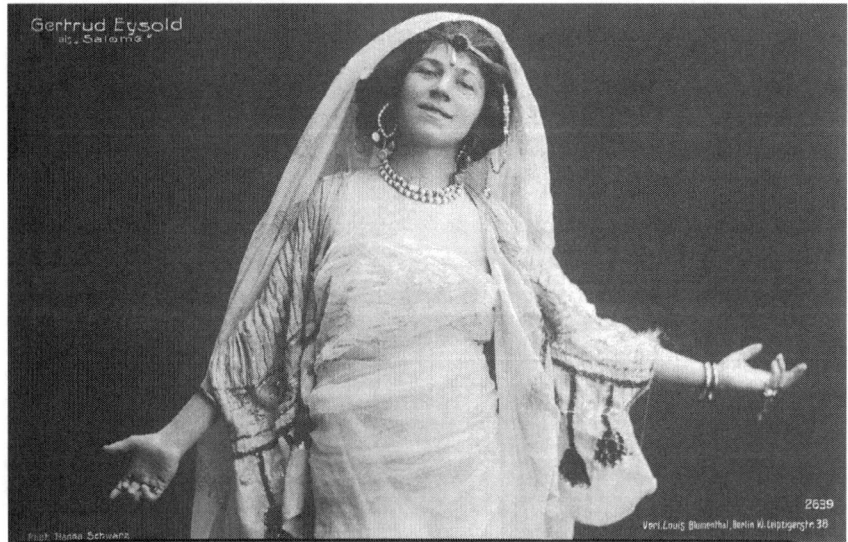

Image 20: *Gertrud Eysoldt [as Salome]*, Louis Blumenthal - Berlin, ca. 1903, Wikimedia Commons.

Eysoldt's performance won praise, with one critic stating she perfectly captured "the pathological persistence of a spoiled child . . . as well as the perverse, erotic, and vengeful lust of a scornful woman."

Reinhardt's production technique was also a significant factor in the production's success. He departed from a traditional bare-bones, naturalistic approach in favor of "total artwork" (Gesamtkunstwerk): elaborate sets, lighting, music, and dance. Audiences embraced this "operatic" style, and the presentation strongly influenced subsequent stagings of *Salome*.

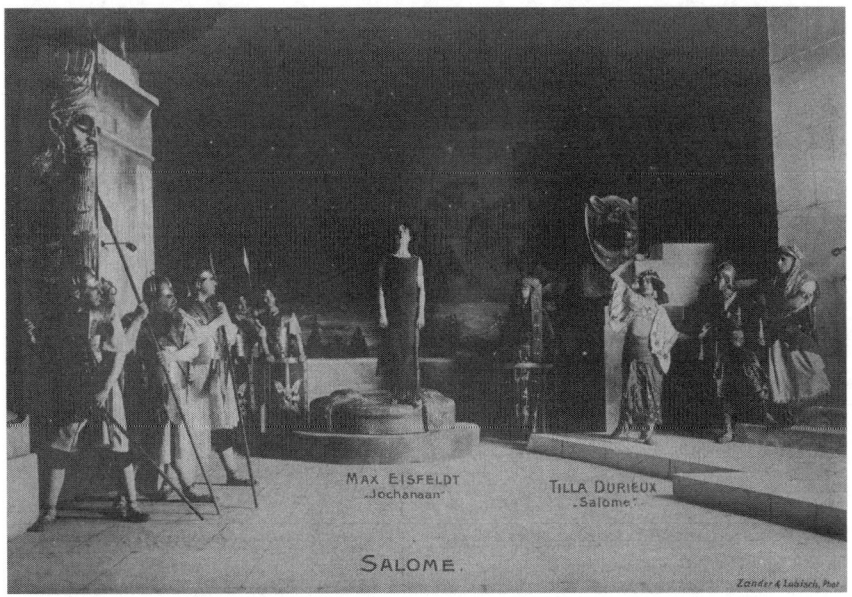

Image 21: *Inszenierungsfotografie "Salome" in Berlin [with Tilla Durieux as Salome]*, Zander & Labisch - Berlin, 1903, Theaterwissenschaftliche Sammlung, University of Cologne (used with permission).

Many of Germany's leading actresses played Salome during the long run of Reinhardt's production, including Tilla Durieux. The role brought Durieux great recognition, drawing the attention of well-known artists, including Auguste Renoir, Max Slevogt, Lovis Corinth, and Franz von Stuck, all of whom painted her portrait.

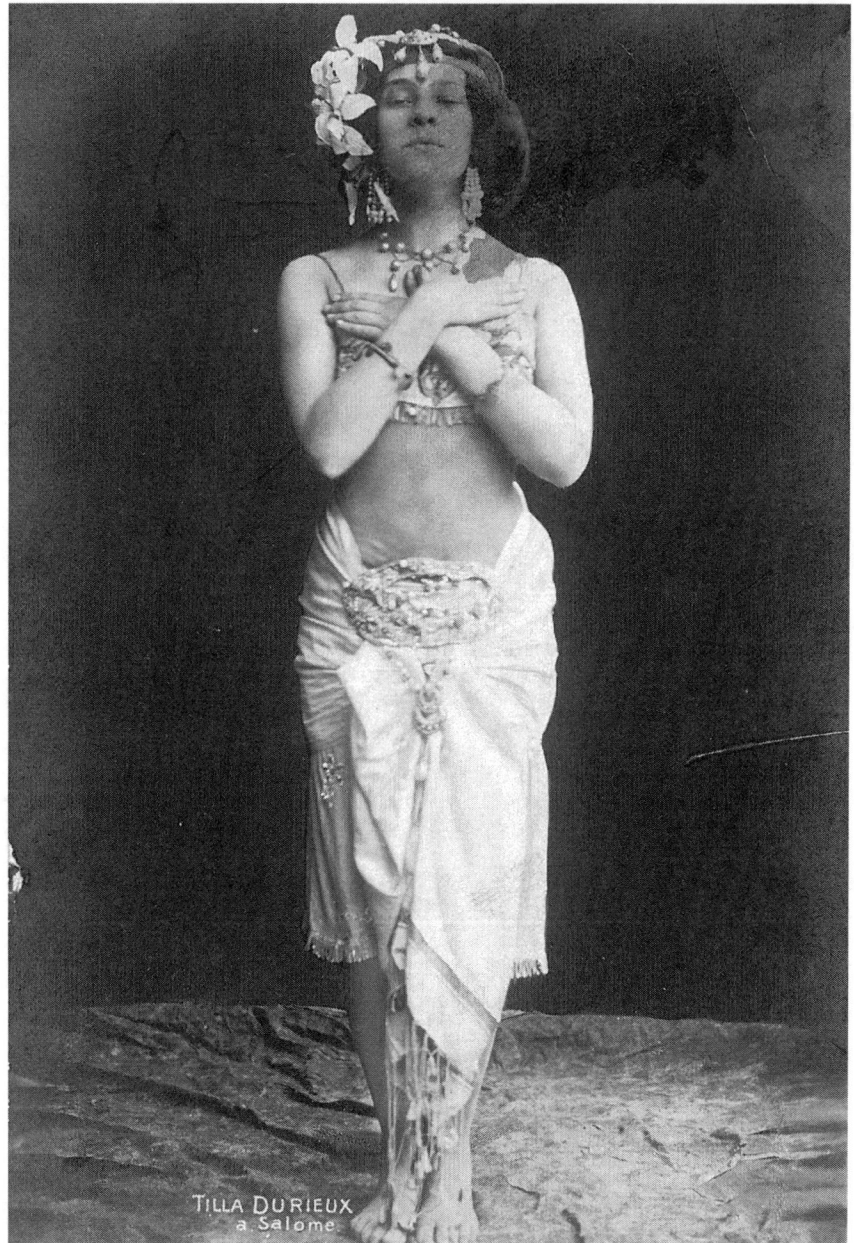

Image 22: *Tilla Durieux als Salome*, Otto Becker & Maass, 1903, Deutsche Fotothek, Europeana.

Reinhardt later enlisted Austrian actress Irene Triesch. A reviewer described her as "the triumphal incarnation of Salome's sensuality . . .

through her scantily clad, girlish form, coy virginity, and ecstatic fervor."

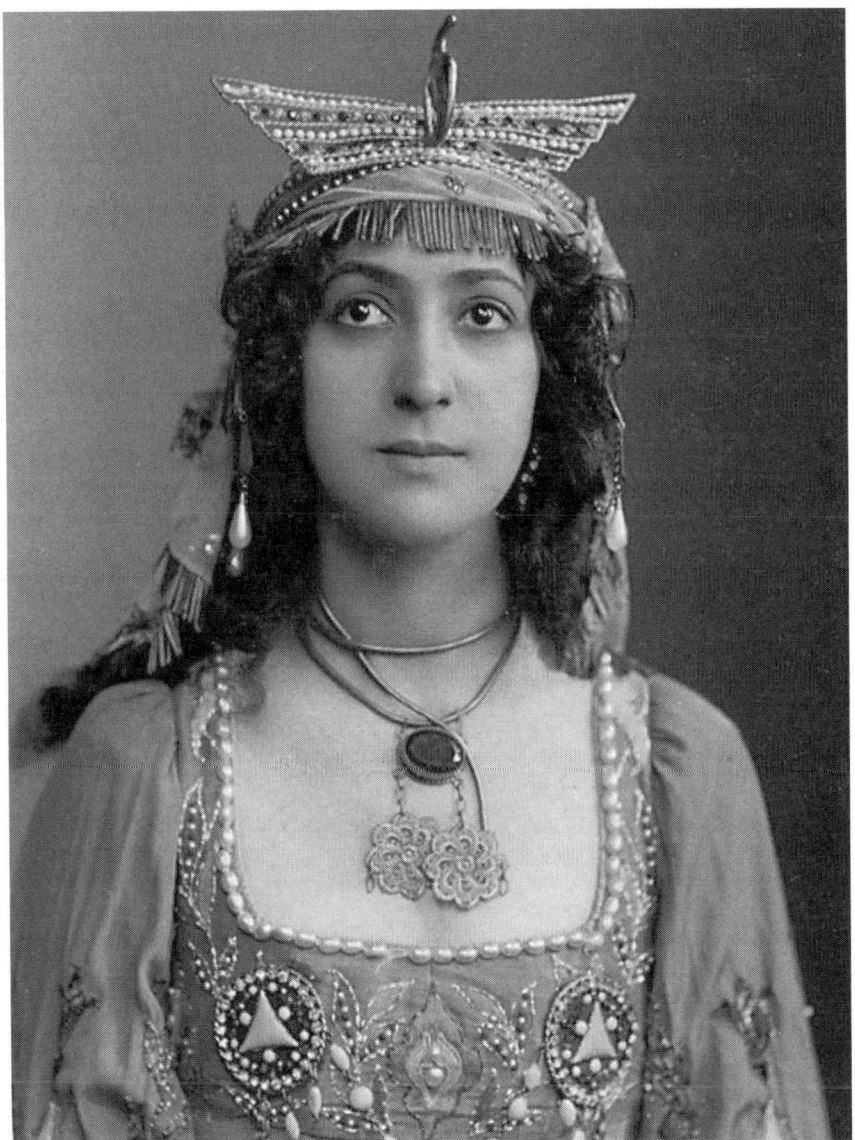

Image 23: *Rollenporträt: Irene Triesch*, J. C. Schaarwächter - Berlin, 1903, TheaterMuseum (used with permission).

Lili Marberg also played Salome for Reinhardt to widespread acclaim. The German magazine *Bühne und Welt* noted her exceptional ability to portray a "brilliant evildoer."

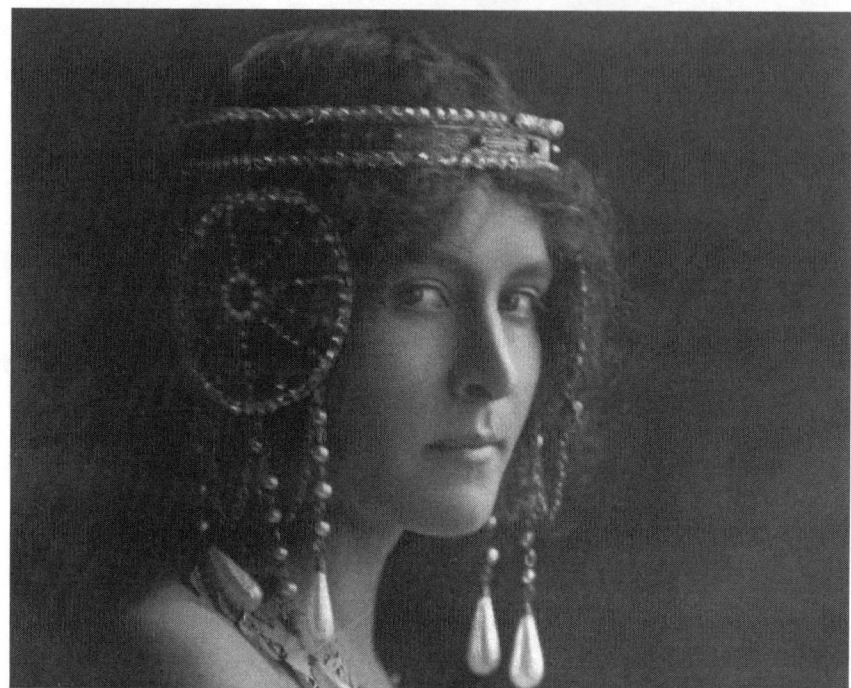

Image 24: Left - *[Lili Marberg]*, [Franz Grainer photographer], 1905, Österreichischen Nationalbibliothek.

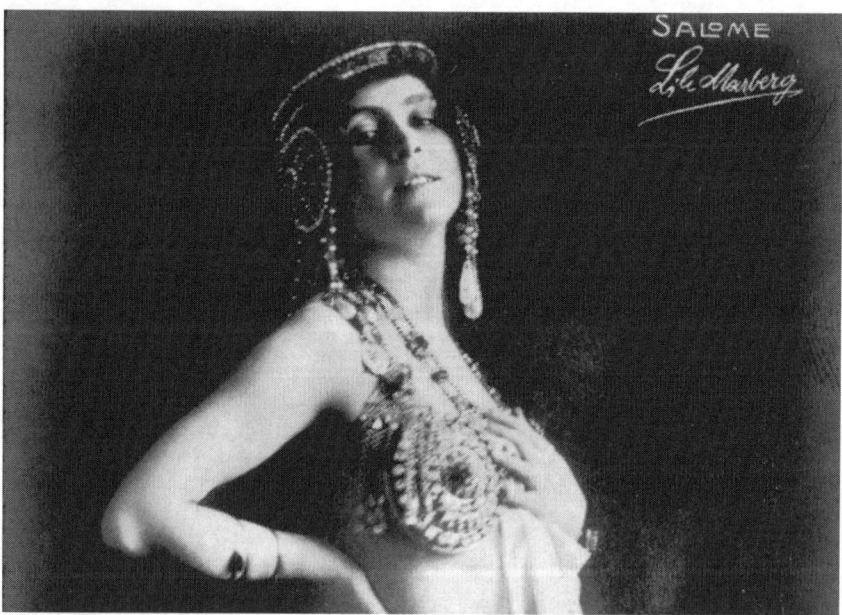

Image 25: *Lili Marberg as Salome*, [Franz Grainer photographer], ca. 1905, collection of the author.

Hedwig Reicher took on the role early in a career that would go on to include many Broadway shows and more than a dozen motion pictures.

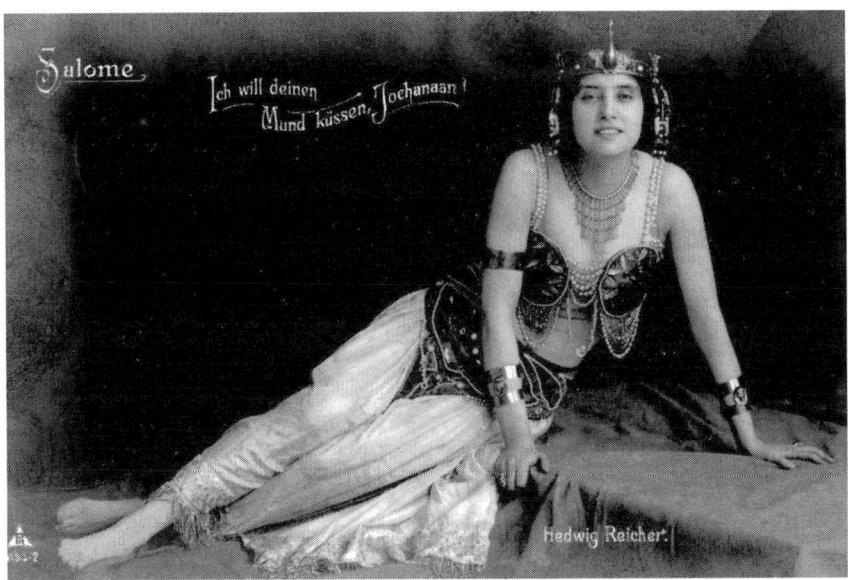

Image 26: *Hedwig Reicher as Salome*, ca. 1906, collection of the author.

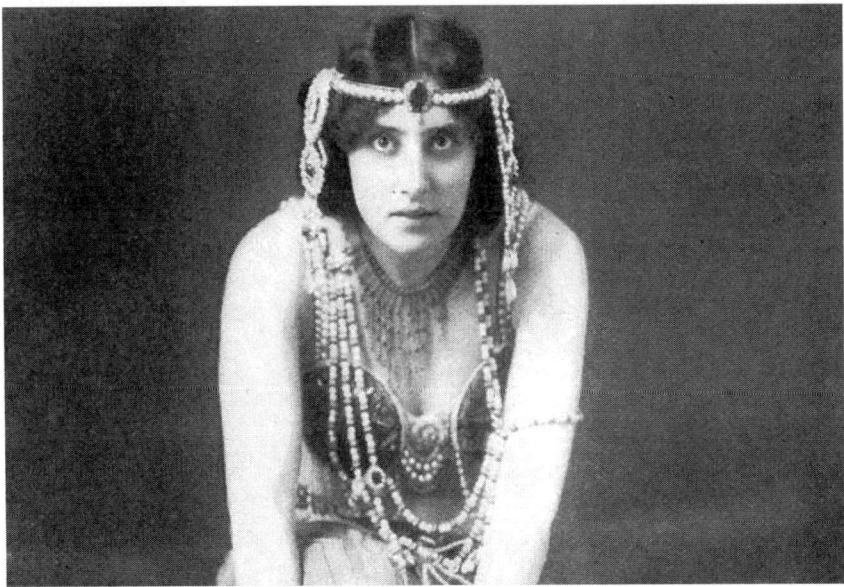

Image 27: *Mlle. Hedwig Reicher, Smith's Magazine*, 1911, American Vaudeville Museum Collection (MS 421), University of Arizona Libraries, Special Collections.

Friederike (Fritzi) Schaffer was a Munich actress who portrayed Salome after about 1905.

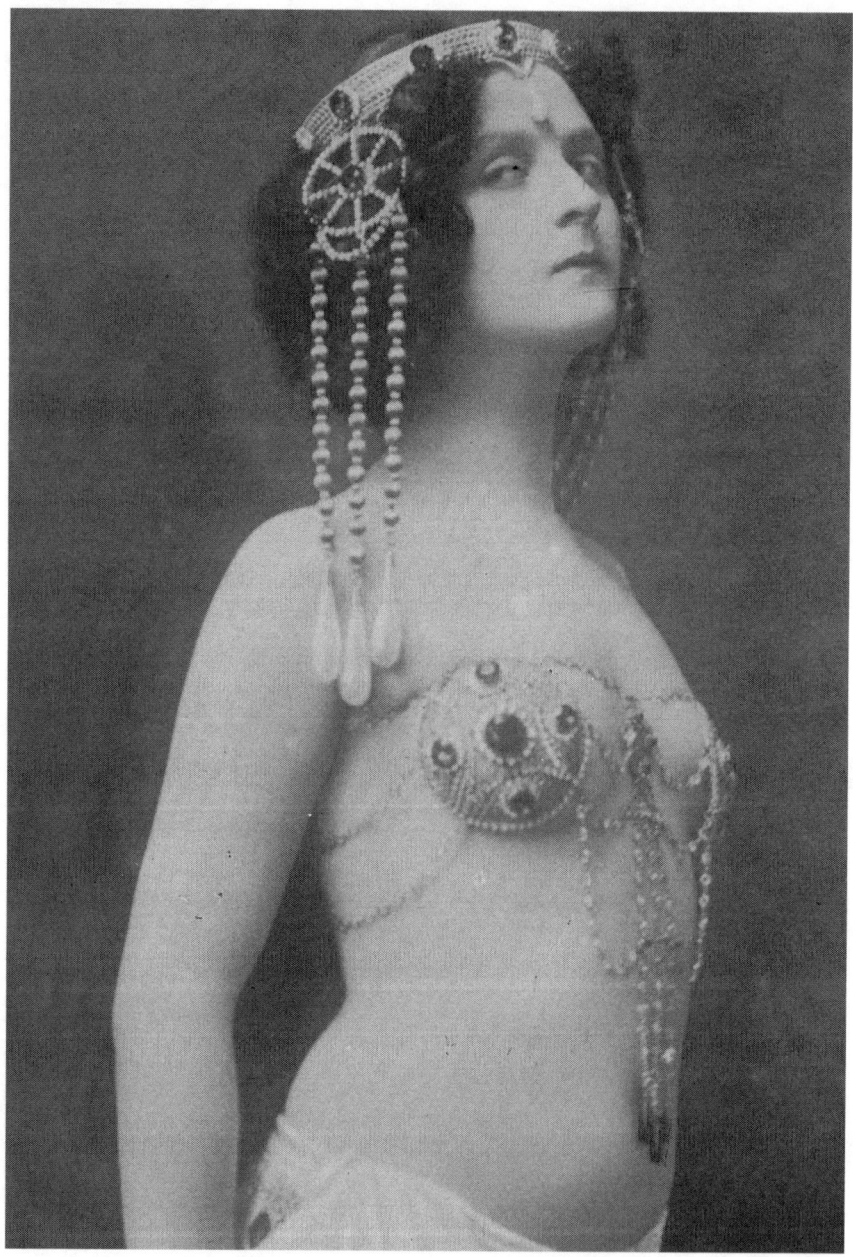

Image 28: *Fritzi Schaffer as Salome*, Bain News Service, ca. 1906, Library of Congress.

Angelina Gurlitt was a "graceful and brainy" actress and dancer who played Salome on stages in Berlin and Dusseldorf.

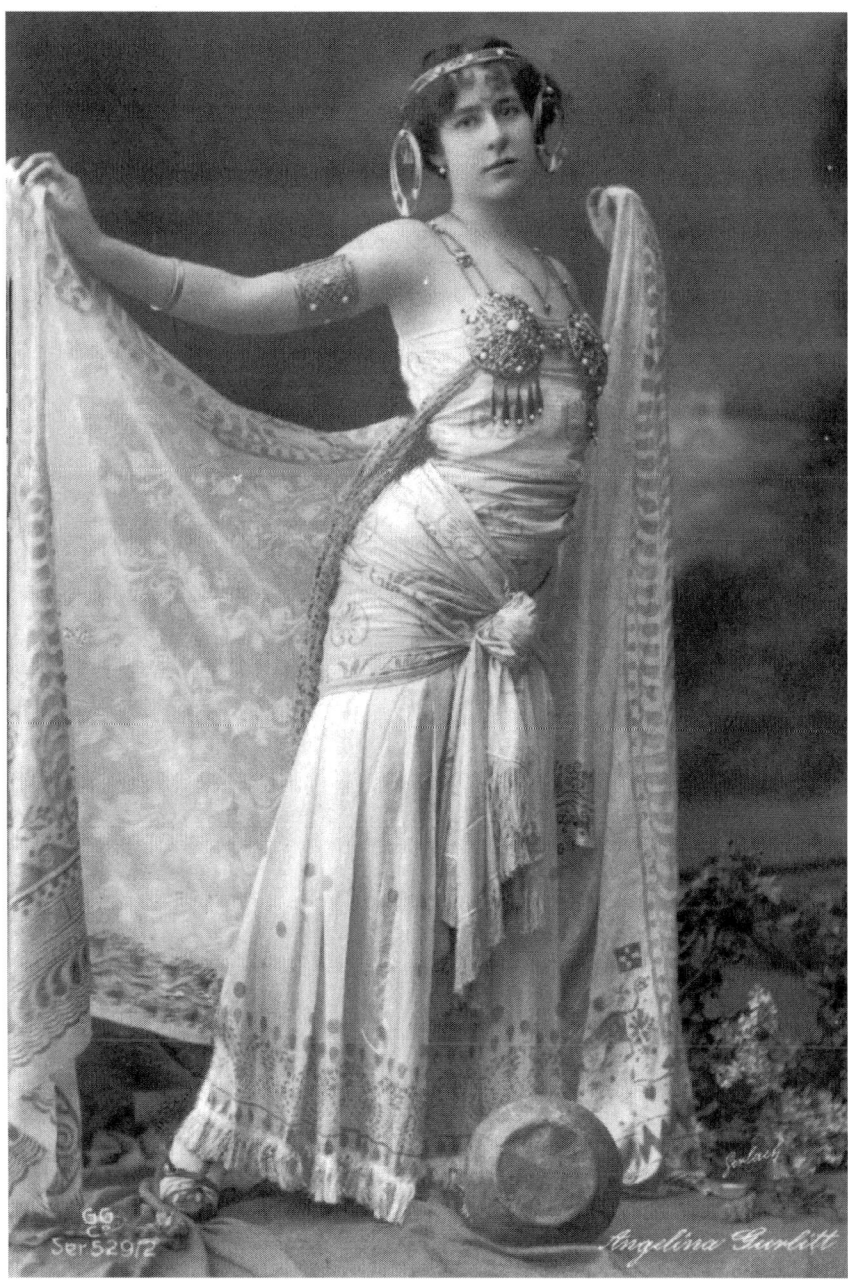

Image 29: *Angelina Gurlitt*, Georg Gerlach & Co., ca. 1905, collection of the author.

The Bucharest National Theatre presented the play in 1910 with Marioara Voiculescu as Salome; she reprised the role in 1922 Bucharest with her own theater company.

Known as "Marshal of the Romanian Theater," Voiculescu was the first female Romanian filmmaker, having directed and acted in several films from 1913-1914.

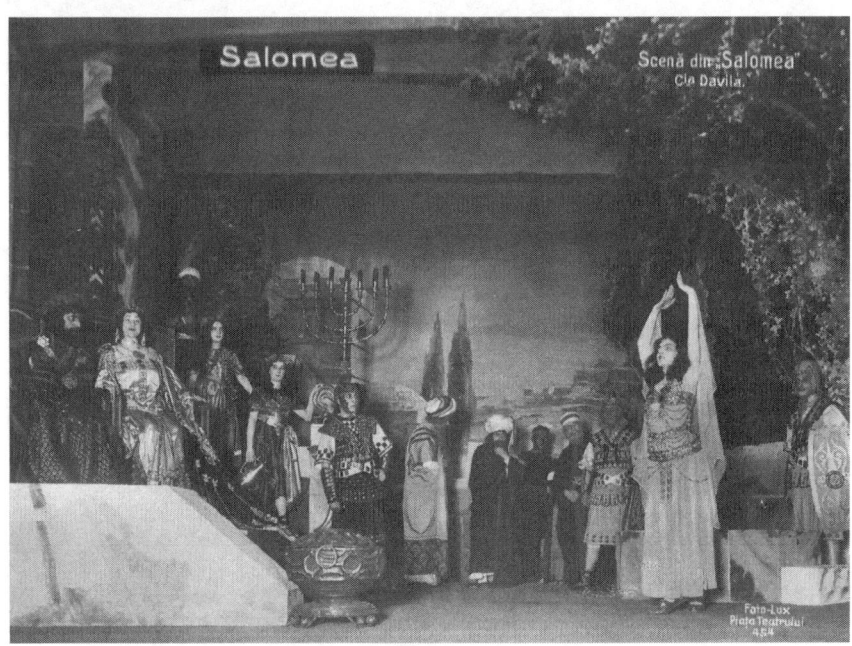

Image 30: *Salomea*, Editura Ad. Maier & D. Stern - București, 1910, Muzeului Național de Istorie a României, (used with permission).

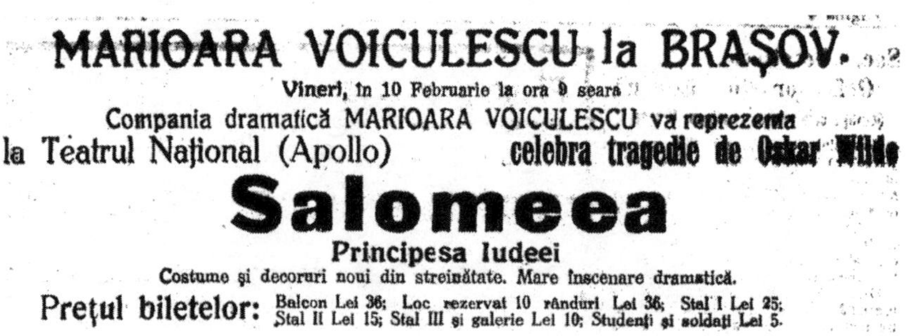

MARIOARA VOICULESCU la BRAȘOV.

Vineri, în 10 Februarie la ora 9 seară

Compania dramatică MARIOARA VOICULESCU va reprezenta

la Teatrul Național (Apollo)   celebra tragedie de Oskar Wilde

Salomeea

Principesa Iudeei

Costume și decoruri noui din streinătate. Mare înscenare dramatică.

Prețul biletelor: Balcon Lei 36; Loc rezervat 10 rânduri Lei 36; Stal I Lei 25; Stal II Lei 15; Stal III și galerie Lei 10; Studenți și soldați Lei 5.

Image 31: Advertisement, *Gazeta de Transilvania*, 1922, Biblioteca Digitala BCU Cluj.

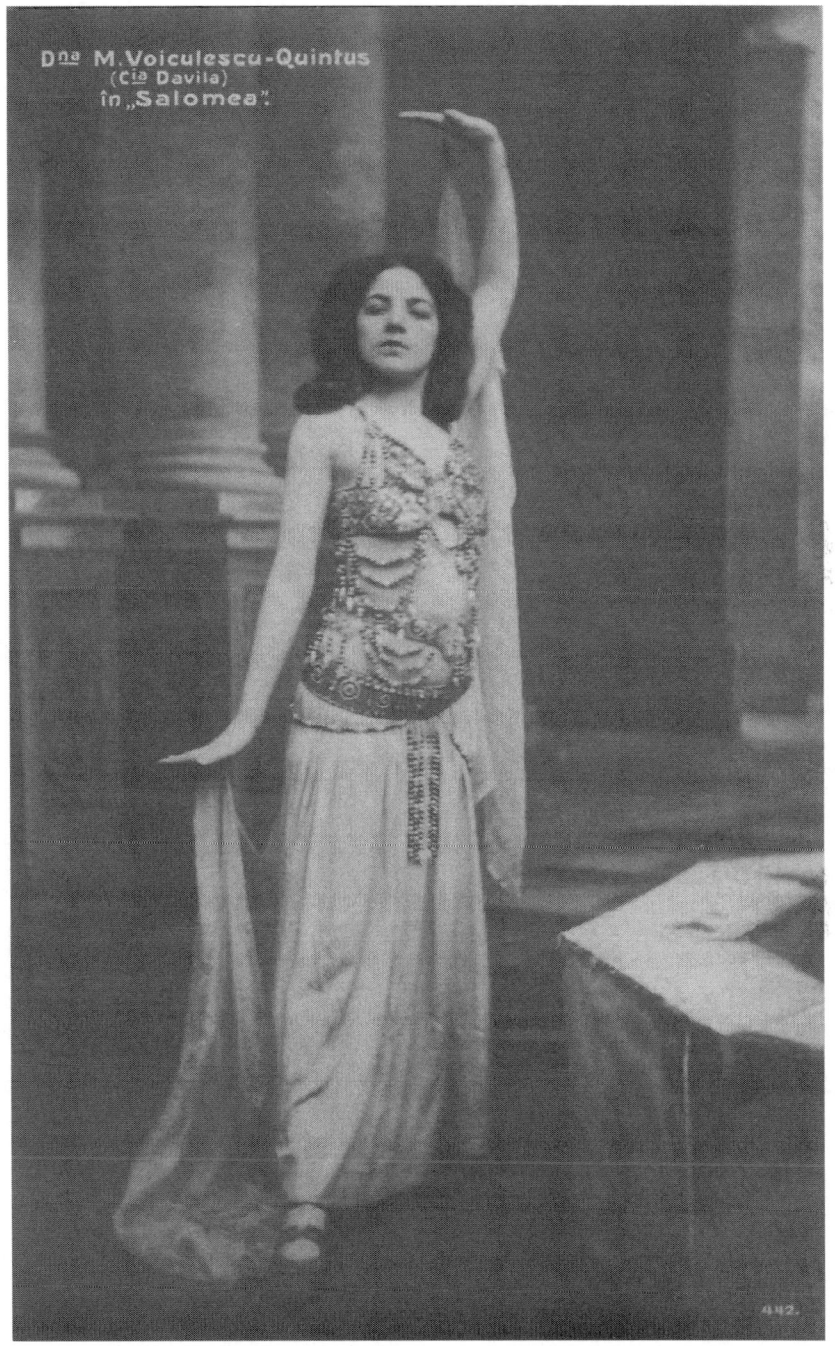

Image 32: *Artista Marioara Voiculescu*, Editura Ad. Maier & D. Stern - București, 1910, Muzeului Național de Istorie a României (used with permission).

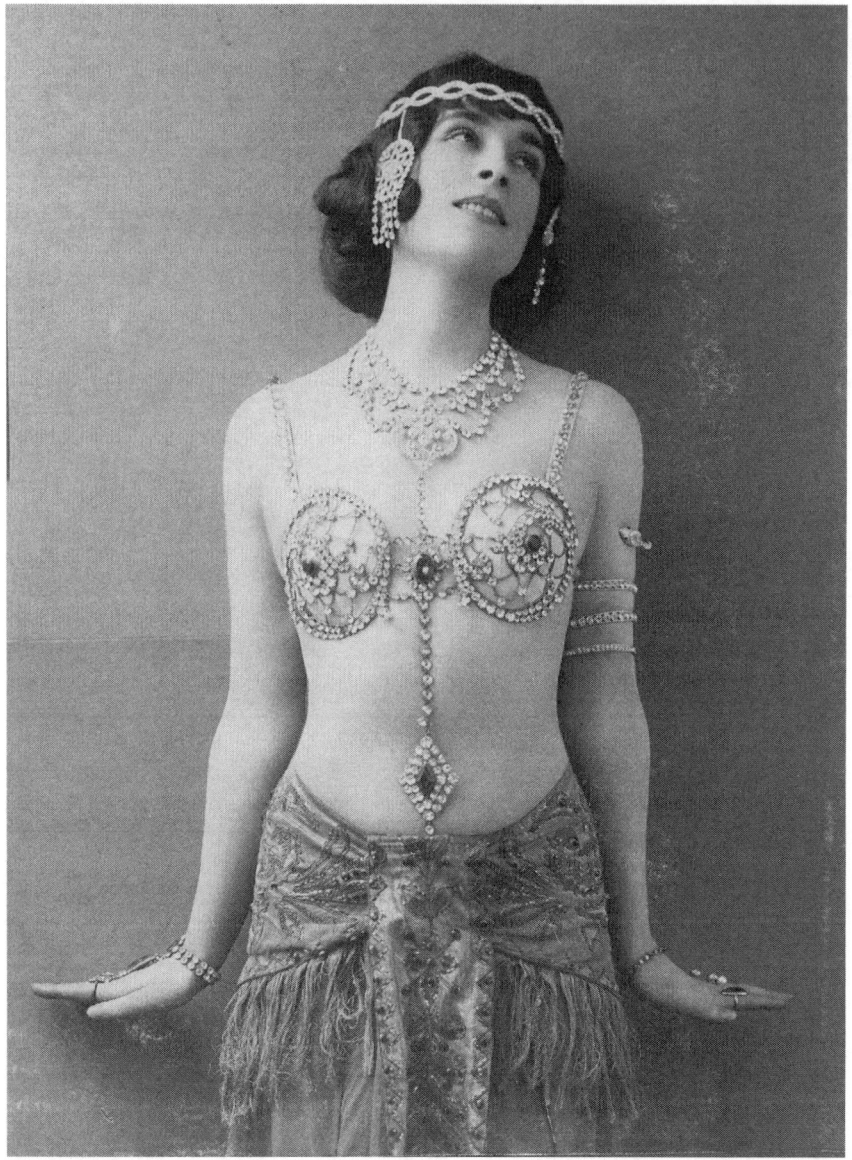

Image 33: [*Magde Lanzy*], Jean Reutlinger photographer, ca. 1910, Gallica, Bibliothèque nationale de France.

The well-known theatrical photographer Jean Reutlinger captured French actress Magde Lanzy in a Salome costume about 1910.

Italian actress Lyda Borelli played Salome with particular gusto.

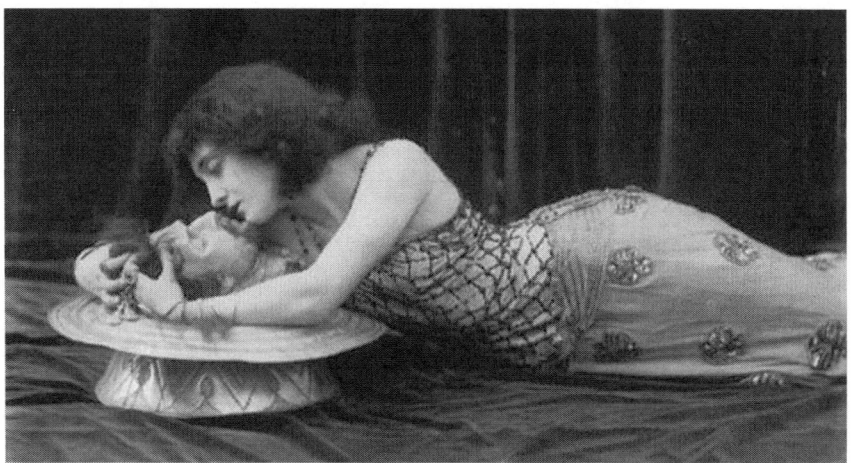

Image 34: *Lyda Borelli in costume da Salomé*, Mario Nunes Vais photographer, ca. 1911, Wikimedia Commons.

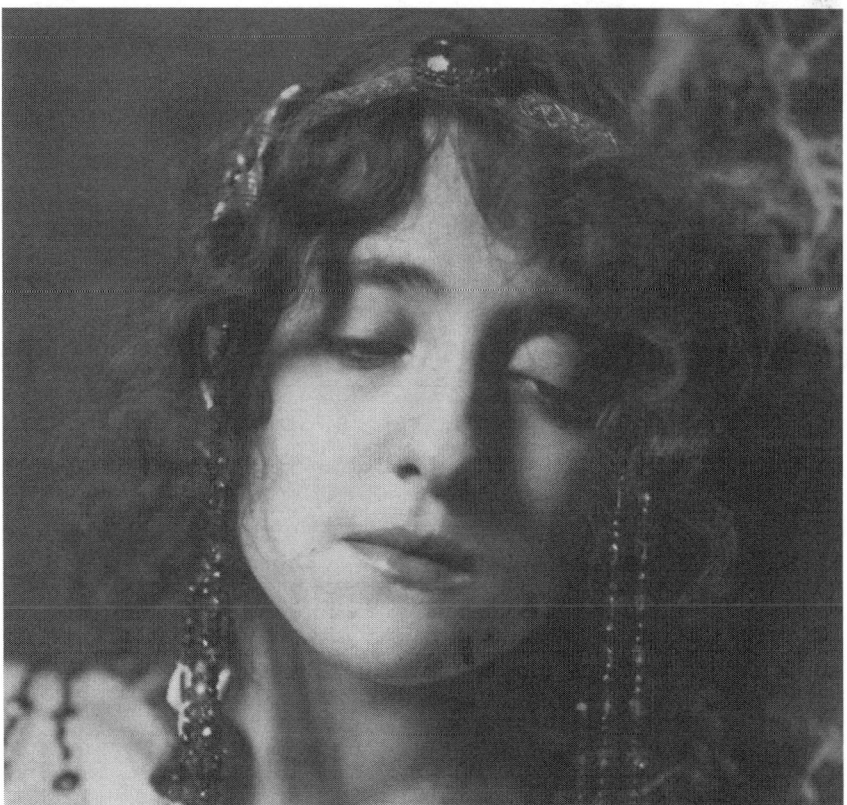

Image 35: *Ritratto di Lyda Borelli in abito da Salomé*, Emilio Sommariva photographer, ca. 1911, Braidense National Library, Europeana.

29

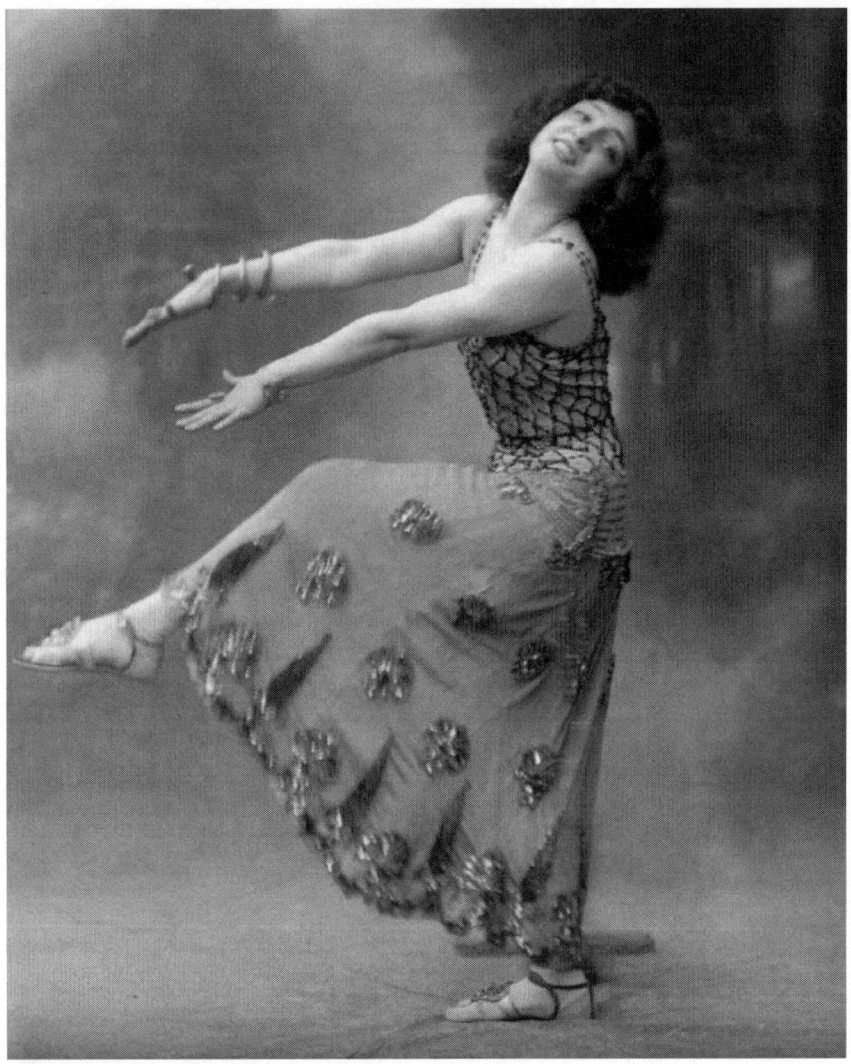

Image 36: *Lyda Borelli*, Mario Nunes Vais photographer, ca. 1911, Wikimedia Commons.

Vanity Fair noted that Borelli's great popularity likely stemmed from her spectacular lifestyle, which supposedly included driving several suitors to suicide. The article praised her "strange, exotic beauty" and noted that "she is an actress of modern methods, possessed of extraordinary power and charm."

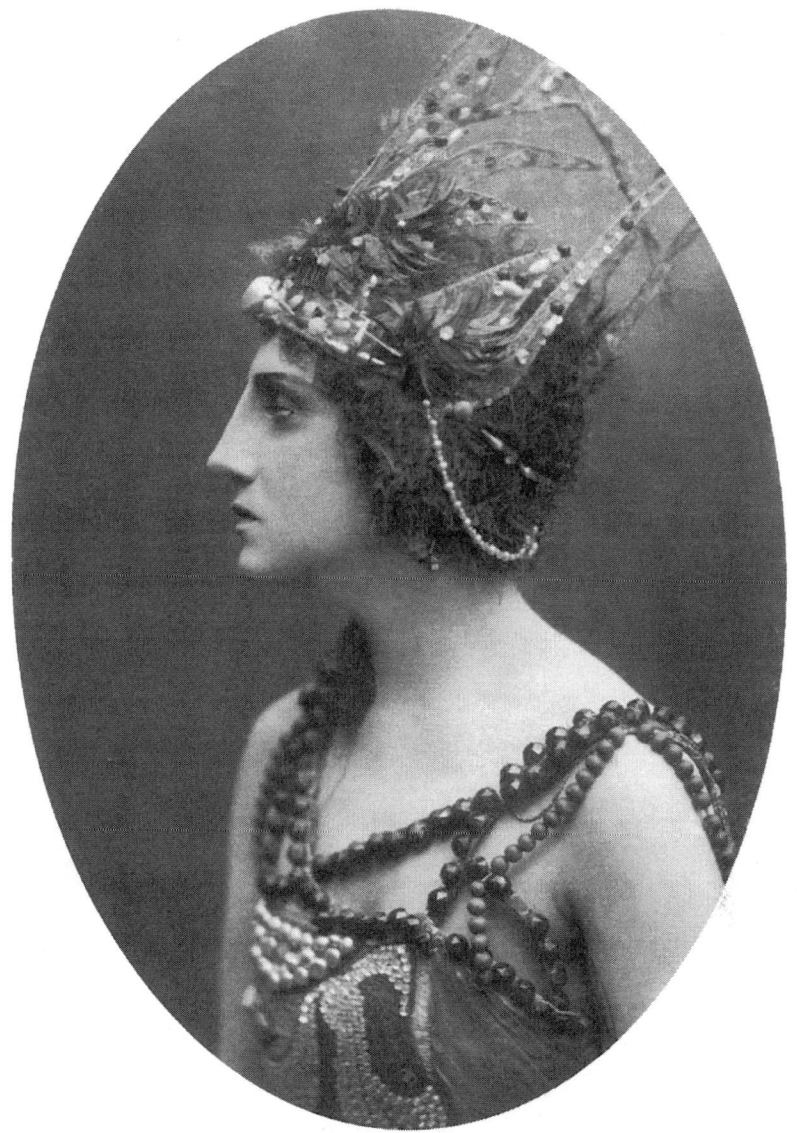

Image 37: *Alice (Alisa) Koonen as Salome*, Kamerny Theater, 1917, Wikimedia Commons.

Actress Alice (Alisa) Koonen presented a "passionate, aggressive Salome" in a 1917 staging at Moscow's Kamersky Theater. Known as the "Cubo-Futurist" production, the costumes and sets were unique.

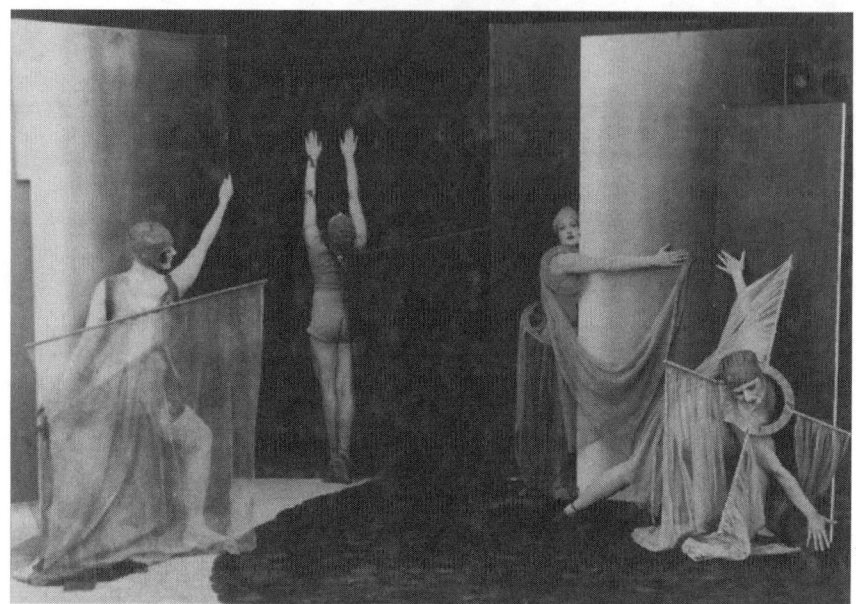

Image 38: *Production Designed by Alexandra Exter*, [Kamerny Theater], ca. 1917, New York Public Library.

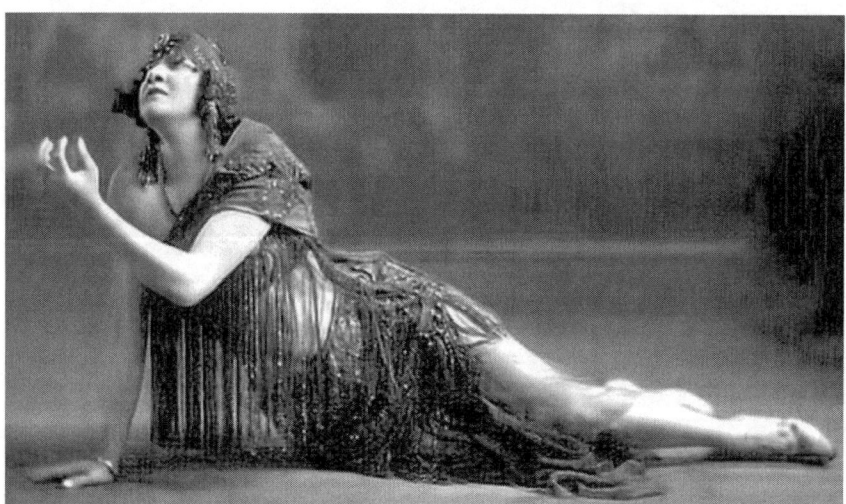

Image 39: *Evelyn Preer, the Gifted Negro Actress in Salome, The Crisis*, 1923-1924, HathiTrust.

During the 1920s, a troupe of African-American actors known as The Ethiopian Art Theater performed Wilde's play across the United States.

Evelyn Preer starred in the production and received excellent reviews. The *Chicago Tribune* stated, "Salome is an opulent beauty named Evelyn Preer. She understands the denouement of passion and there is more than a hint of fire in her acting."

Preer made over a dozen motion pictures and was known among African- Americans as "the First Lady of the Screen."

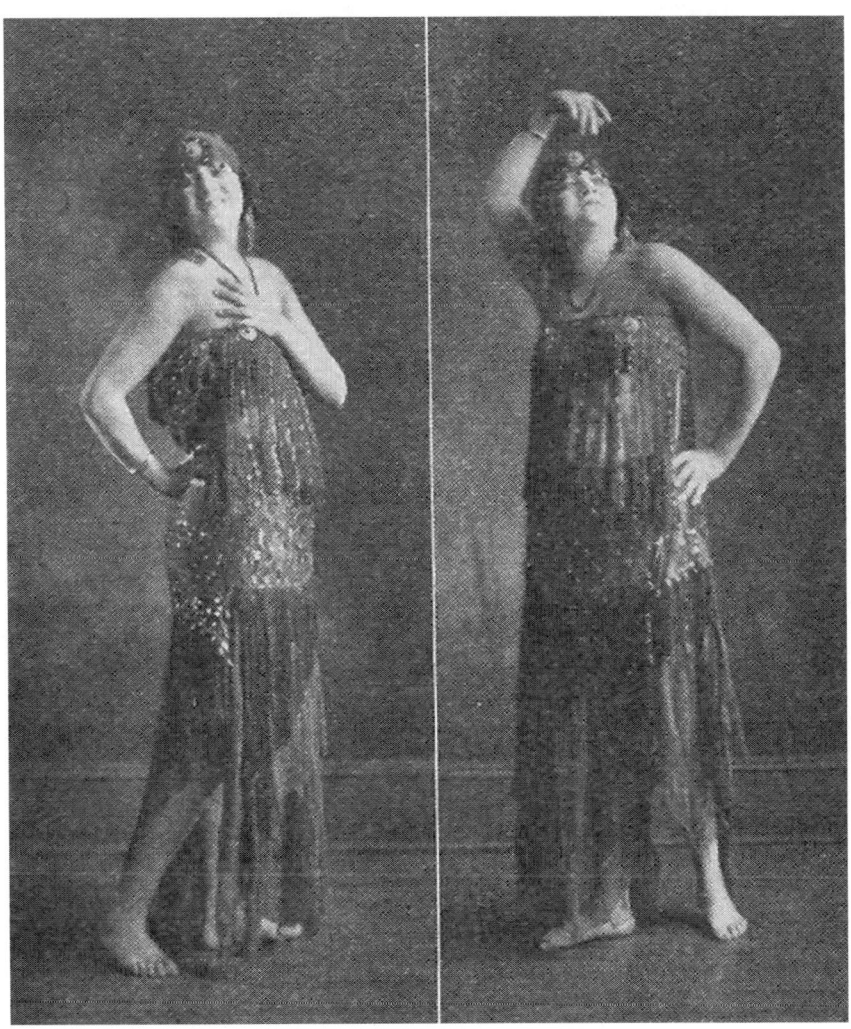

Image 40: *Two Striking Poses of Miss Preer, The Crisis*, 1923-1924, HathiTrust.

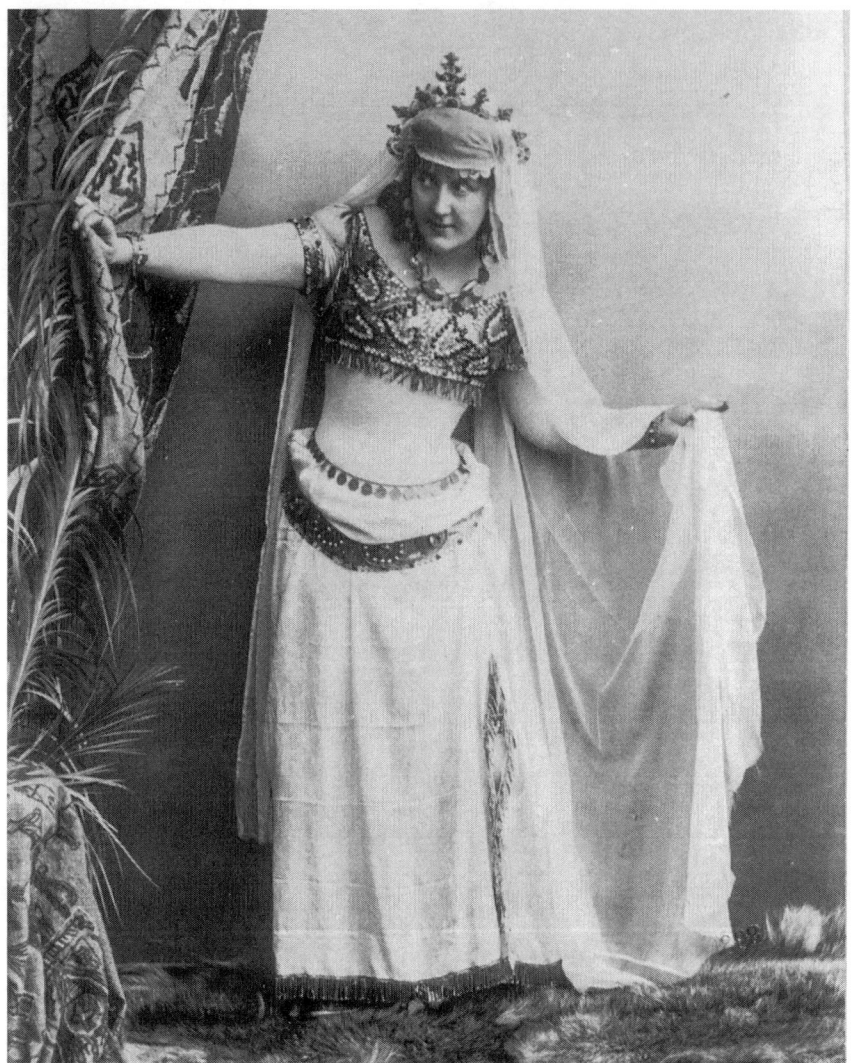

Image 41: *Charlotte Basté als Salome in dem Schauspiel "Johannes der Täufer,"* Wilhelm Höffert, 1898, Deutsche Fotothek, Europeana.

Wilde's play is the best-known featuring Salome, but other playwrights also took up the story. In 1898, for example, Hermann Sudermann wrote *Johannes der Täufer (John the Baptist)*. Charlotte Basté premiered the role in 1898 Dresden.

CHAPTER 3 - OPERA: RICHARD STRAUSS AND THE DIVAS

When Richard Strauss attended the *Salome* theater production in 1903 Berlin, he felt the play "cried out for music."

In choosing the provocative story for operatic treatment, Strauss courted controversy—perhaps with hope of drawing an audience. Still, as Alex Ross notes, the composer "felt drawn to sexually charged material throughout his life. Women dominate his operas; men tend to be weak and shallow in comparison."

Whatever his motivation, Strauss had trouble finding a venue to launch his creation. The grand opera houses of Vienna refused to host what they saw as a shocking, immoral work. Dresden finally agreed to stage the opera in 1905.

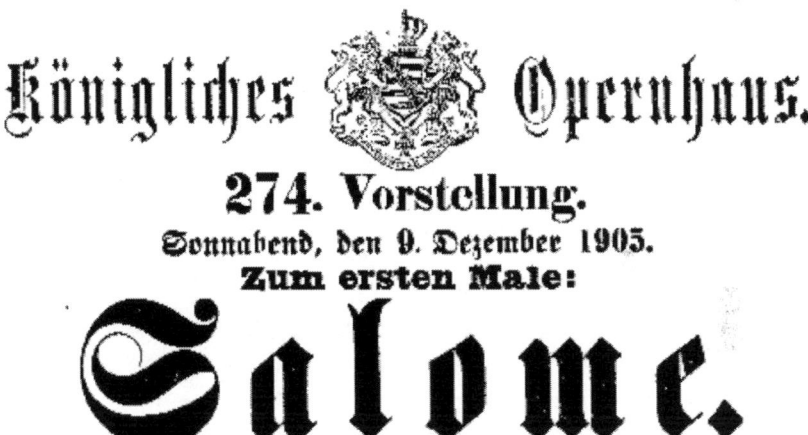

Image 42: *Salome by Richard Strauss, Playbill of 1905 premiere*, 1905, Wikimedia Commons.

Strauss cast Marie Wittich, a well-known soprano, as his first Salome. He reportedly doubted the matronly Wittich's ability to portray the lithesome Salome but decided her voice was more important than her appearance.

Wittich initially refused the role, declaring, "I won't do it; I'm a decent woman." She eventually relented, with a ballerina taking her place for the erotic Dance of the Seven Veils. Wittich was undoubtedly glad to have participated, as she got thirty-eight curtain calls on opening night.

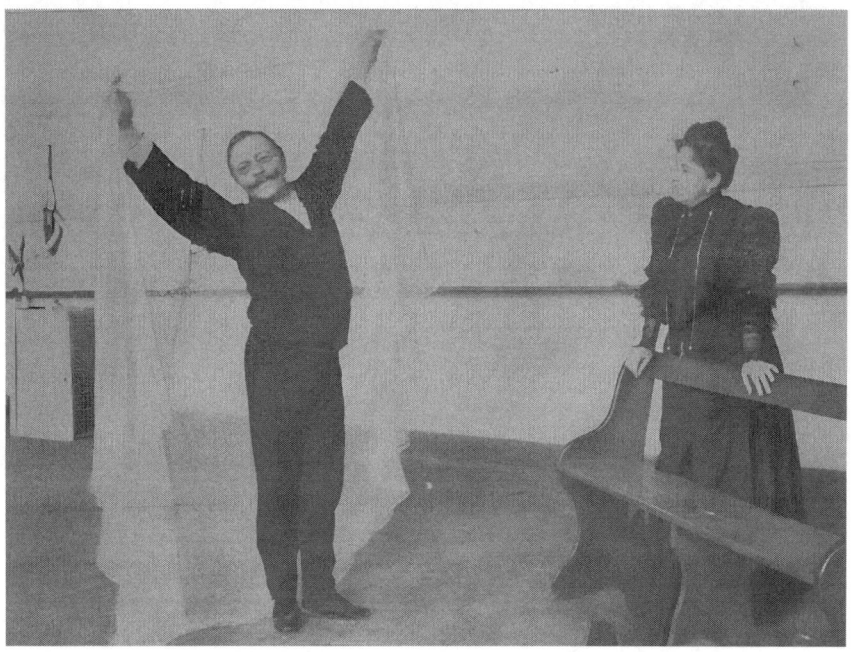

Image 43: *Balletmeister August Berger Studiert mit Marie Wittich den Tanz in "Salome,"* 1905, *Die Woche, Moderne Illustrierte Zeitschrift*, HathiTrust.

Strauss took a chance in presenting the opera, as German censors were quick to block any performance judged immoral. *Salome* had plenty of shock value, not the least of which was its association with Oscar Wilde, notorious for his same-sex orientation. German law banned gay relationships, and the subject was especially touchy due to rumors that such activity existed in circles close to Kaiser Wilhelm II.

Some critics were quick to sound the alarm. "We are no fans of censorship," wrote Adam Röder in the Wiesbaden *Rheinischer Kurier*. "But if the sadists, masochists, lesbians, and homosexuals approach us demanding that we understand their crazy world of thought and sensibility as expressions of art, then we have to intervene in the name of the healthy."

Nevertheless, the show was a huge critical and box office triumph that lifted Strauss into the top ranks of composers. *Salome* made Strauss rich, allowing him to build a lavish villa and enjoy the high life. At least fifty productions of the opera took place in Europe over the next two years, and many more took place worldwide over the following thirty years.

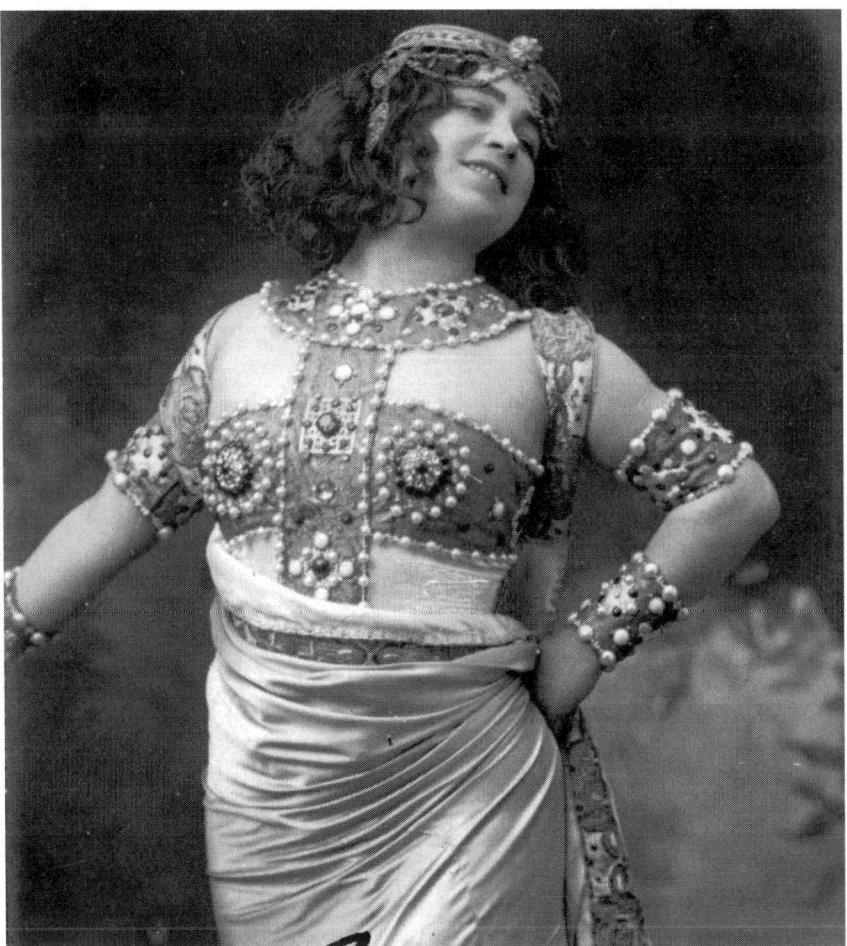

Image 44: *Claire Friché*, ca. 1909, collection of the author.

Subsequent stagings of the opera often followed the original model of casting one performer to sing and one to dance. This was the case in 1909 Belgium when soprano Claire Friché did the singing while "Mlle. J. Cesny" did the Dance of the Seven Veils.

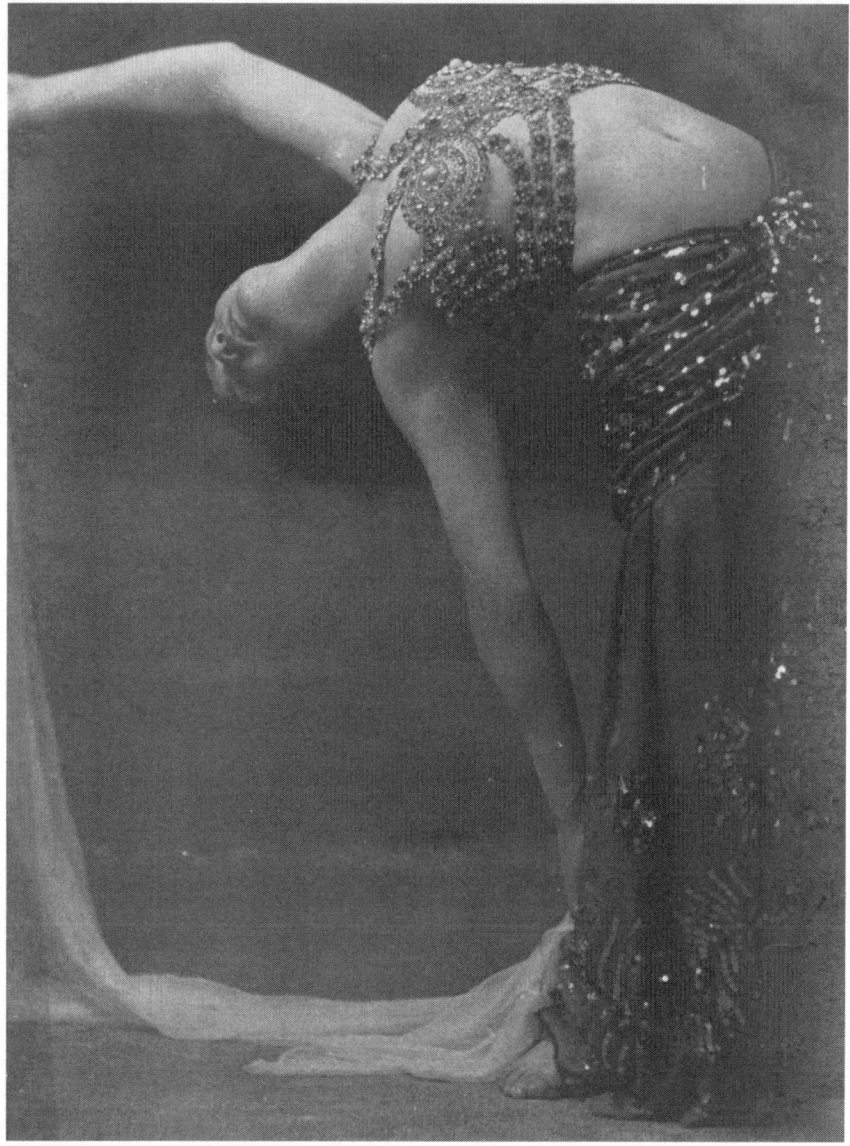

Image 45: *Cesny als Salome*, ca. 1909, Frankfurt am Main: Stadt- und Univ.-Bibliothek, collection F. N. Manskopf (used with permission).

Many of the most famous European sopranos of the day took on the role, including Emmy Destinn, who performed across Germany.

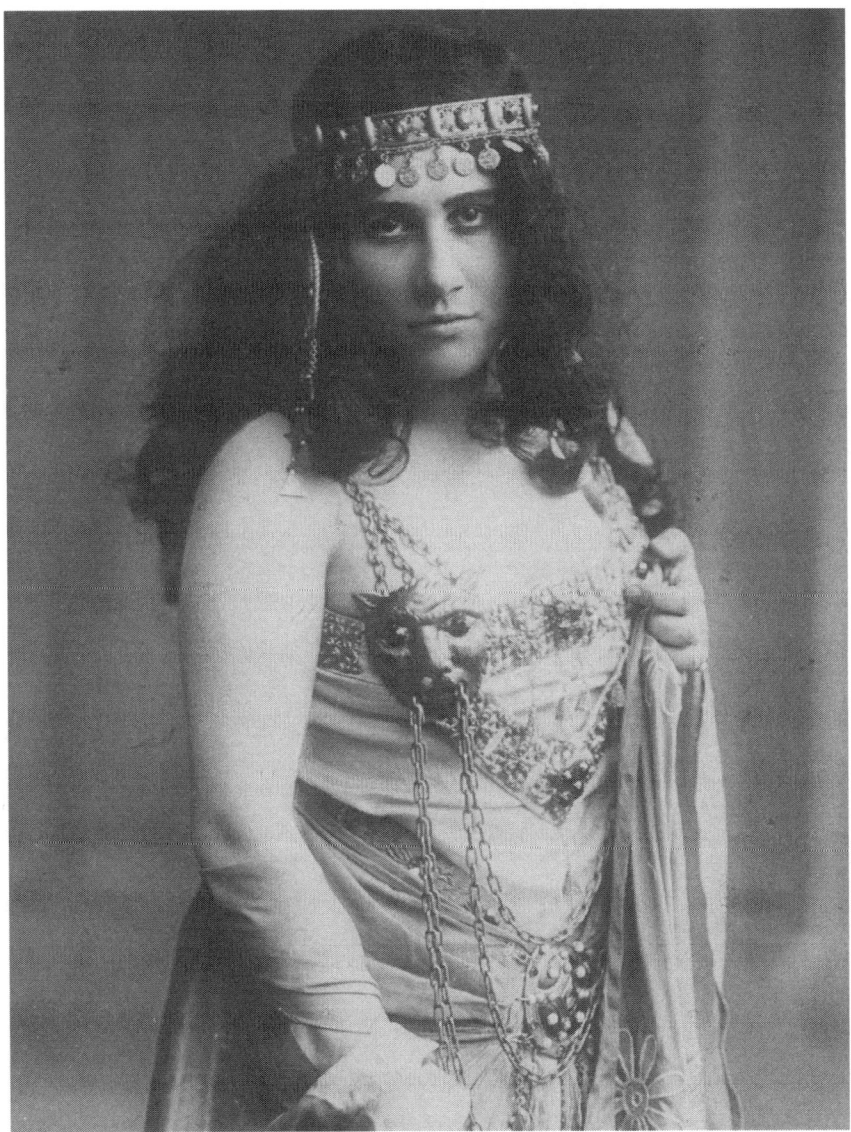

Image 46. *Ema Destinnová als Salome*, ca. 1907, Frankfurt am Main: Stadt- und Univ.-Bibliothek, collection F. N. Manskopf (used with permission).

Other stagings featured the Swiss Anna Sutter, who died in Stuttgart at the hands of a lover in 1910. Sutter's obituary compared her life to that of Salome, claiming "She was a natural, full of unmediated, effervescent temperament; she lived the roles she played."

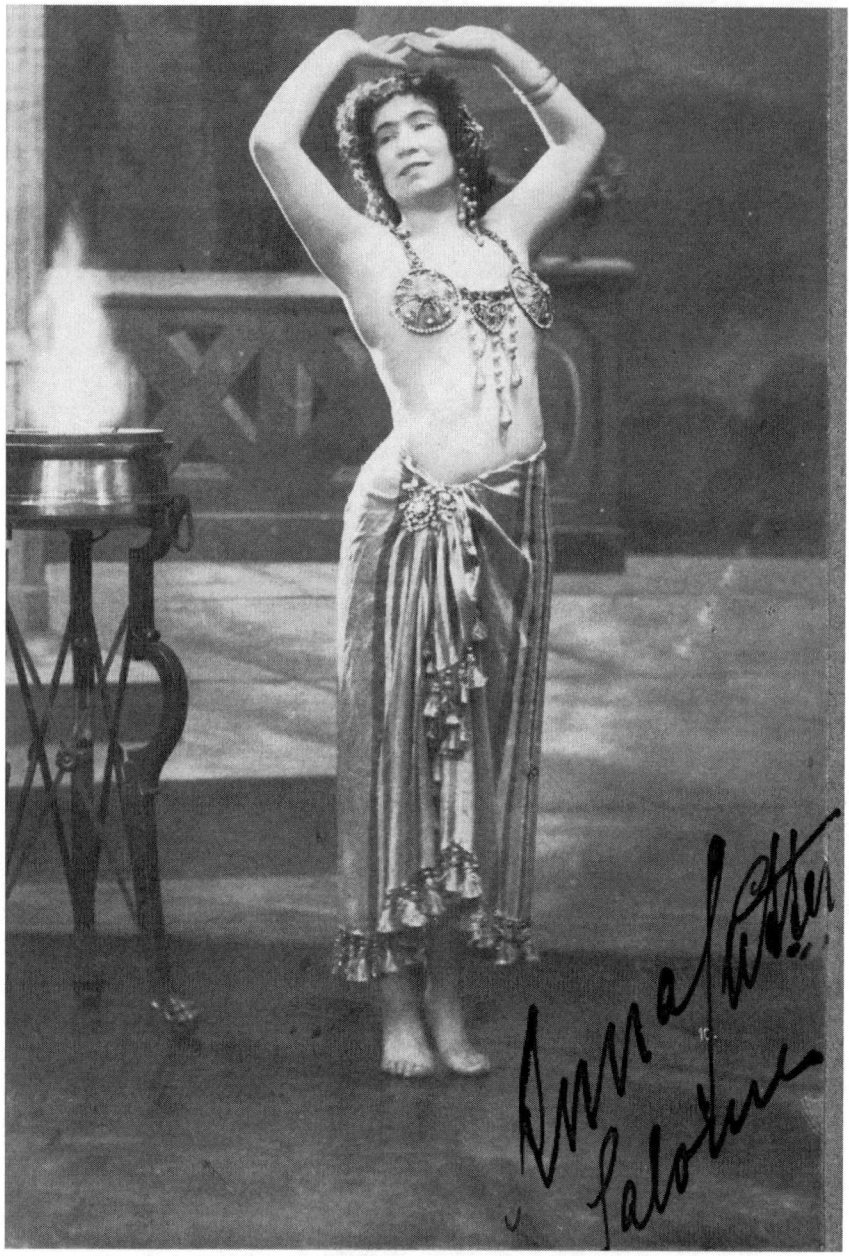

Image 47: *Anna Sutter als Salome,* ca. 1907, Frankfurt am Main: Stadt- und Univ.-Bibliothek, collection F. N. Manskopf (used with permission).

Thyra Larsen, "the Munich Salome," was widely praised for her expressive performances during the early 1900s.

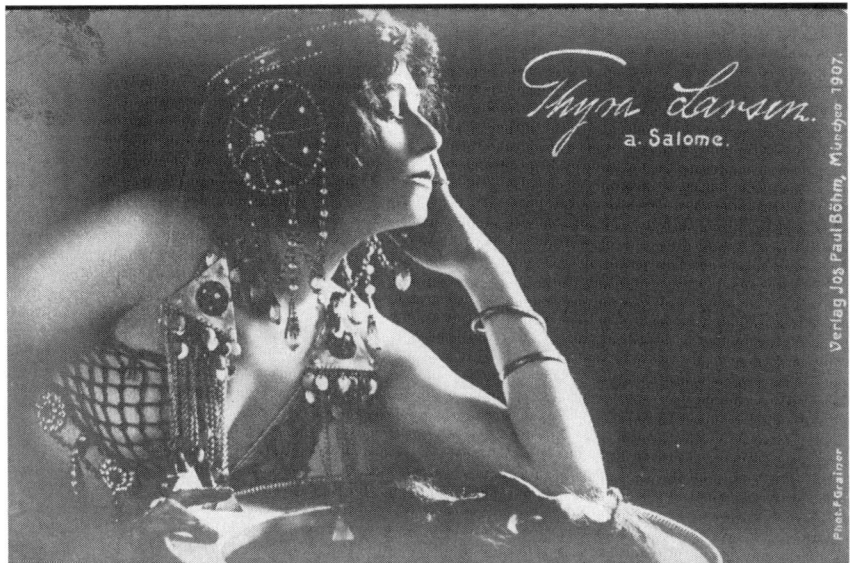

Image 48: *Thyra Larsen als Salome*, ca. 1910, Frankfurt am Main: Stadt- und Univ.-
Bibliothek, collection F. N. Manskopf (used with permission).

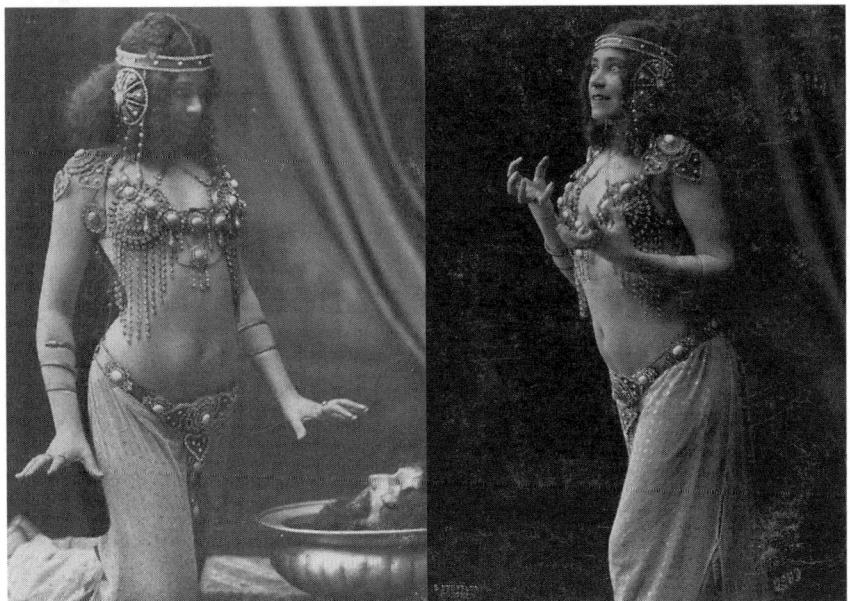

Image 49: Left - *Thyra Larsen*, ca. 1901, by Adolf Baumann, TheaterMuseum,
Europeana; right - same as left, Europeana (used with permission).

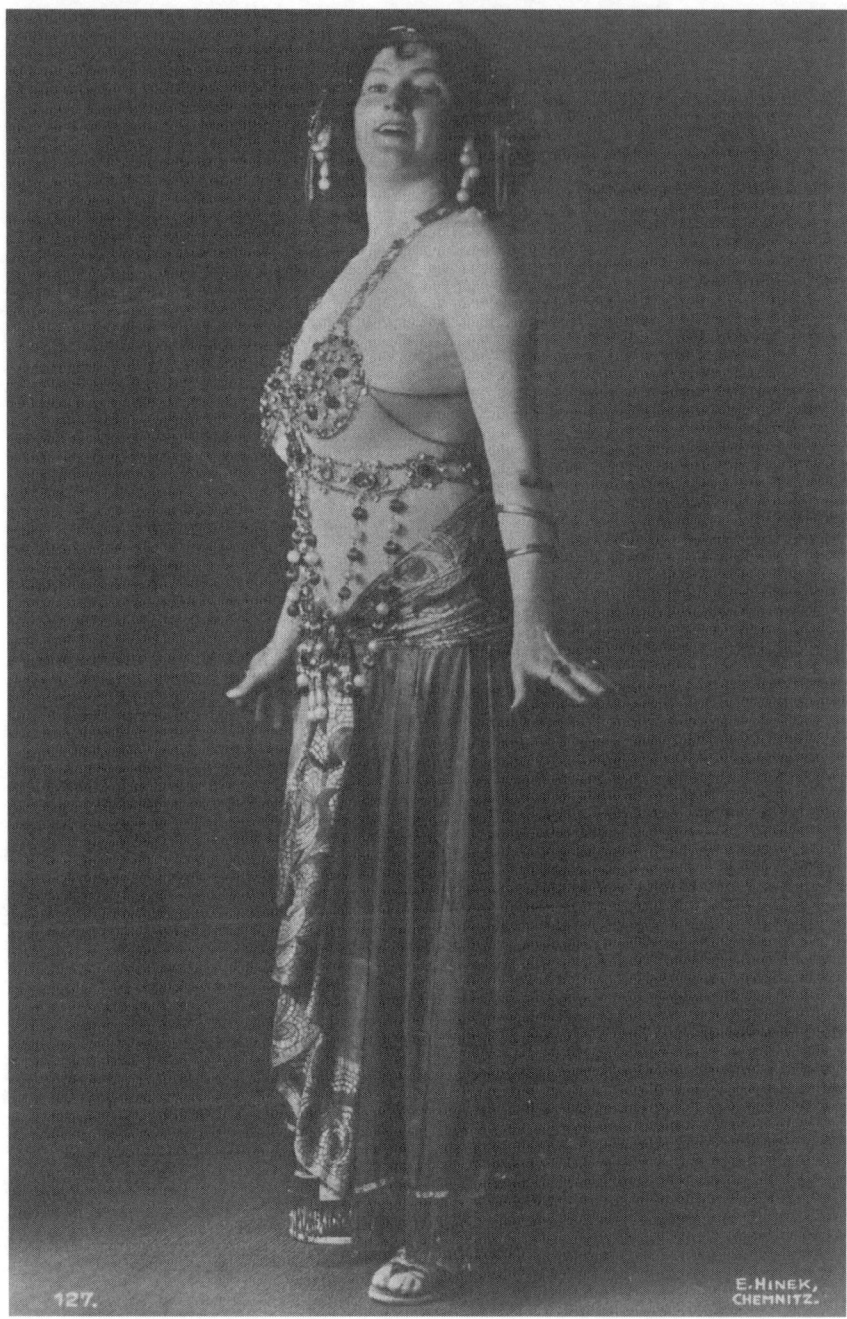

Image 50: *Gerta Barby als Salome*, ca. 1912, Deutsche Fotothek, Europeana.

Gerta Barby won praise for playing a Salome with "sensuous beauty."

Aline Sanden, a soprano known for her emotionally gripping and erotically intense portrayals, played Salome in various European cities, including Berlin, Leipzig, and Copenhagen.

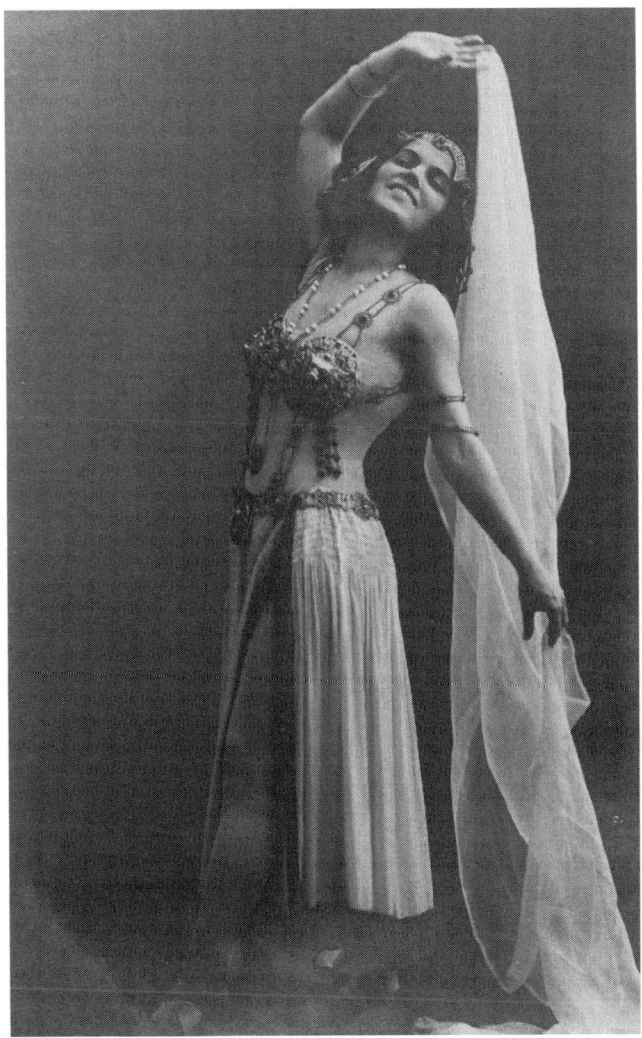

Image 51: *Aline Sanden als Salome*, Neues Theater Leipzig, 1910, Europeana.

A 1907 review of the Hungarian singer Alice Guszalewicz said she "Sang Salome with captivating dramatic fire and impeccable euphony while displaying a great deal of grace."

43

Unfortunately for the legacy of Ms. Guszalewicz, a photograph of her was for many years mistakenly assumed to depict Oscar Wilde in drag. A 1992 commentary noted, "The picture is almost too eloquent. His . . . flowing locks adorned with an 'Oriental' headdress, a jewelled [sic] belt at his ample waist . . . It is Oscar Wilde in the costume of Salome."

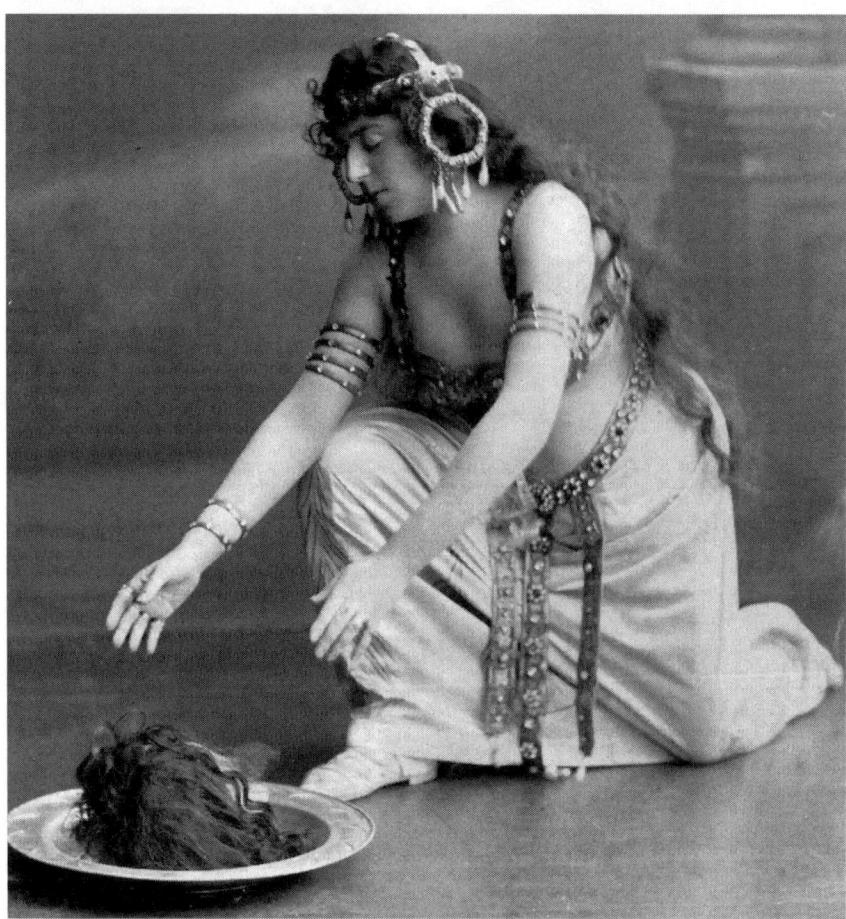

Image 52: *Alice Guszalewicz as Salome*, ca. 1906/1907, Wikimedia Commons.

One writer cited the misidentified photograph as proof of Salome's "veiled homosexual desire;" another author used it to illustrate the idea that Salome was, in fact, a male-to-female cross-dresser. Researchers identified Ms. Guszalewicz as the true subject of the photo in the mid-1990s.

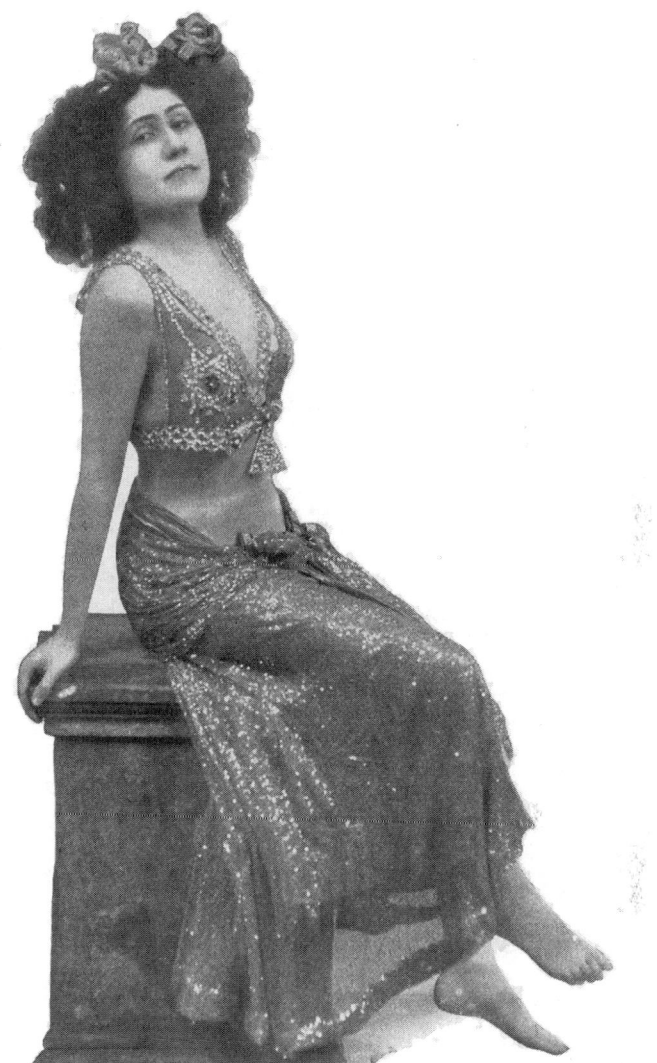

Image 53: *Aino Ackté as Salome*, 1910, *The Bystander*, HathiTrust.

In 1910, the Finn Aino Ackté sang and danced as Salome for the opera's debut in England. *The Nation* applauded her performance, stating that she was "an imperious princess, a spoilt child, and a woman intoxicated with sensuousness."

Ackté managed to excel in spite of a censorship requirement to keep the severed head covered with a cloth during the performance. The intent was to protect the audience from any unseemly representation of intimacy between Salome and John's detached body part.

Also in 1910, *The Sketch* magazine illustrated "Twelve Famous Salomes of the Continent (Images 54 and 55). One hundred years later, the performers pictured here are a mix of the remembered and the nearly forgotten.

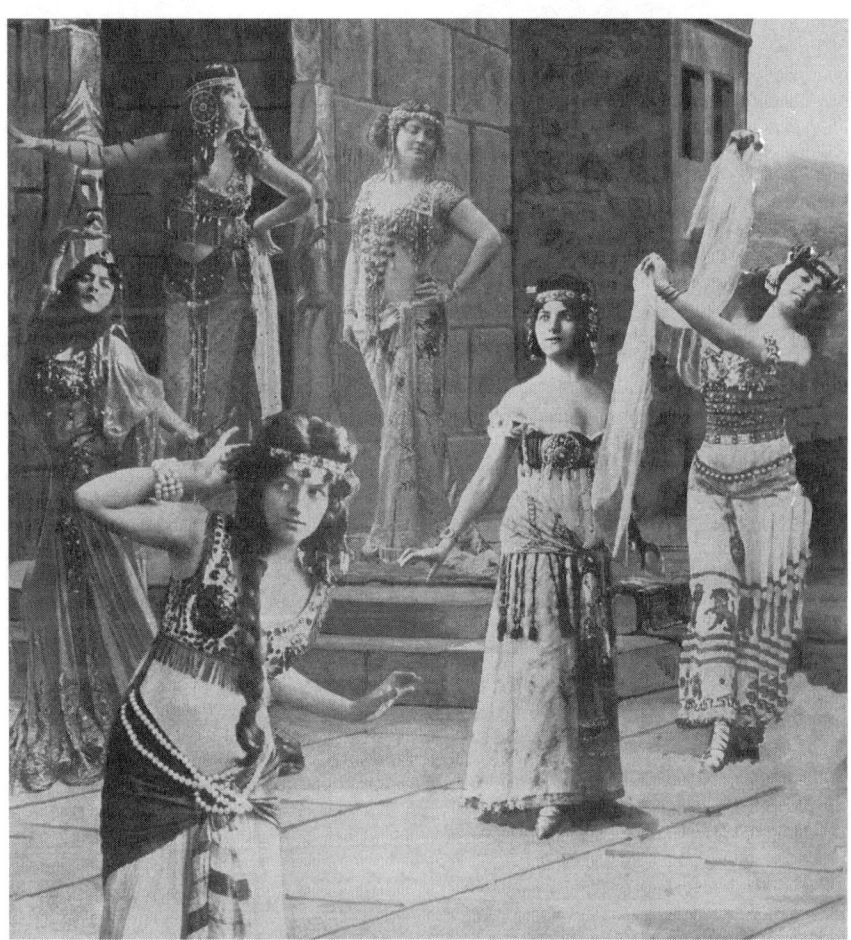

Image 54: *Twelve Famous Salomes of the Continent [Clockwise from far left: Lucy Isnardon, Henny Dima, Josephine von Hubbenet, Salomea Kruszelnicka, Malvine Kann, and Agnes Klebe], The Sketch*, 1910, National Library of Finland (this is part 1 of the original; note also the Kruyszelnicka figure has been moved in this version of the image).

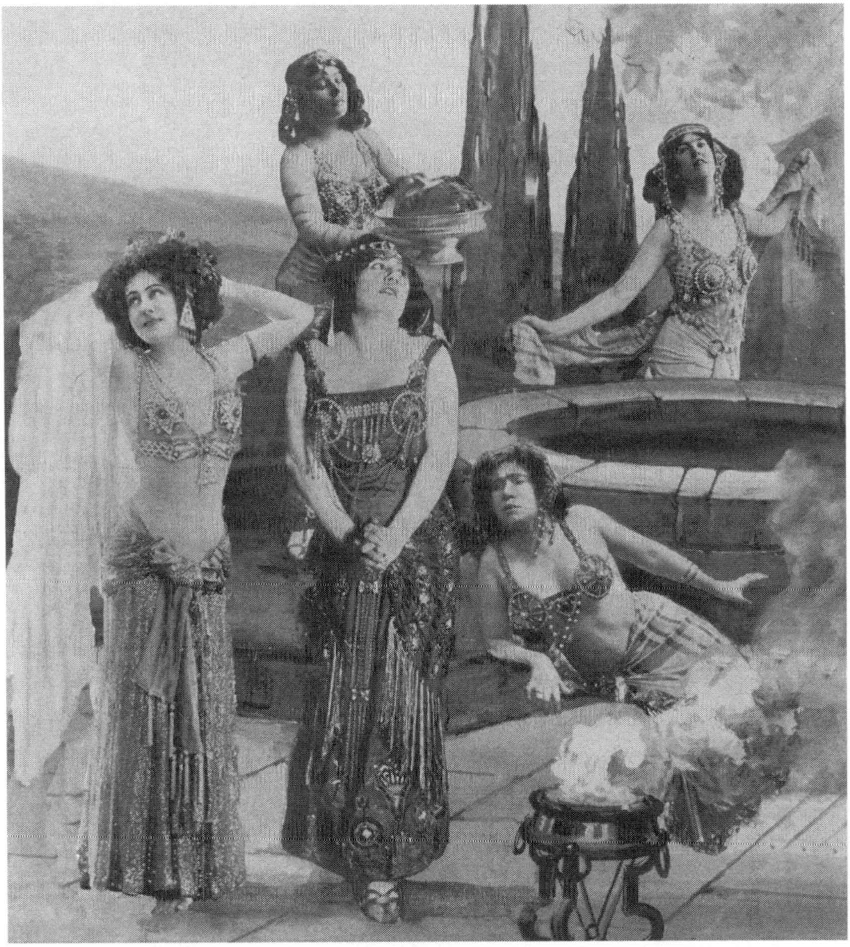

Image 55: *Twelve Famous Salomes of the Continent [From left, Aino Ackté, Emmy Destinn, Fanchette Verhunk, Anna Sutter, and Singe von Rappe]*, *The Sketch*, 1910, National Library of Finland (this is part 2 of the original; note also Thyra Larsen has been removed from this version of the image).

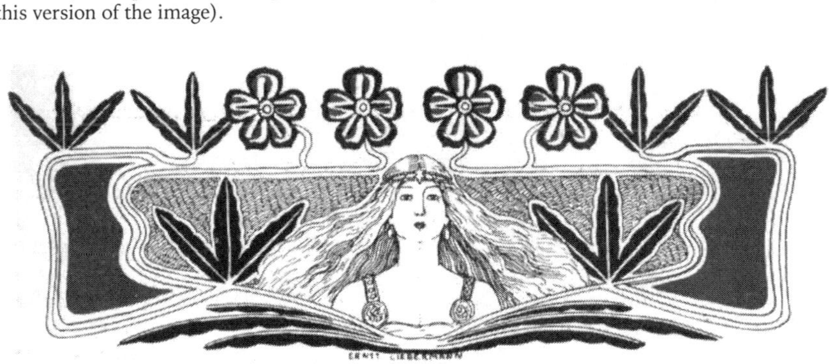

Image 56: *[Drawing of Salome]*, *Bühne und Welt*, 1902, HathiTrust.

French soprano Alice Baron had a successful career in Europe and America. She often sang at the Manhattan Opera House as Salome.

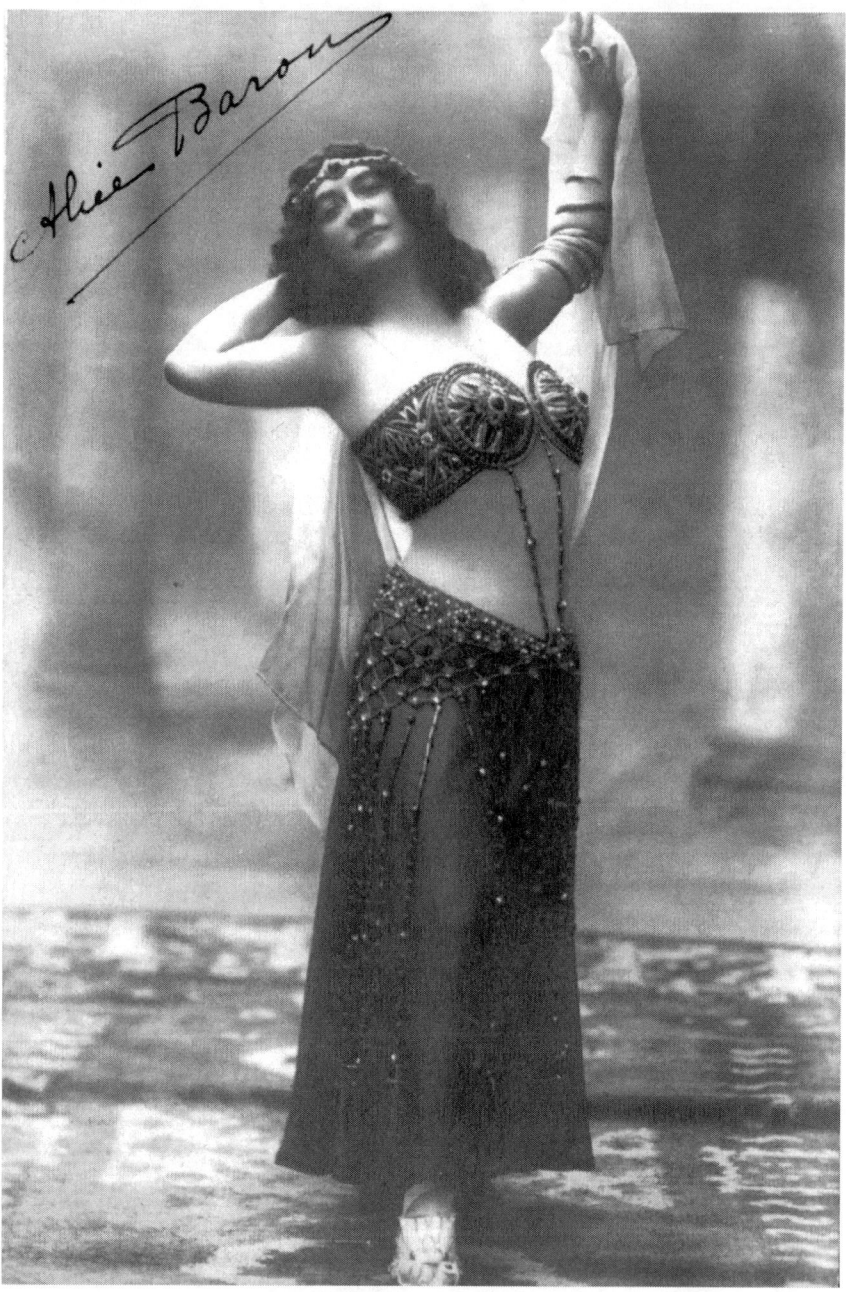

Image 57: *Alice Baron*, ca. 1908, collection of the author.

The New York Metropolitan Opera staged the U.S. premiere in 1907, with Olive Fremstad in the title role. But J. P. Morgan, a major financial backer, demanded the Met shut down the show. The opera house complied, citing the work's "moral stench." *Salome* did not reappear on the Met's stage until 1934.

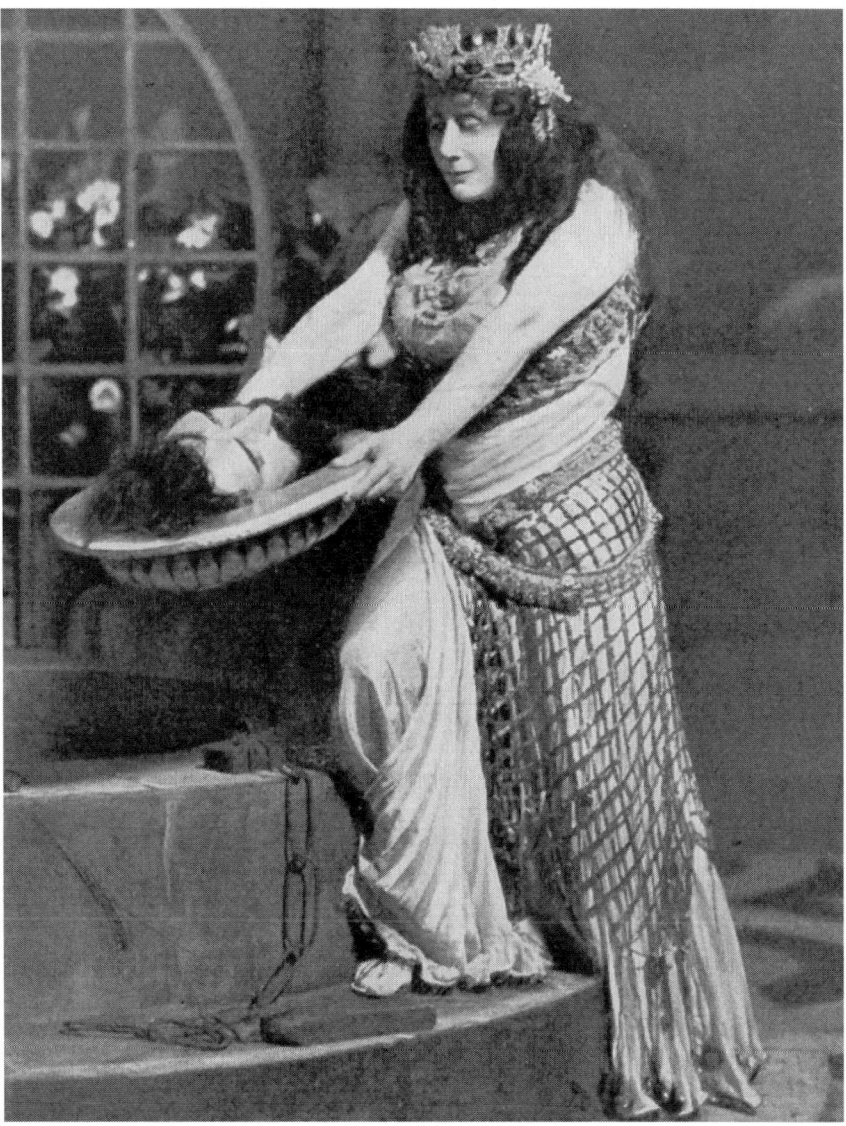

Image 58: *Fremstad Salome*, 1907, Wikimedia Commons.

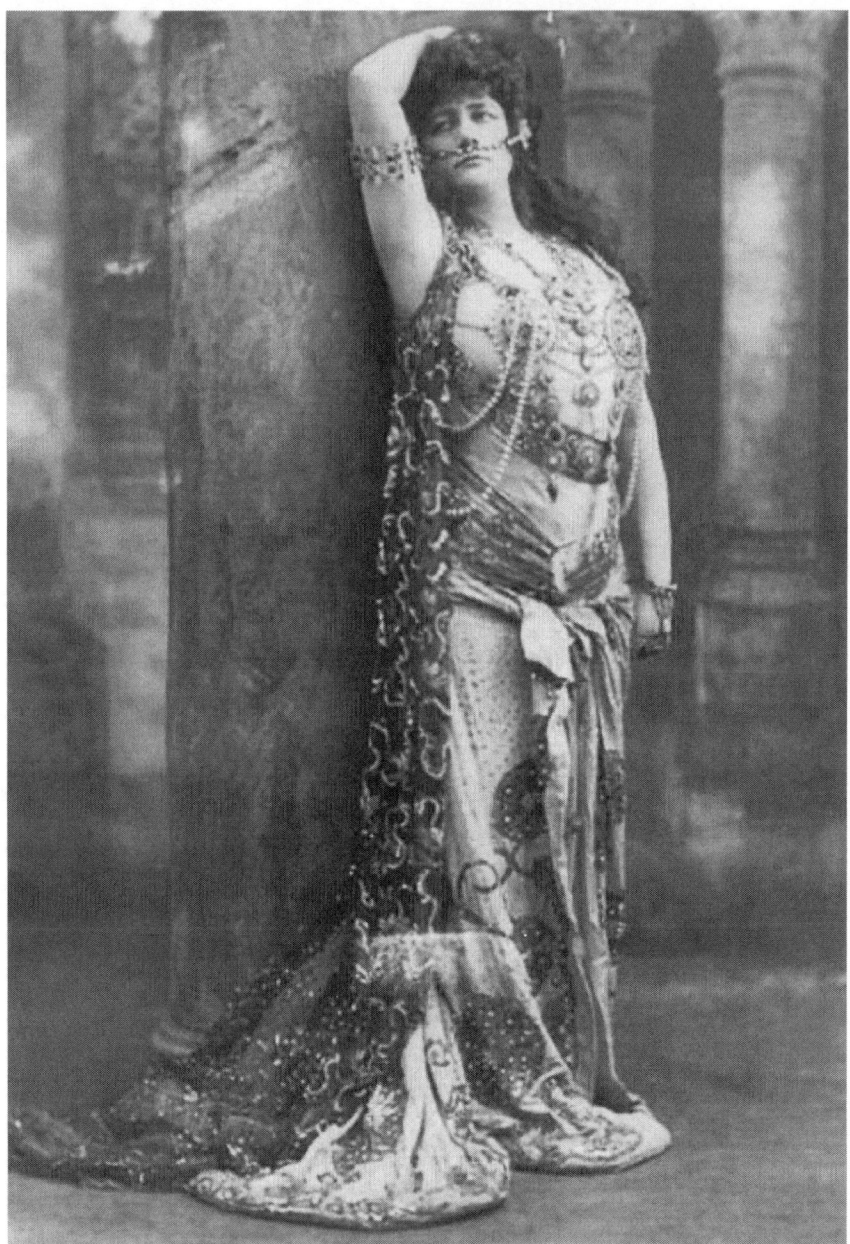

Image 59: *Olive Fremstad as Salome*, Byron photographer, 1907, The Sembrich Collection
(used with permission).

In 1909, Mary Garden sang and danced as Salome at the Manhattan
Opera House. She was a smash hit and was soon touring the country.

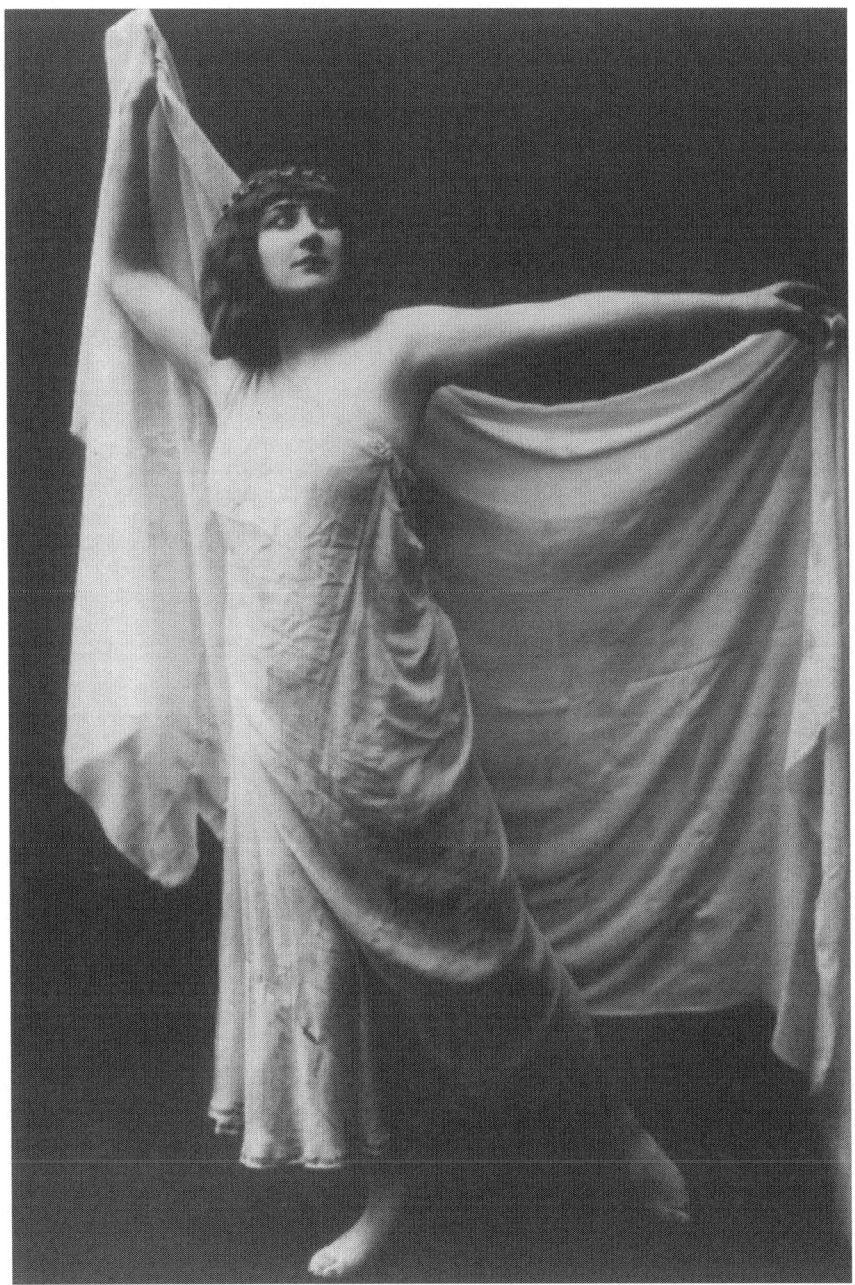

Image 60: *Mary Garden*, ca. 1909, Miscellaneous items in high demand, Library of Congress.

Garden's lusty 1910 Salome portrayal in Chicago astonished the city. The *Chicago Tribune* reported that the audience "filed out of the theater with but slight evidence of approval or appreciation . . . they were oppressed and horrified." Regardless, Garden remained in high demand to perform Salome for many years.

Marcella Craft is among the most famous of the American Salomes. Strauss himself sought her out for the role, and she performed it with great brio and a flair for the dramatic.

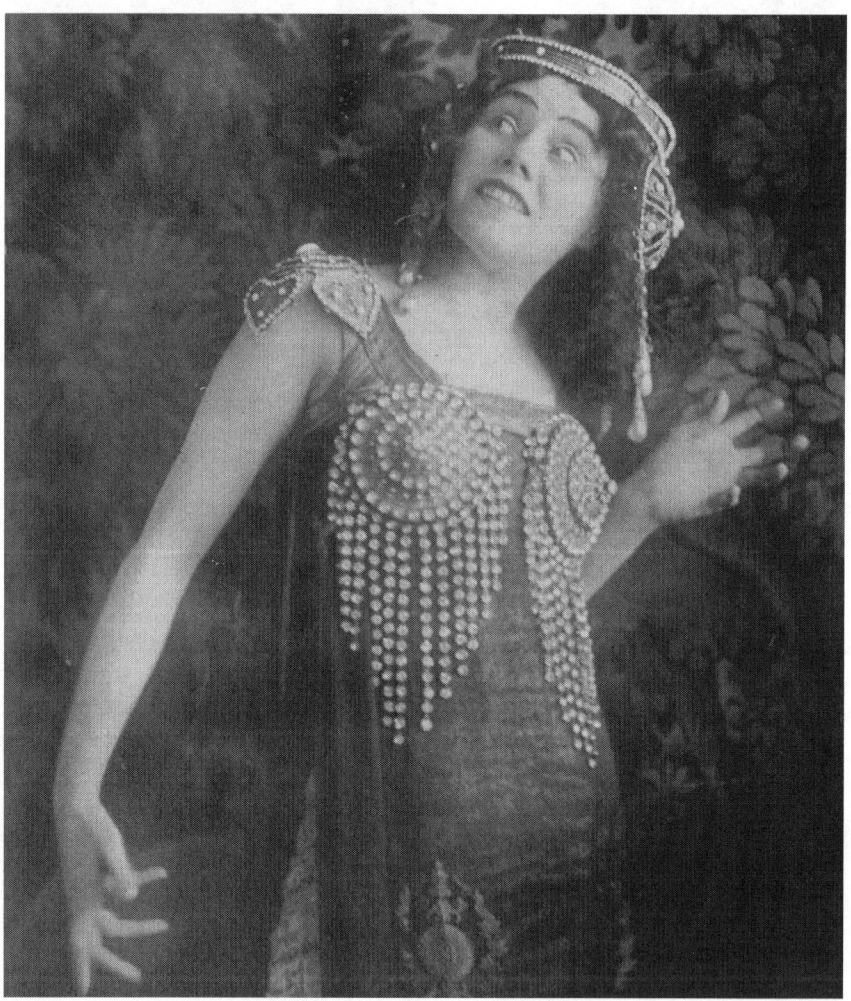

Image 61: *Marcella Craft as "Salome,"* ca. 1910, Bain News Service, Library of Congress.

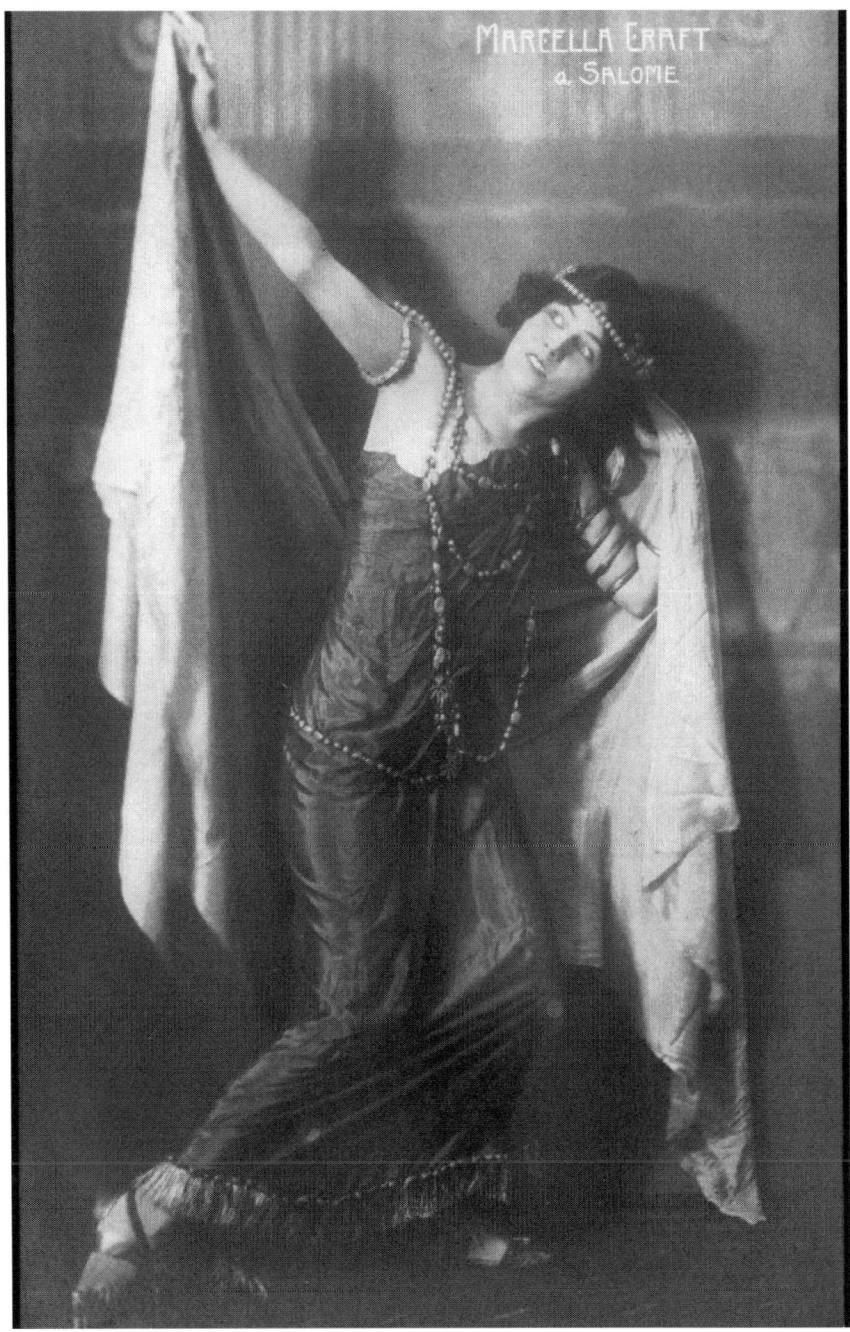

Image 62: *Marcella Craft als Salome,* ca. 1910, Frankfurt am Main: Stadt- und Univ.-
Bibliothek, collection F. N. Manskopf (used with permission).

While the Strauss composition is the most famous Salome operatic vehicle, at least two other composers tackled the story. In 1881, Jules Massenet wrote *Hérodiade,* which features a Salome said to be more spiritual than sensual.

Antoine Mariotte created *Salomé* in 1908, also based on Wilde's play. Described as "less sexually charged" than Strauss's work, the opera's staging history is not extensive.

The Swiss Lucienne Bréval is perhaps the most famous singer associated with both works.

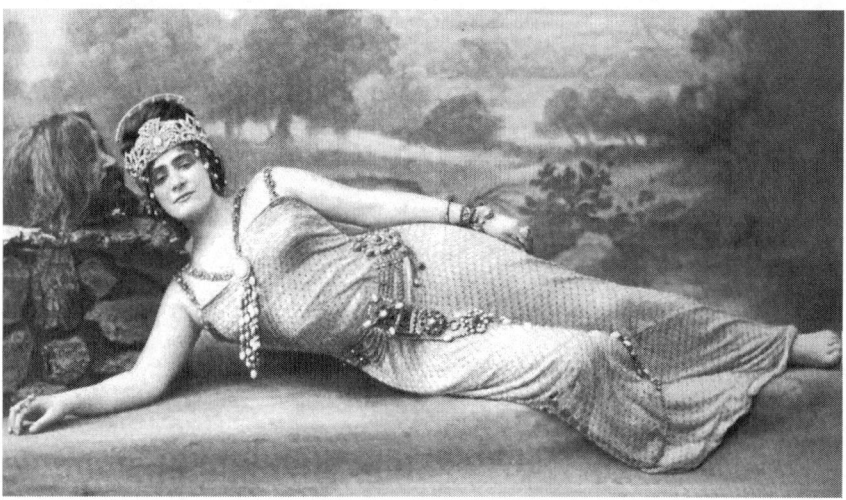

Image 63: *Salome - Mlle. Lucienne Bréval,* ca. 1910, *Le Theatre,* HathiTrust.

CHAPTER 4 - ART DANCE: MAUD ALLAN AND CONTEMPORARIES

A self-taught Canadian dancer, Maud Allan, raised Salomania to a fever pitch after her 1908 London debut, dancing barefoot to Marcel Rémy's musical composition, *Vision of Salome*. Allan is now largely forgotten, a fate that seemed unimaginable at the height of her fame.

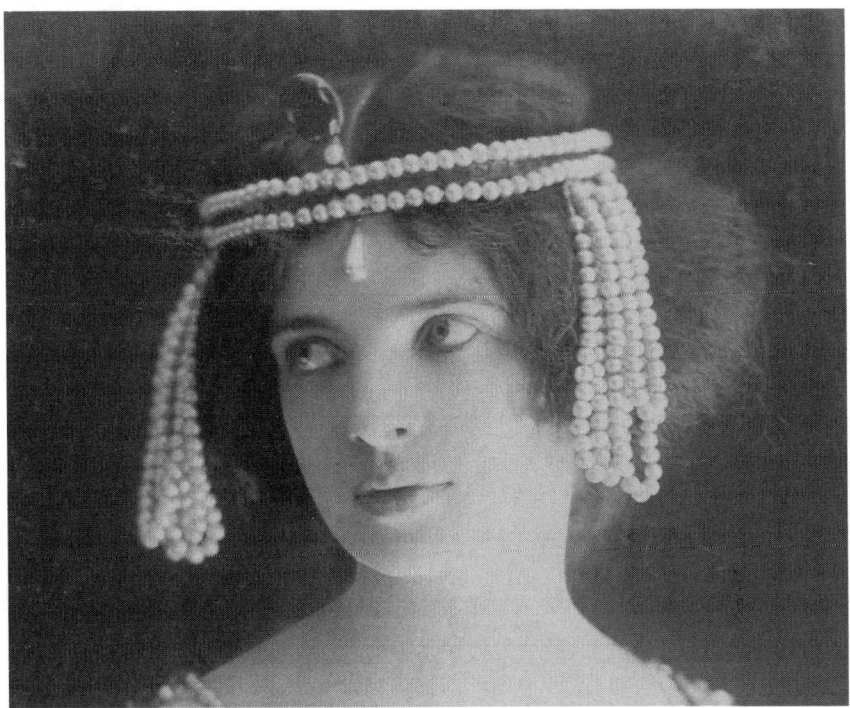

Image 64: *[Maud Allan]*, ca. 1910, Gallica, Bibliothèque nationale de France.

"Exotic dancing" such as Allan's had a history of controversy. The World's Columbian Exposition in 1893 Chicago introduced the public to belly dancers supposedly from the mysterious Orient (at least one was from New Jersey).

Anthony Comstock, a crusading government inspector, branded the belly dance as indecent and tried, without success, to suppress it. The act was so popular that cabarets soon offered dancers doing a variant dance known as the hoochie-coochie.

In 1895 Paris, the American Loie Fuller was among the first to present a Salome-inspired dance. Famous for her skirt-swirling "serpentine dance," Fuller's Salome failed to impress critics who found her performance devoid of a necessary "aura of unreality, ineffability, and mystery."

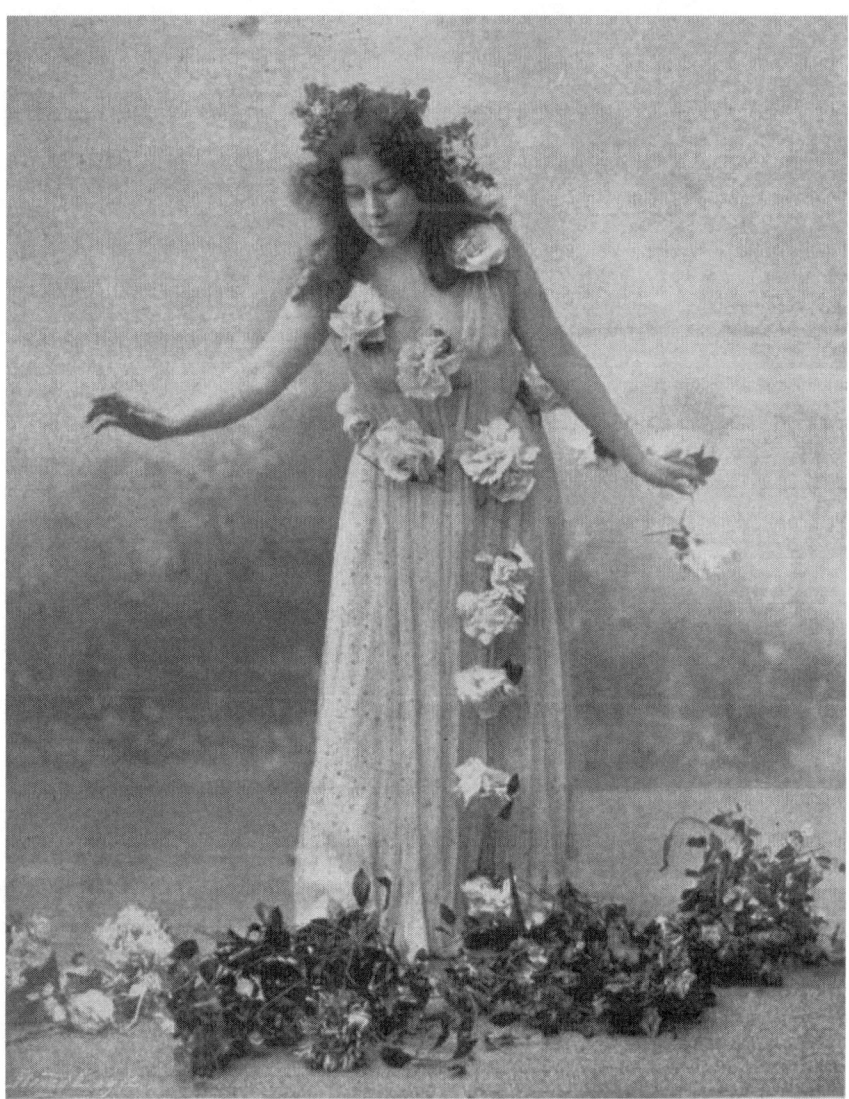

Image 65: *Loie Fuller in Salome costume*, 1895, Jerome Robbins Dance Division, New York Public Library.

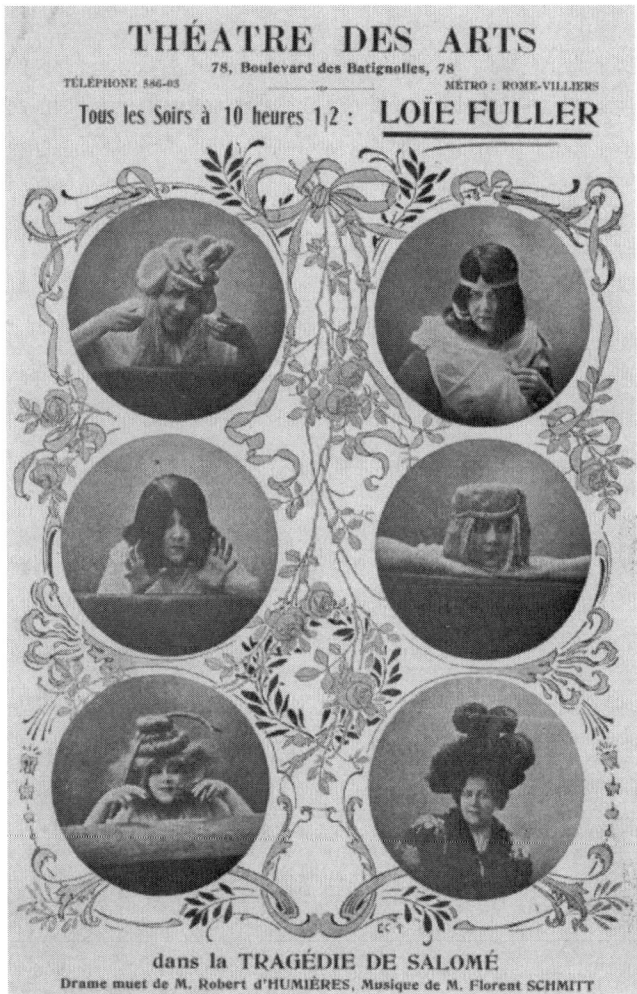

Image 66: *Programme Théâtre des Arts Loie Fuller*, 1907, Wikimedia Commons.

Fuller reprised Salome in 1907 Paris, dancing to Florent Schmitt's ballet *Tragédie de Salomé*. Reviews were lukewarm, although the *Les Annales du théâtre et de la musique* wrote:

"Under colors of various lights . . . in which she seems to swim like in a fluid, the dancer of charm and grace, waving supple arms and fast legs, evolves sometimes with languor, sometimes with violence, always in fair and harmonious rhythms."

At the time of Allan's 1908 triumph, Isadora Duncan was the best-known practitioner of what was known as barefoot dance. She pioneered "art dancing," a style apart from the conservative strictures of classical ballet. Dressed as a Grecian goddess in a flowing toga, she danced with startling freedom and expressive variety.

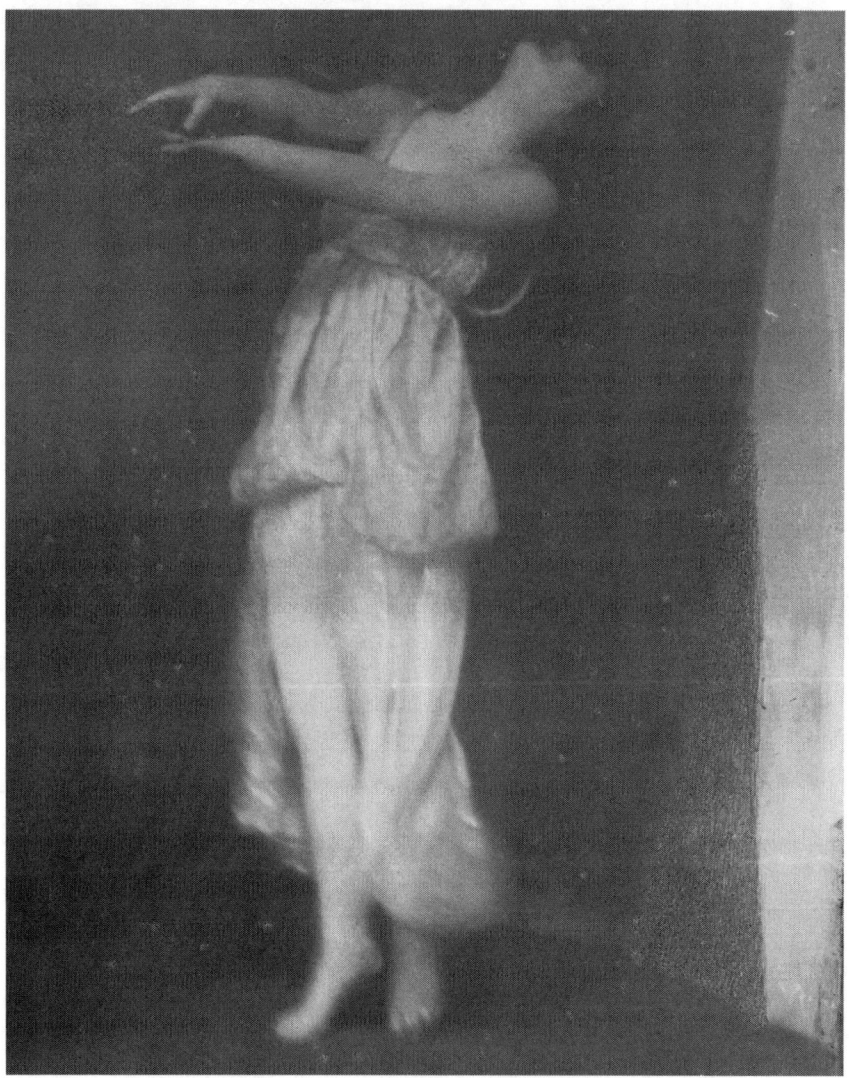

Image 67: *Isadora Duncan Dancer*, ca. 1915-23, Genthe Photograph Collection, Library of Congress.

Duncan initially received a mixed reception. Critics debated her artistic merits; some saw her as brilliant and transformative, while others dismissed her as a crackpot.

Maud Allan had things going for her that Duncan did not. King Edward VII had previously endorsed Allan's dancing with great enthusiasm after a private show. The king had enormous influence among the fashionable London elite, and his stamp of approval automatically put her in demand.

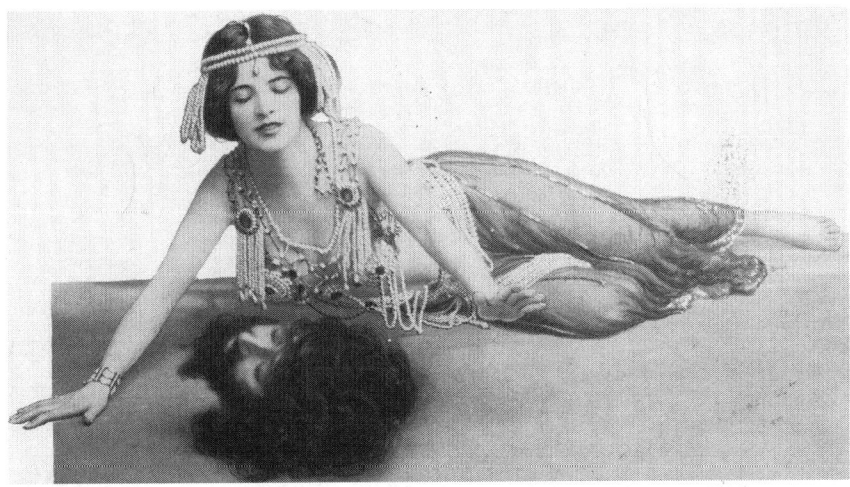

Image 68: *Maude* [sic] *Allan A Stage Dancer*, University of Washington Libraries, Special Collections, JWS26200 (used with permission).

Allan also danced in a "Salome costume" of beads and sheer fabric, drawing upon the popularity of the exotic Orient in general and Strauss's opera in particular.

Allan's performance drew a rapturous response from many. One reviewer piled on the purple prose:

> Her naked feet, slender and arched, beat a sensual measure. The pink pearls slip amorously about her throat and bosom as she moves, while the long strands of jewels that float from the belt about her waist float languorously apart from the sheen of her smooth hips . . . The desire that

flames from her eyes and bursts in hot gusts from her scarlet mouth infect the very air with the madness of passion. Swaying like a white witch, with yearning arms and hands that plead, Maud Allan is such a delicious embodiment of lust that she might win forgiveness for the sins of such wonderful flesh. [As Salome, she twists] her body like a silver snake eager for its prey, panting with hot passion, the fire of her eyes scorching like a living furnace.

While Allan was not a political rebel, she served as a change agent. Petra Dierkes-Thrun writes:

As Salomé, she also inhabited a dangerously assertive and forceful femininity . . . [some] identified Allan as a feminist and as an artist whose *Vision of Salomé* encouraged ladies and ordinary women to break codes of modesty in clothes and behavior at a time when the suffragettes were marching in the streets.

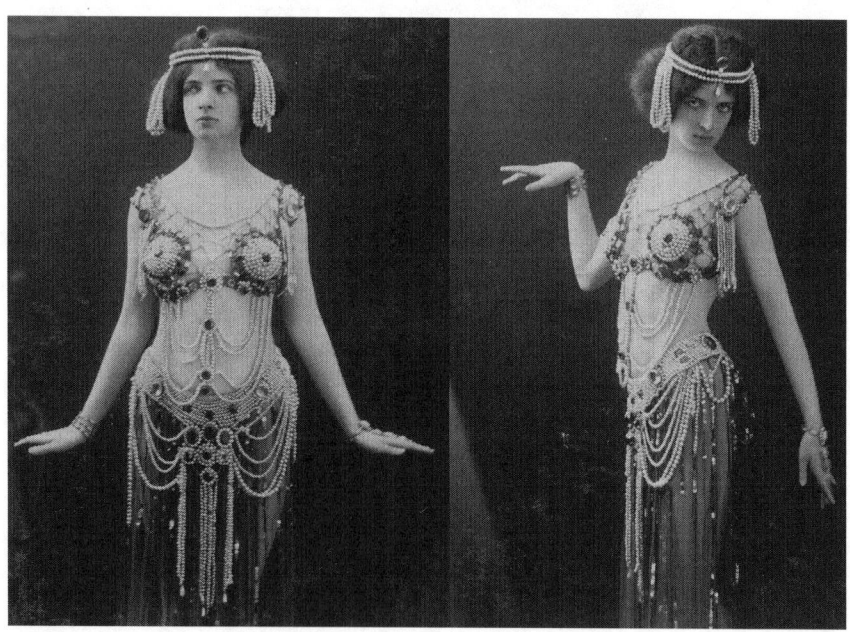

Image 69: *[Maud Allan]*, ca. 1910, Gallica, Bibliothèque nationale de France.

Others judged her act less favorably from an artistic standpoint. In *The Saturday Review of Politics, Literature, Science and Art,* Max Beerbohm observed that Allan did not convey much, if any, lust. "I cannot imagine a more lady-like performance," he wrote.

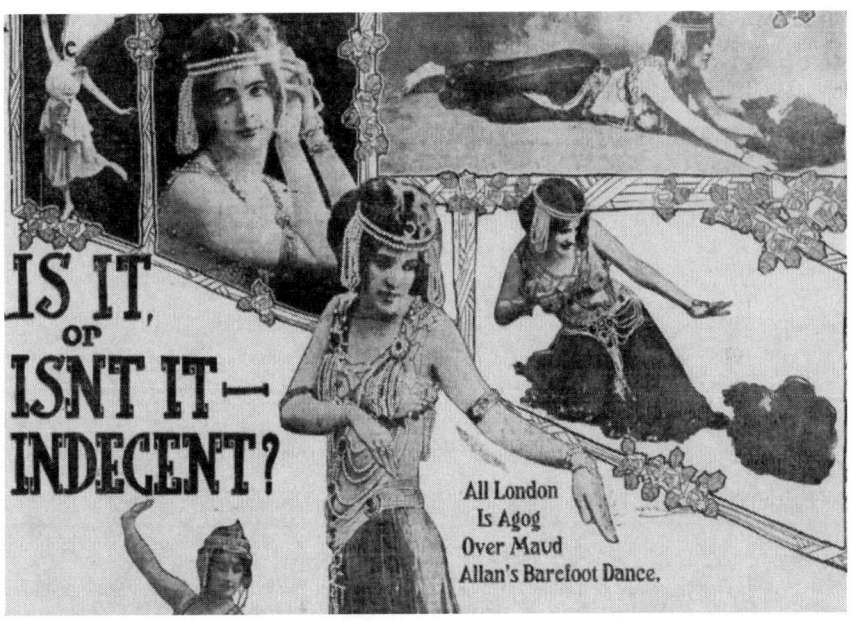

IS IT, or ISNT IT— INDECENT?

All London Is Agog Over Maud Allan's Barefoot Dance.

Image 70: *Photo Montage, The San Francisco Examiner,* 12 July 1908, Newspapers.com.

Beerbohm went on to say that "Some six or seven years ago, there arrived in London a certain Miss Isidora [sic] Duncan . . . who did not succeed in obtaining a public engagement." Noting that Duncan originated Allan's dance style, he writes that those who have seen both perform agree "that Miss Allan's dancing is by far the less remarkable." That Allan succeeded where Duncan did not "is as an amusing instance of the power of mere fluke in human affairs."

Whatever the merits of Allan's dancing, her fame was brief. Her popularity was already in decline when, in 1918, an English gadfly accused her of membership in "the cult of the clitoris." This odd phrase was an oblique reference to lesbianism, and Allan sued for libel. But, like Oscar Wilde twenty years before, she lost in court and her career faltered.

Europe generally had a more tolerant view of how much skin a dancer could show. But the enigmatic Adorée (or Viola) Villany—who was either French (born in Rouen), Hungarian ("The Pearl of the Puszta"), or a German Jew (born in Danzig as Erna Reich)—pushed the limit with nudity on stage.

The *Grazer Volksblatt* states she began performing in the Berlin Überbrettl cabaret (perhaps in 1902) as "a Duncan imitator." Karl Toepfer writes that she first came to public notice in 1905, performing the Dance of the Seven Veils while simultaneously speaking Salome's final monologue from Wilde's play.

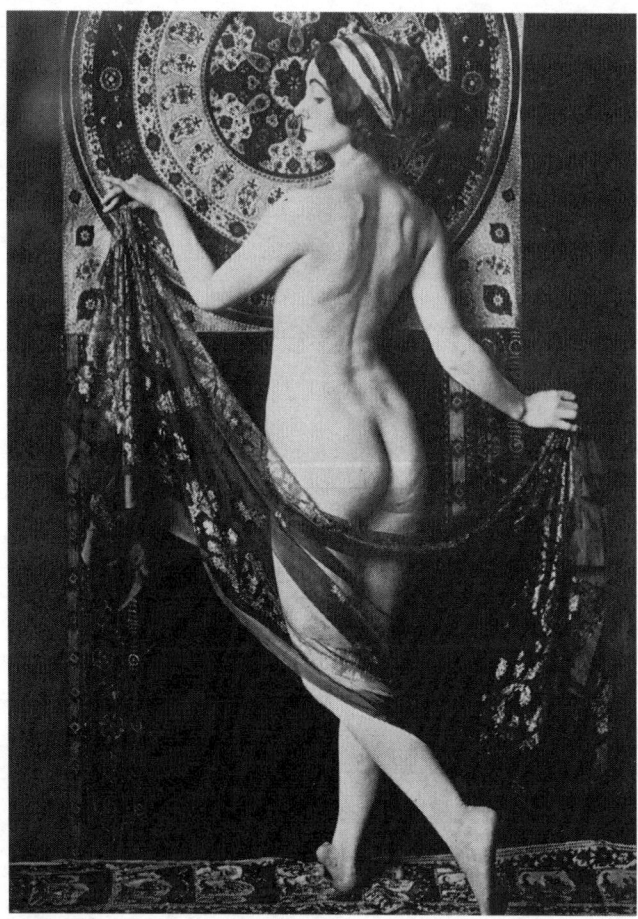

Image 71: *Adorée Villany*, ca. 1914, Bain News Service, Library of Congress.

SEX, ART, and SALOME

In 1911, Munich police arrested Villany for indecent exposure after various exotic dances, including one as Salome. Villany defended herself as a "reform dancer," claiming "my unveiled body reveals my soul." Various artists came to her defense, and a jury acquitted her based on "the higher interests of art."

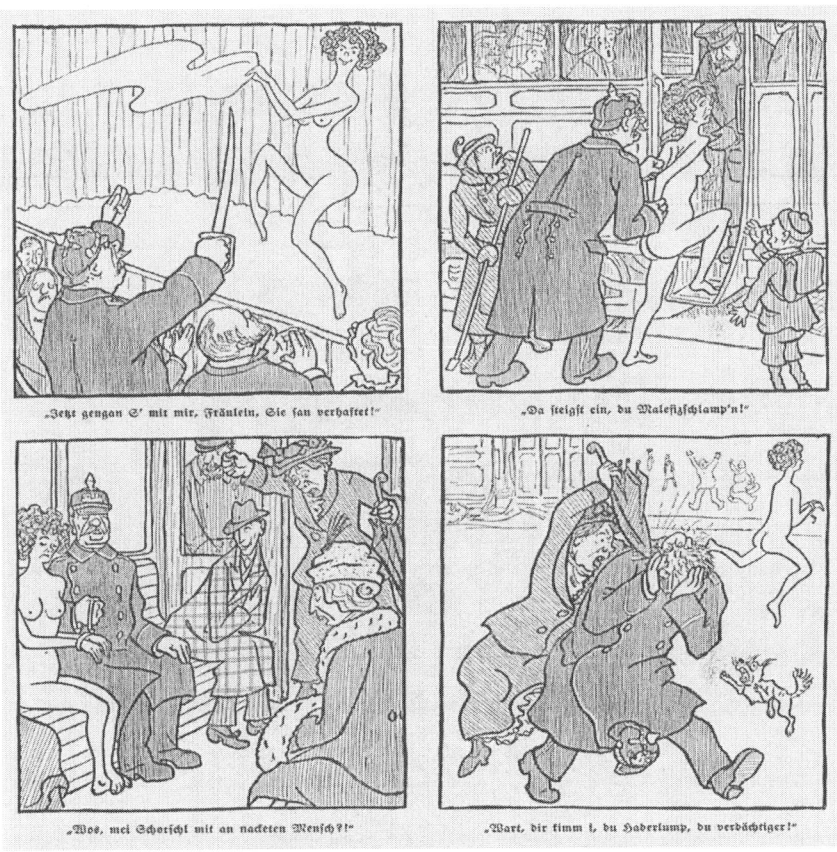

Image 72: *Die Nachttänzerin [satirizing Villany's Munich arrest]*, *Simplicissimus*, 1911, Simplicissimus 1896 to 1944 Online Project.

Villany wrote in 1912 that hers was the only authentic Dance of the Seven Veils, as she performed it as "Huysmans dreamed, as Regnault painted, and as Oscar Wilde imagined." She denounced other interpretations as "tame Salome dancers" who showed "thoughtless movement" by confining "their emotions into squiggly pirouettes."

Villany appeared quite often in the German press from about 1911 to 1914, but I found no mention of her after 1927.

The Russian actress and dancer Ida Rubinstein also broke the rules of decorum. She started in 1908 Saint Petersburg, performing as Salome in Wilde's play. Rubinstein also staged the Dance of the Seven Veils as a separate show, in which she reportedly danced naked.

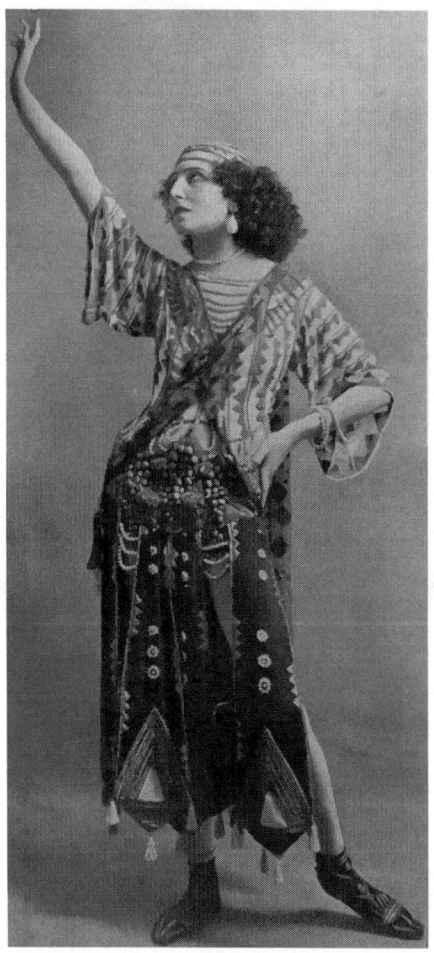

Image 73: *Ida Rubinstein as Salome*, 1912, Wikimedia Commons.

Tall and boyishly thin, Rubinstein made a striking visual impact on stage. She came to the attention of Sergei Diaghilev, manager of the

Ballets Russes. Despite Rubinstein's limited formal training, she danced in several Ballets Russes productions. She performed as Salome on multiple occasions, including in Florent Schmitt's *Tragédie de Salomé* with the Paris Opera in 1919.

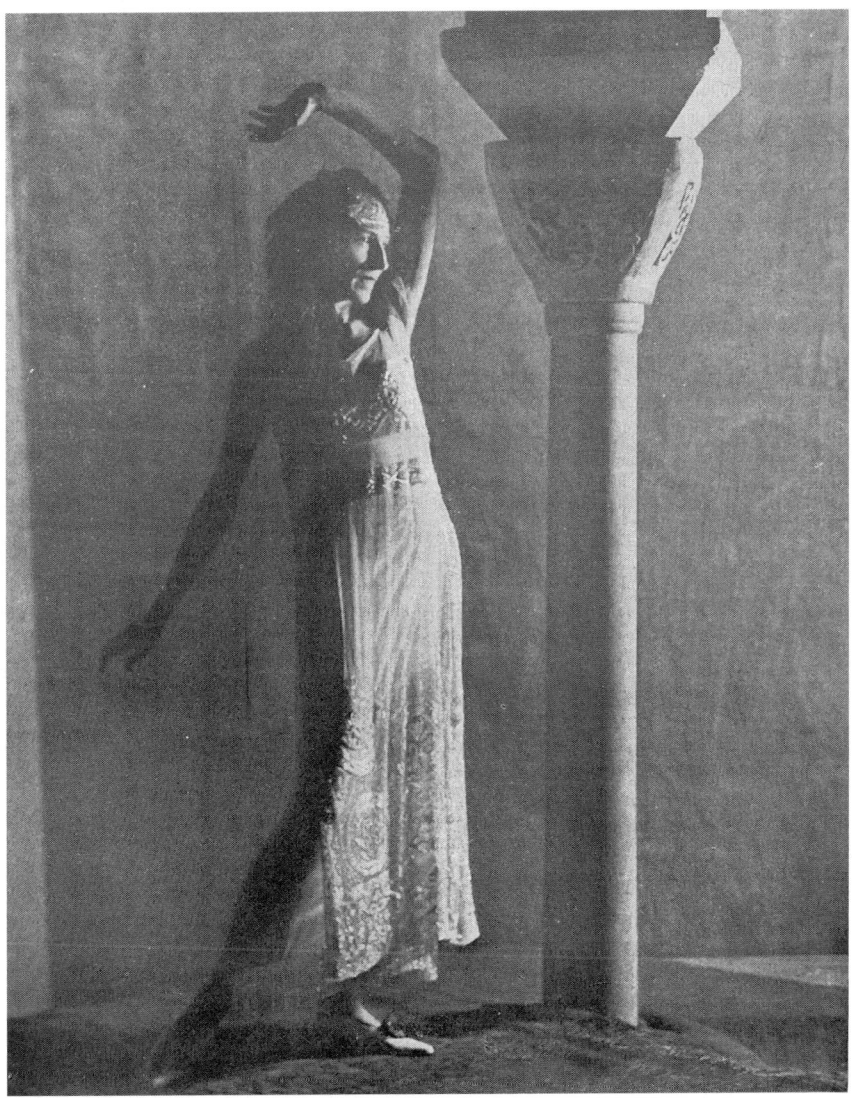

Image 74: *Ida Rubenstein as Salome with Paris Opera*, 1919, collection of the author.

Schmitt reworked his 1907 version of *Tragédie de Salomé*, cutting its length in half and intensifying the music and choreography. Apart from

Rubinstein's performance, memorable stagings of the revised ballet (sometimes termed a "mute drama") took place in 1912 and 1913.

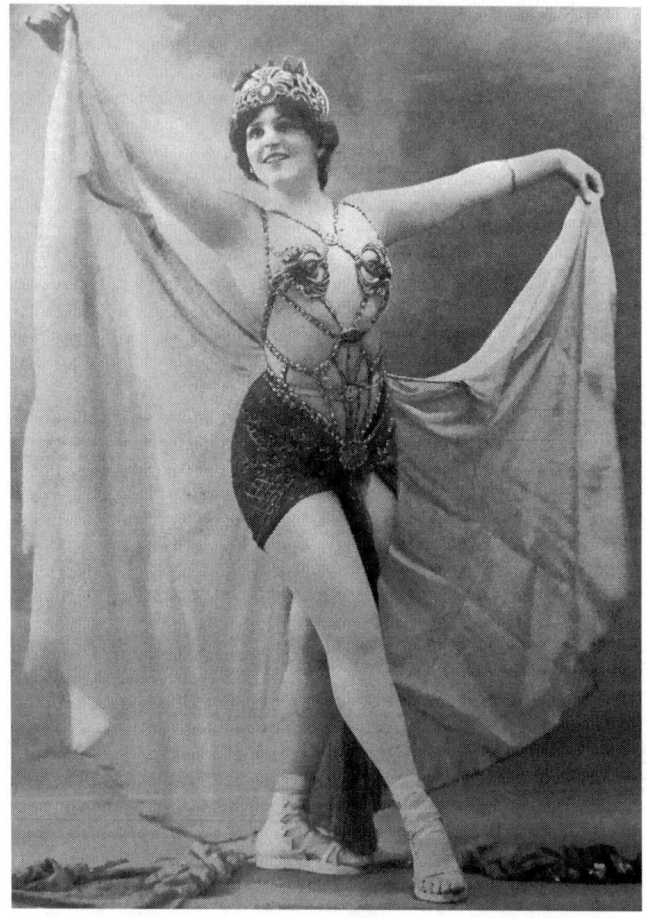

Image 75: *Mlle. Natacha Trouhanowa dans sa danse des "Sept Voiles" de "Salome,"* 1912, *Comœdia Illustré*, HathiTrust.

The 1912 Paris production of *Tragédie de Salomé* starred prima ballerina Natasha Trouhanova. She drew praise for her beauty and graceful movement, which "softened everything into Venus."

Tamara Karsarvina and the Ballets Russes staged Schmitt's work again in Paris the next year. Despite sets and costumes that conjured "a spectacular Art Nouveau aesthetic," most critics regarded the show as an overly experimental flop. One reviewer, however, found Karsarvina "a majestic Salome" with "extraordinary qualities of grace, lightness and power."

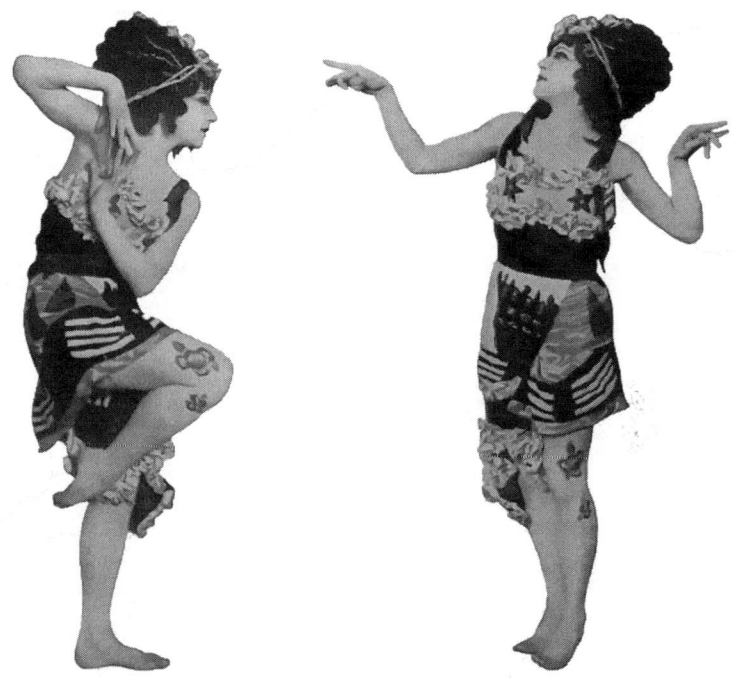

Image 76: *Mlle. Karsarvina*, 1913, *Comœdia Illustré*, HathiTrust.

Salomania also figured in the life of modern dance pioneer Ruth St. Denis. An interpreter of Eastern dance, St. Denis performed in Salome-mad 1909 New York. According to Elizabeth Kendall, St. Denis, "whose commercial instinct never failed," wore "Salomé's jeweled harness" and inspired one reviewer to proclaim "Out-Saloméing all the Salomés, Miss St. Denis burst upon dazzled audiences."

Late in her life, St. Denis choreographed and danced as Salome. The *Los Angeles Times* quoted her concept of Salome as:

> A child-woman, a young girl just beginning to be aware of her body but enough of a child to lose herself in the fantasies of games. Her dance involves imaginative transformations into various creatures—a peacock, a butterfly—to beguile Herod's mind as well as his senses.

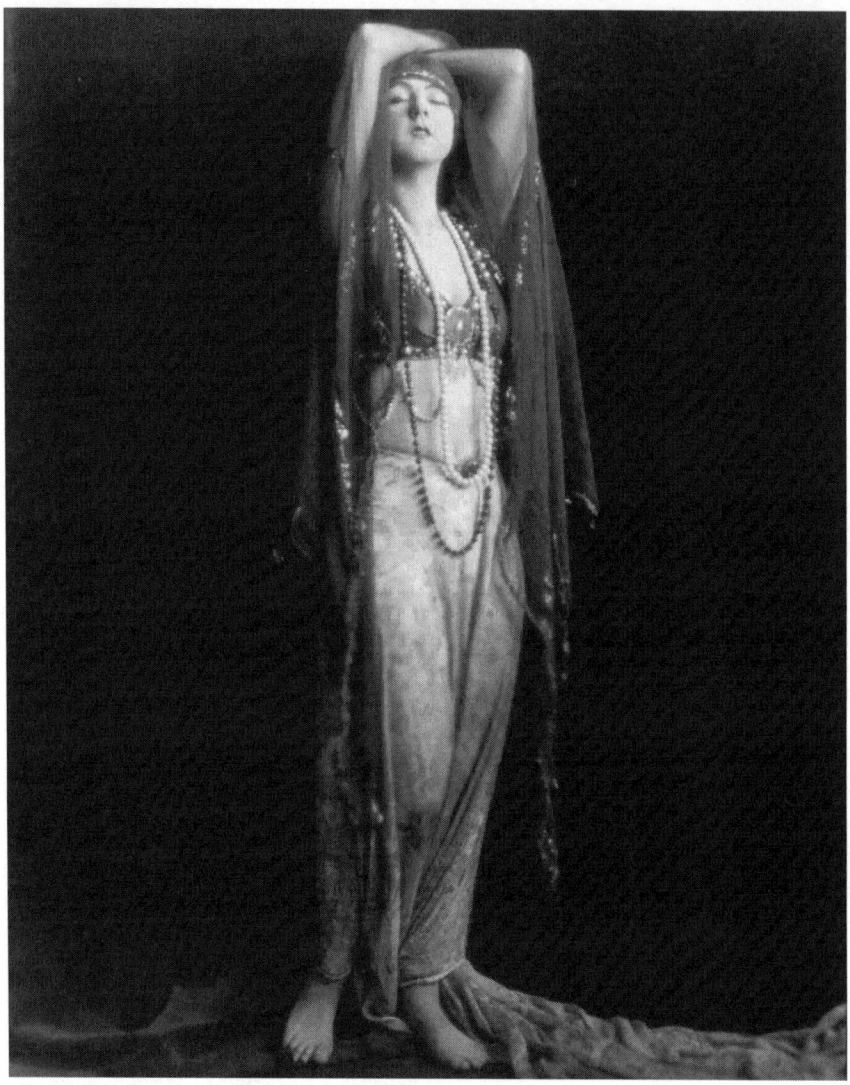

Image 77: *Ruth St. Denis*, by Orval Hixon, 1918, Wikimedia Commons.

St. Denis danced the role in 1938 and again in 1948 at age 69.

RUTH ST. DENIS
in "SALOME"

Image 78: *Advertisement, Asheville Citizen-Times, 5 July 1938, Newspapers.com.*

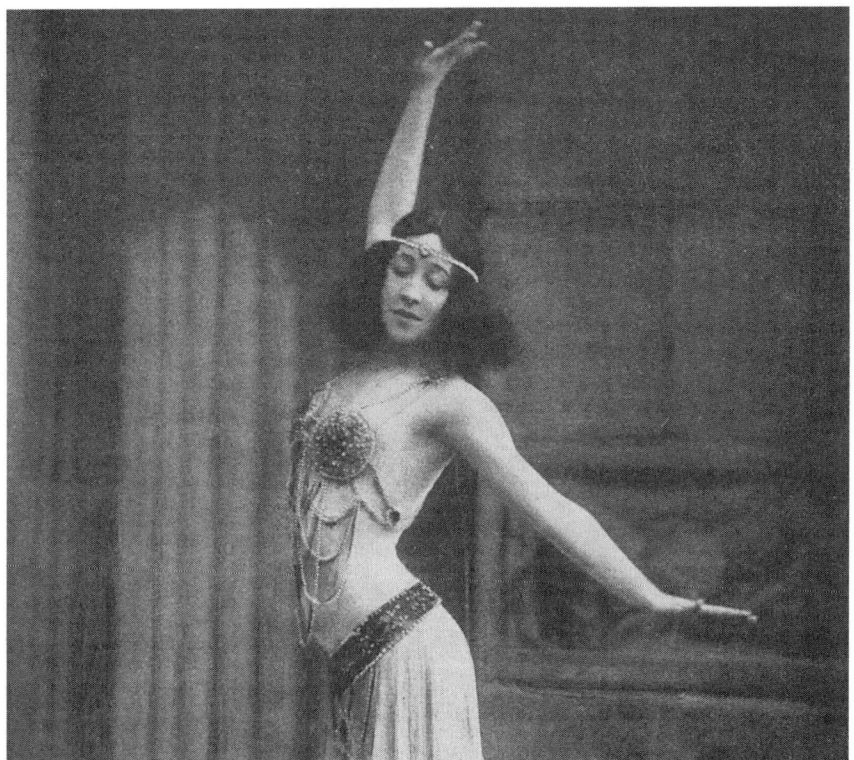

Image 79: *A Dansarina Belga, Actualmente no Municipal, Felyne Verbist, na Salomé*, 1915, Ibero-Amerikanisches Institut - Preußischer Kulturbesitz.

The Belgian ballerina Felyne Verbist also danced as Salome.

Verbist was among the first European prima ballerinas to visit South America, and she may have influenced the Afro-Cuban dancer Dulce Maria Morales Cervantes, stage name La Perla Negra. In 1913, Morales moved to Valencia, Spain, to perform cakewalks, classical dance, and rumbas.

La Perla Negra's repertoire also included "Visión de Salomé (Cuchipanda)." As Kiko Mora explains, "cuchipanda" is a dance related to tango, rhumba, and fandango. Morales's Salome interpretation would have been a remarkable blend of Orientalist art dance and contemporary Afro-Cuban dance.

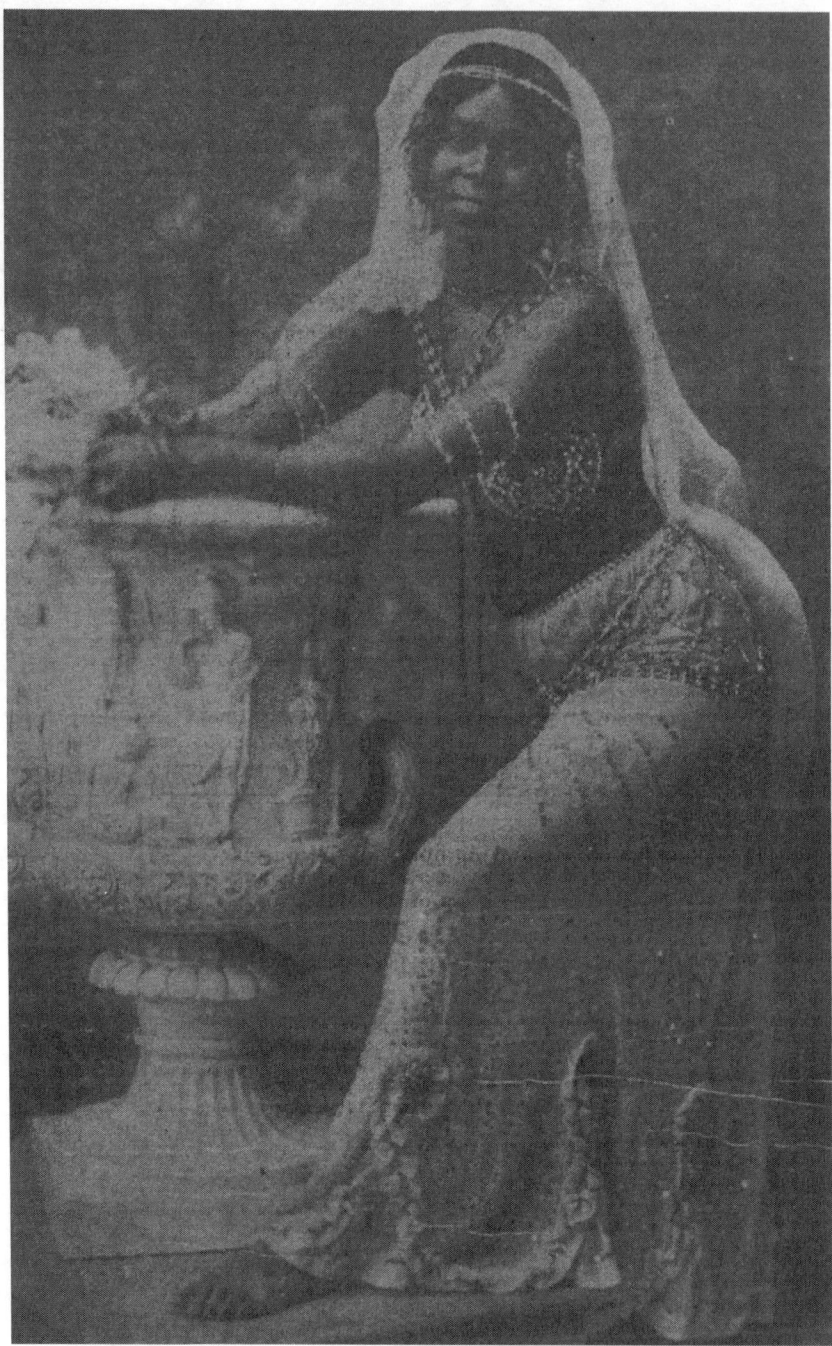

Image 80: *[Maria Morales - La Perla Negra]*, 1917, *La Nación*, La Biblioteca Nacional de España.

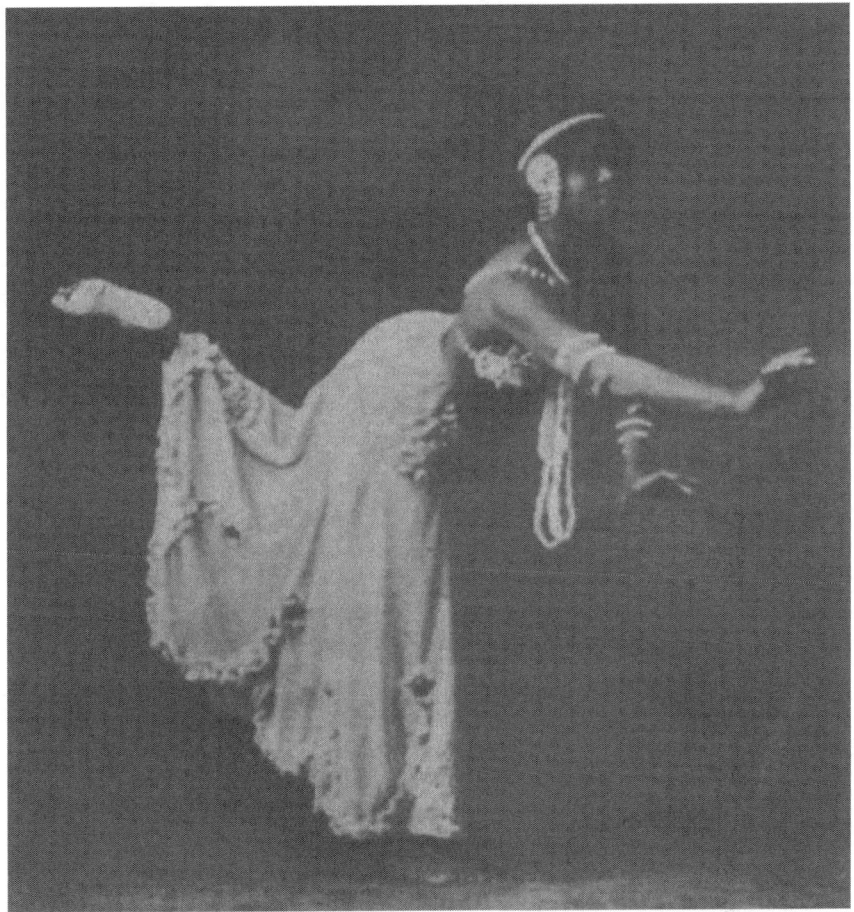

Image 81: *[Maria Morales - La Perla Negra]*, 1915, *Eco Artistico*, La Biblioteca Nacional de España.

Morales was hugely popular upon her arrival in Spain and, according to Mora, was "The first Afro-American to perform on a Valencian stage and, quite possibly, the first in the entire country in the 20th century."

Morales is also notable for bridging multiple styles, including authentic Cuban dance (such as the rhumba), the Spanish variety-show version of Cuban dance, and avant-garde modern dance.

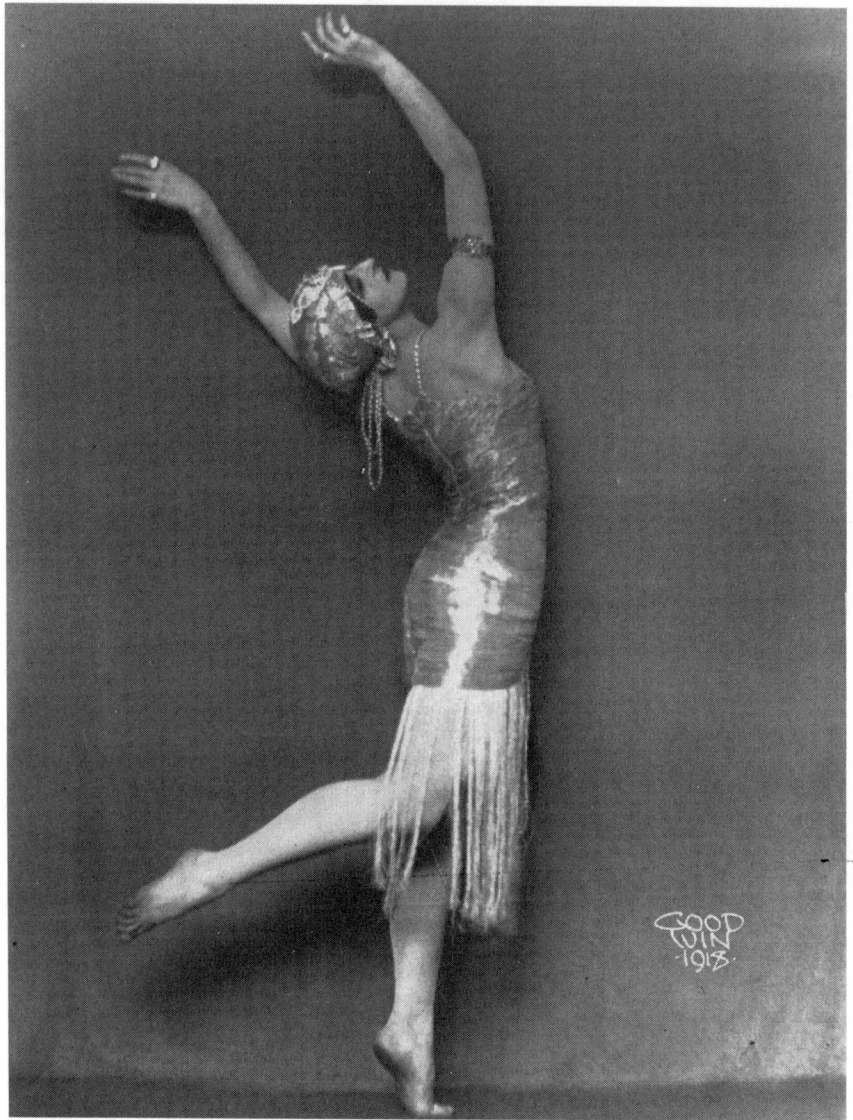

Image 82: *Vera Fokina [dans "Salomè"]*, Good Win photographer, ca. 1919, Gallica, Bibliothèque nationale de France.

Theatrical interpretations of Salome continued to evolve after World War I. During 1919-20, ballerina Vera Fokina performed as Salome in Europe and America. The New York *Daily News* hailed her performance as "closely approximating genius" as well as "poignant and subtle."

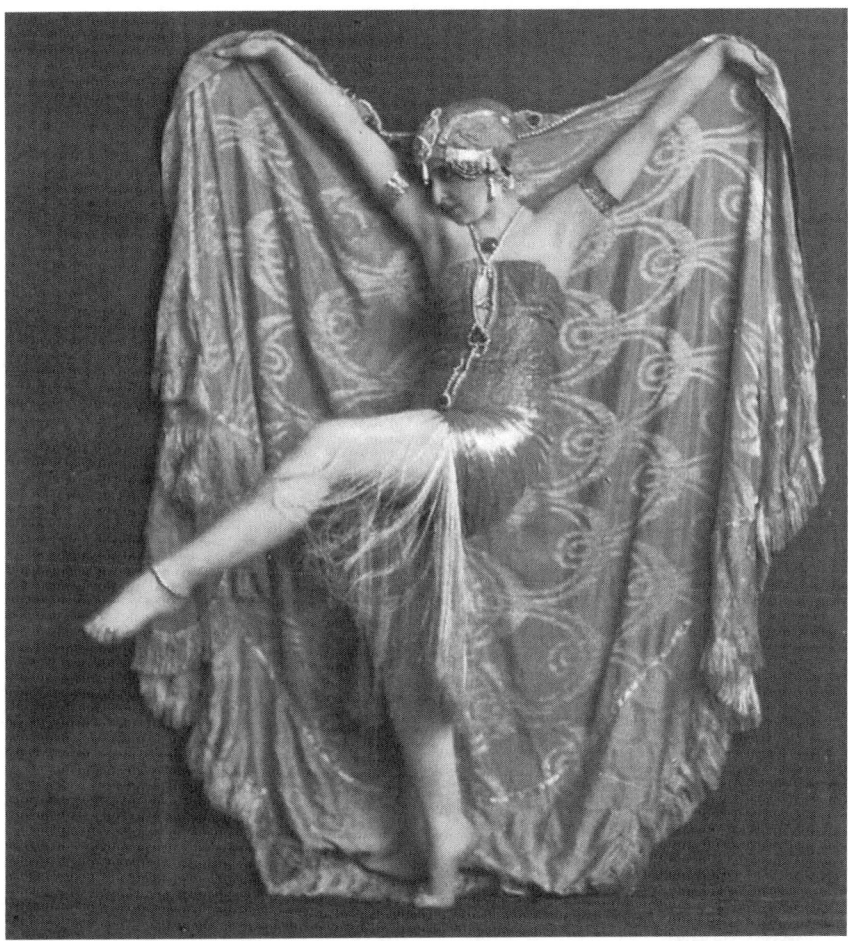

Image 83: *Dance of Salome [Vera Fokina]*, Waldemar Eide photographer, ca. 1920, Internet Archive.

Fokina's husband, dancer and choreographer Mikhail Fokine, originally developed the ballet for Ida Rubinstein and the Ballets Russes.

During the 1920s, Weimar Germany hosted radical new Salome dances, including Anita Berber's nude interpretation. Karl Toepfer states Berber began her Salome dance from "a huge urn filled with blood." After "panting orgasmically," she executed several expert ballet steps before finishing with a crawl back into the urn.

Berber declared that "If everyone had a body like me, everyone would walk around naked." She was infamous for her open bisexuality, drug use and outrageous behavior. "She needed scandal like her daily bread," wrote her contemporary Klaus Mann. "Post-war eroticism, cocaine, Salomé, ultimate perversity—such were the terms the mirage of her glory was made of."

Berber reveled in her shock value, and reportedly hung about Berlin nightspots naked except for a sable wrap, a pet monkey, and a silver container filled with cocaine. The revels did not last long, as she died at age 29. Most sources cite tuberculosis as the cause, although there was a rumor that she died amongst used morphine syringes. According to Mel Gordon, Berliners were by then tired of her antics and she died a "carrion soul that even the hyenas ignored."

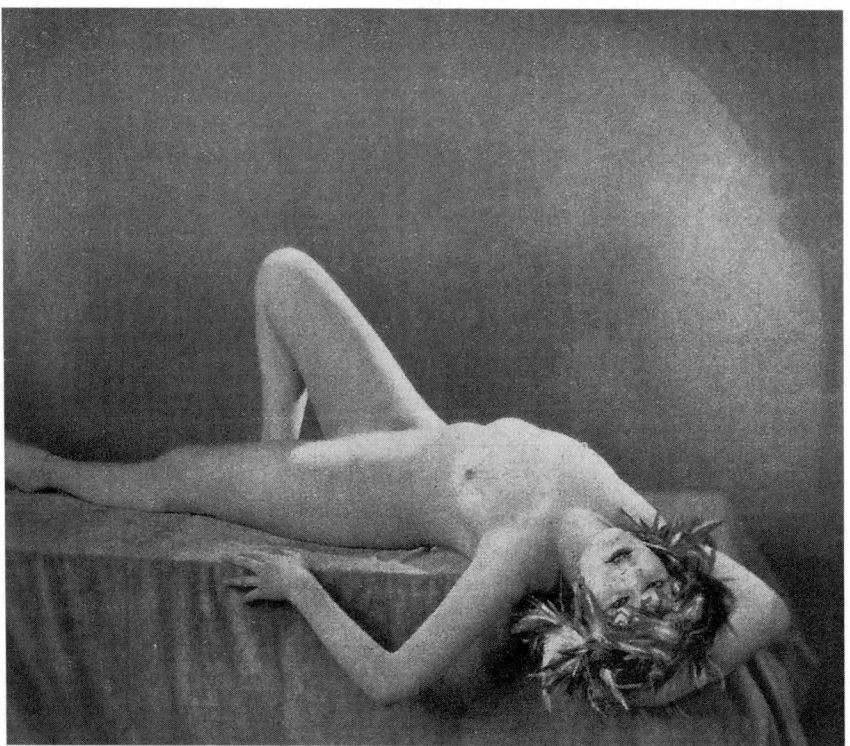

Image 84: *Anita Berber [as Salome]*, Alexander Binder photographer, ca. 1921, Wikimedia Commons.

In 1923, the German dancer and actress Valeska Gert presented a starkly different version of Salome. Gabriele Brandstetter describes it as:

SEX, ART, and SALOME

A new, grotesquely shrill method of representing the physical femme fatale image. In a radically alienated, ruthlessly garish performance, the beautiful, exotic-attractive art nouveau Salome was presented as an outdated cliché of femininity.

Gert danced without music, with women rhythmically howling offstage. Distinct from earlier Salome portrayals, she wore only a simple dress rather than an exotic costume.

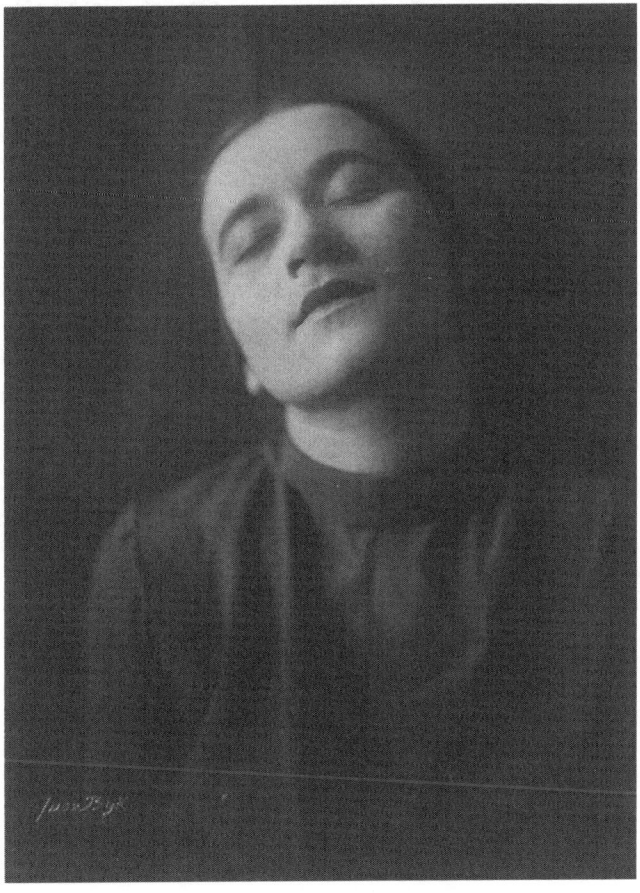

Image 85: *Valeska Gert 'Salome,'* Suse Byk photographer, 1923, Wikimedia Commons.

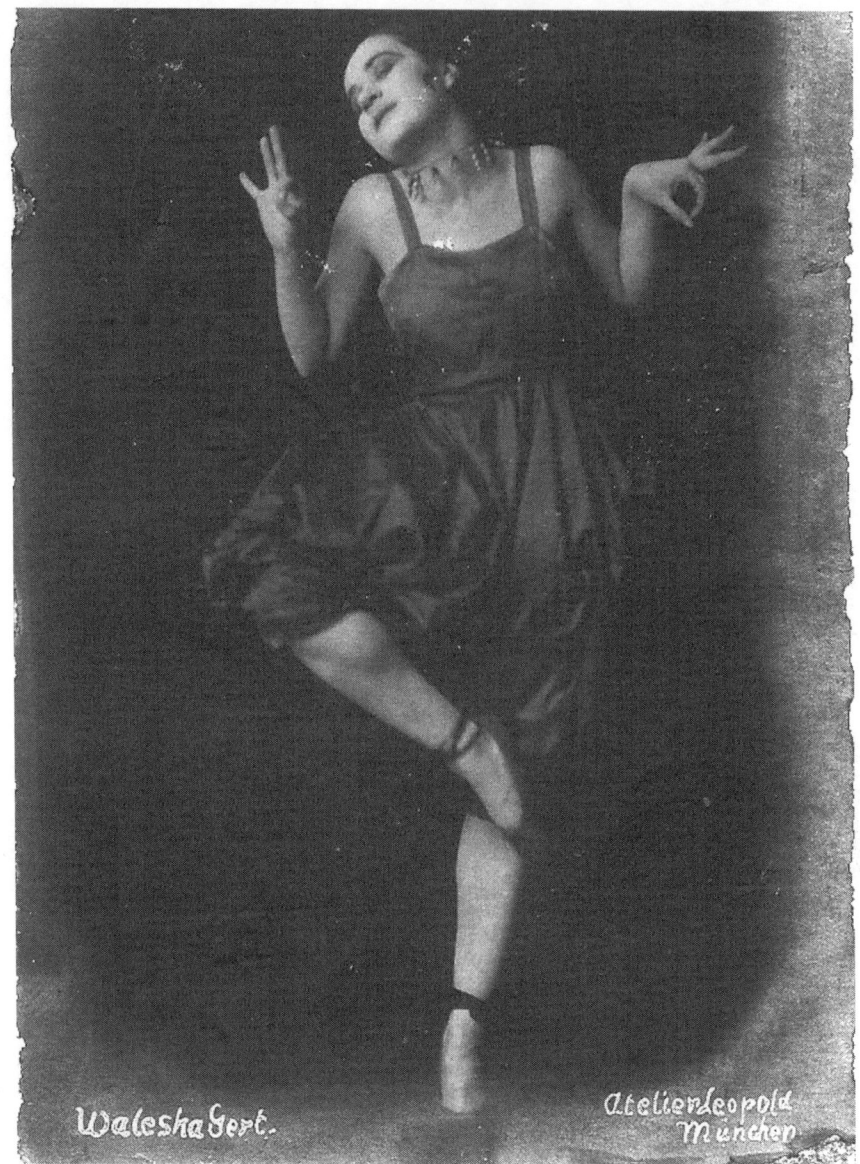

Image 86: *Valeska Gert [Dance in Orange]*, Atelier Leopold, 1918, Wikimedia Commons.

Critics described Gert as "a master of . . . psychological caricature" and her performance as "simultaneously supremely animalistic and supremely divine."

CHAPTER 5 - EXOTIC DANCE: GERTRUDE HOFFMANN, MATA HARI, AND CONTEMPORARIES

In 1905, the New England Watch and Ward Society, an organization devoted to protecting public morals, issued a stern warning in its annual report.

> The advent of Salome has been the debauching agent. It has meant the introduction of a new element of indecency on the stage—the uncovered feet and limbs—and has created a vogue of risqué dances which have tended to deprave public taste. The barriers against the Oriental muscle dances with their bodily contortions and appeal to the baser instincts, have been swept away in a flood of unnatural indecency. Dances hitherto suffered under limitations at our cheaper show houses under a vulgar name have been adopted into polite society under the appellation "Salome Dance."

The problem was long-standing. "For seventeen years," the report noted, "this dance has gone over this country as vaudeville and sideshow to a circus, but now it has risen from its contempt to grand opera."

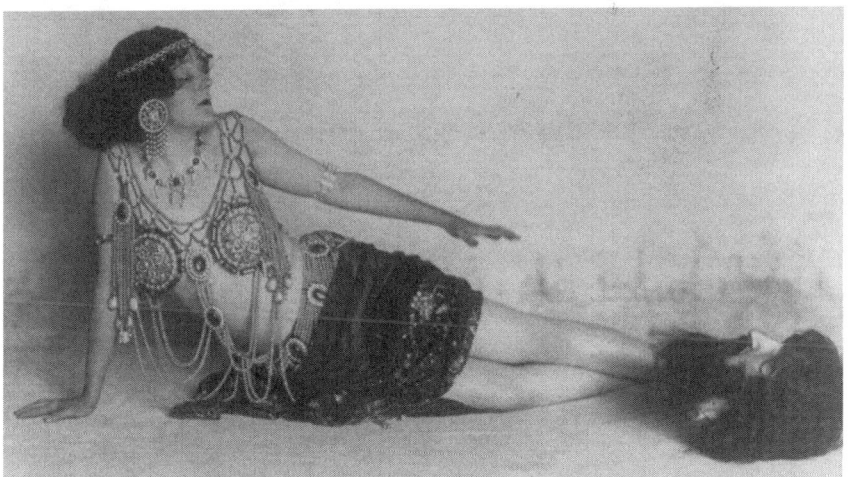

Image 87: *Gertrude Hoffmann*, ca. 1908, Miscellaneous Items in High Demand, Library of Congress.

Little did such groups know how much more Salome-induced indecency was in store.

One of the chief offenders was Gertrude Hoffmann, who rose to fame in 1908 with a salacious "skin Salome" act. Local police arrested Hoffmann more than once for sexy dancing in skimpy beaded costumes.

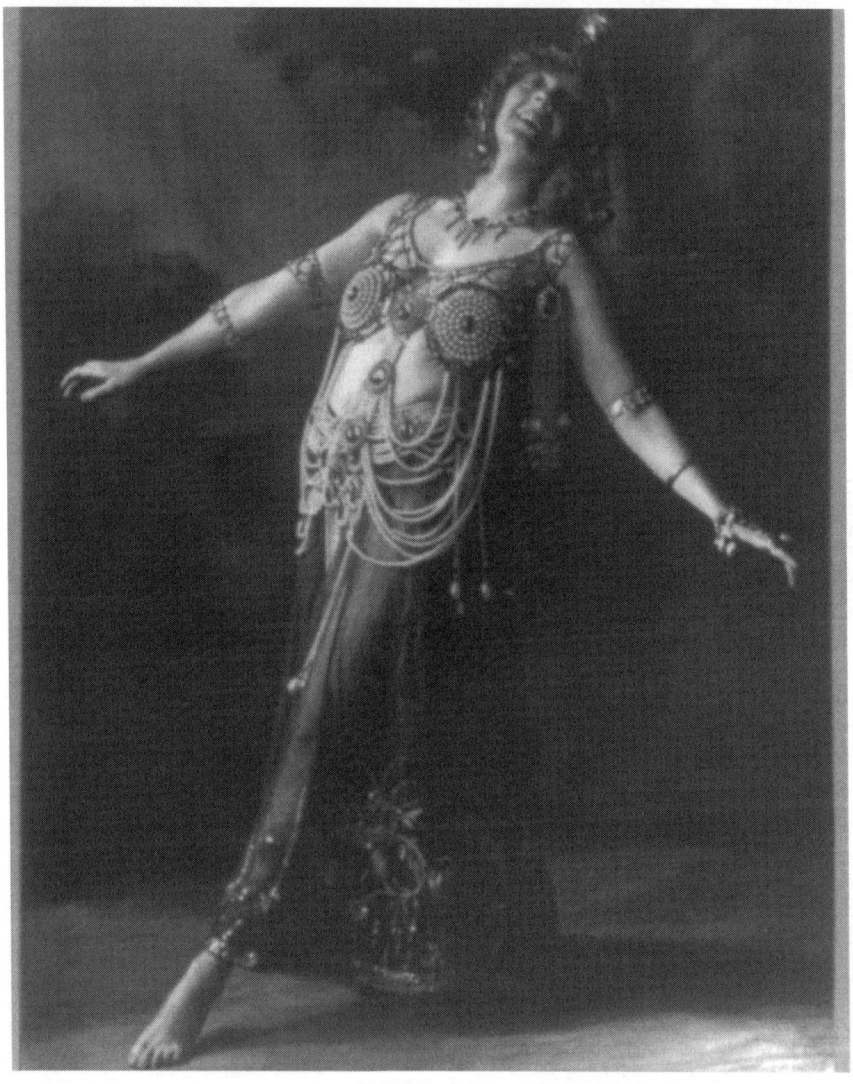

Image 88: *Gertrude Hoffmann*, ca. 1908, Miscellaneous Items in High Demand, Library of Congress.

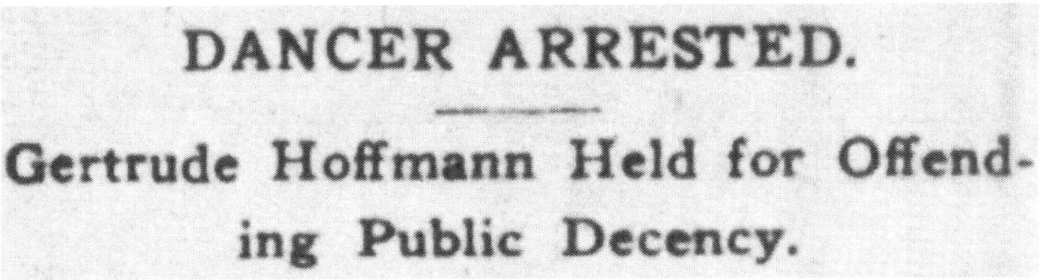

DANCER ARRESTED.

Gertrude Hoffmann Held for Offending Public Decency.

Image 89: Headline, The *Passaic Daily News, 24 July 1909*, Newspapers.com.

Hoffmann, who based her act on Maud Allan's "Vision of Salome," was a sly performer. According to Susan Glenn, Hoffmann used Salome "to enlighten, confound, and satirize the phenomenon of Oriental dancing and her own role in it." Publicity was essential. "Welcoming press coverage that emphasized the orgasmic violence and lust of her performances, Hoffmann was only too happy to see her dances discussed in terms usually reserved for lurid crime reportage."

For added effect, she displayed theatrical indignation when censors intervened. "What kind of a town is this?" she blustered in 1909 to a Kansas City reporter after a judge clamped down on her act. "I have given my dances all over the . . . the United States. I played in the leading cities of New England, where the Puritans came from and where their descendants live and thrive and still preach purity."

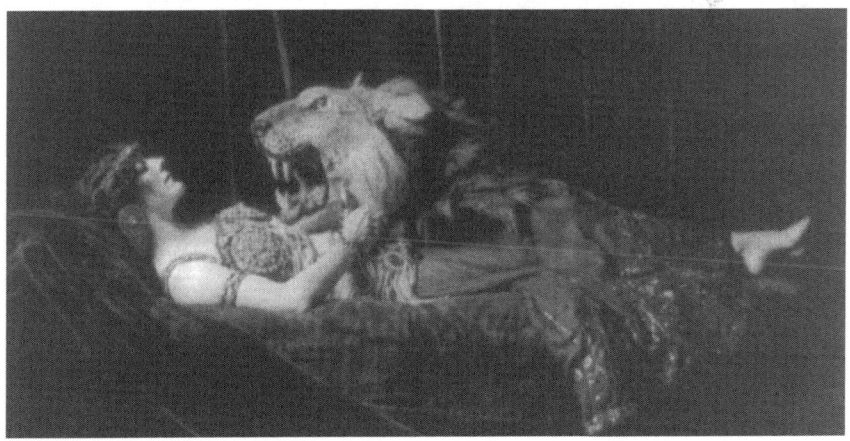

Image 90: *Gertrude Hoffmann*, ca. 1908, Miscellaneous Items in High Demand, ca. 1908, Library of Congress.

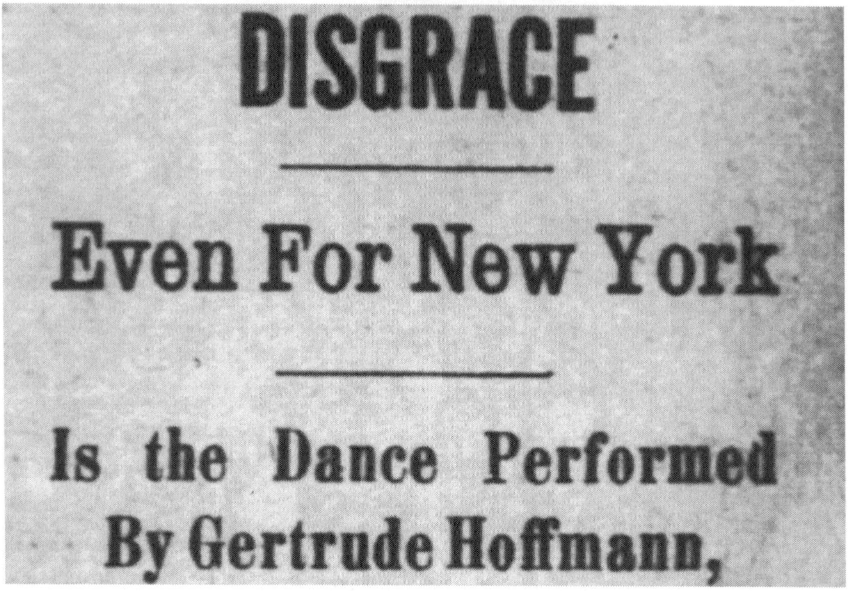

Image 91: Headline, The *Cincinnati Enquirer*, 25 July 1909, Newspapers.com.

Hoffman was far from alone in serving up the outrageous Jewish princess on stages across the nation.

In 1908, *The Sketch* magazine printed a composite photograph showing "A Few of the Multitude of Salomes Now Dancing in America."

Of these, perhaps the most famous was Eva Tanguay, known as "the Queen of Vaudeville" or "The Cyclonic One." Tanguay astutely sought headlines, good and bad. Police arrested her in 1910 for stabbing a stage-hand with a hat pin when he blocked her path. As the man writhed in pain, she supposedly declared, "Now, maybe you'll know how to get along with a lady!"

Tanguay played Salome with similar audacity, boasting hat she was the "real deal" and that everyone else's act was a pale imitation. She enjoyed flaunting her racy outfit, claiming, "I can fit the entire costume in my closed fist." Like the future Mae West, her Salome act involved camp sexuality while giving the audience a knowing wink.

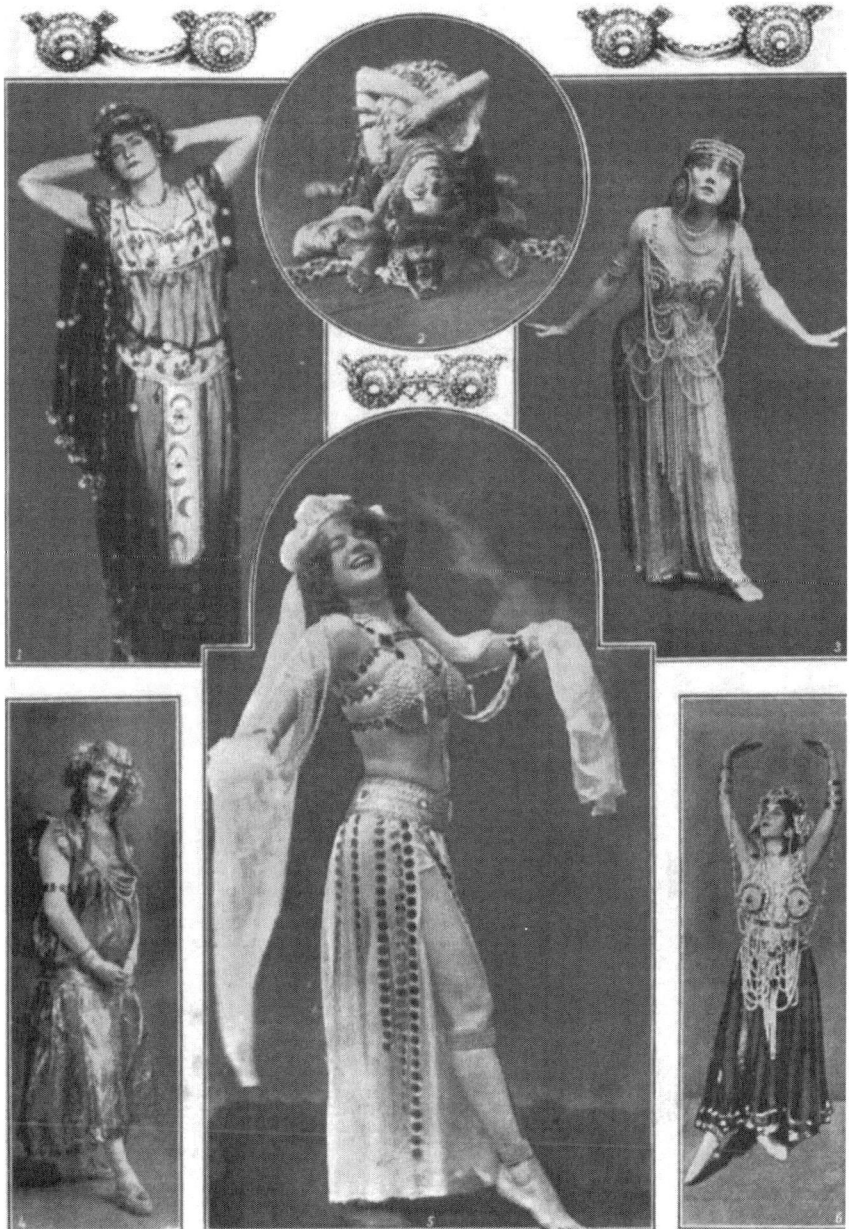

Image 92: *A Few of the Multitude of Salomes Now Dancing in America [Clockwise from bottom left: Vera Olcott, Hilda Caroll, La Sylphe, Lotta Faust, La Belle Zola, and Eva Tanguay], The Sketch*, 1908, HathiTrust.

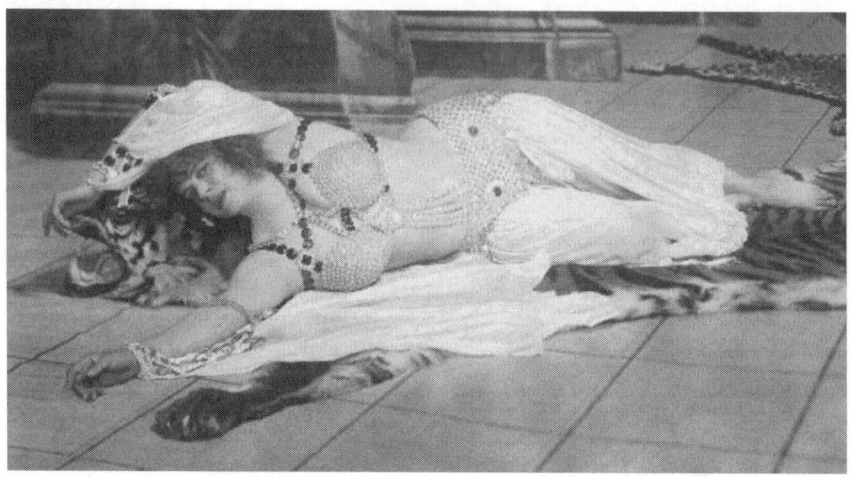

Image 93: *Eva Tanguay as Salome*, ca. 1910, Billy Rose Theatre Division, New York Public Library.

La Sylphe (Edith Lambelle Langerfeld) was notable as a very flexible Salome, and her dance routine included a variety of extreme contortions.

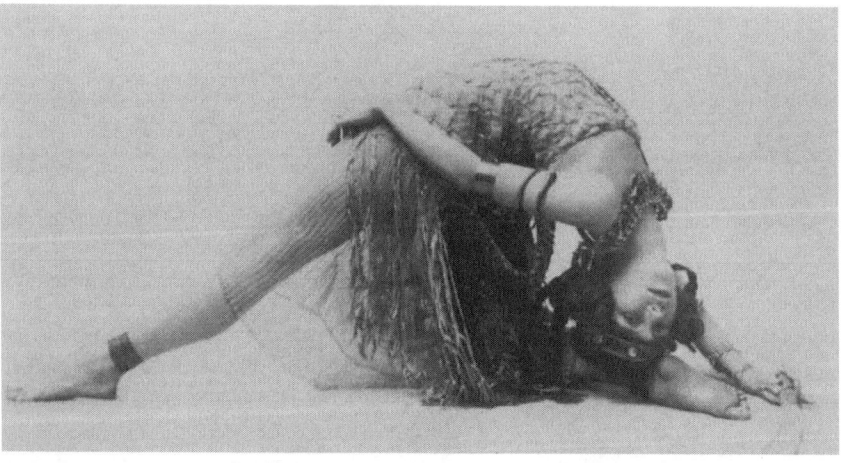

Image 94: *La Sylphe (the Dancer Suffrage) [various postures]*, ca. 1910, Schwimmer-Lloyd collection, New York Public Library.

Lotta Faust also made for a memorable Salome, drawing much attention with her semi-nudity and provocative movements. "Her undulation becomes more riotous as the dance continues," observed the *Chicago Tribune*.

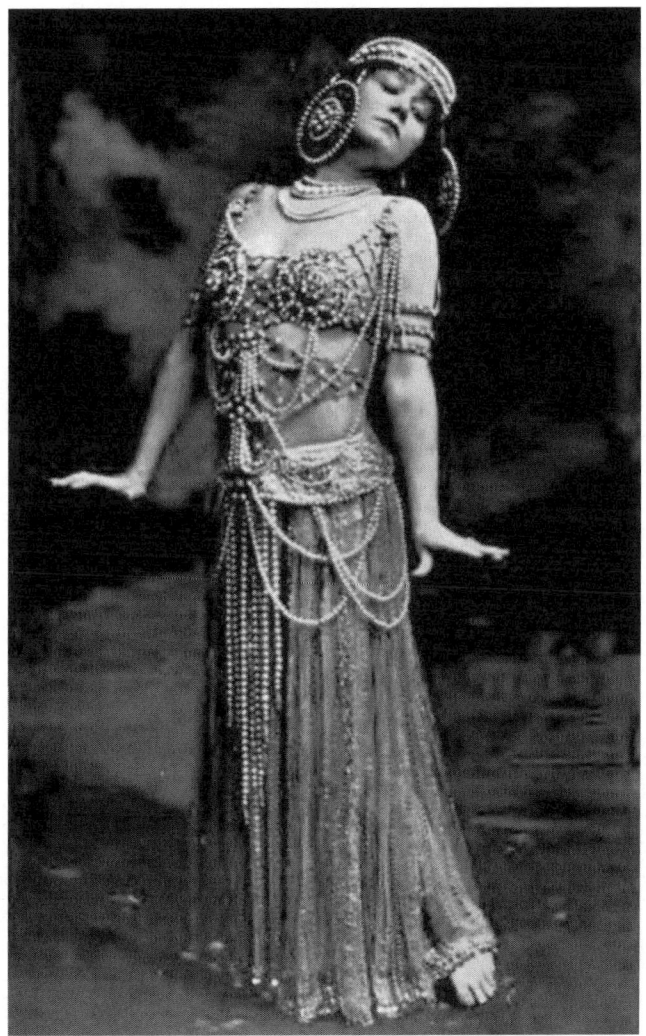

Image 95: *Lotta Faust as Salome*, 1908, Wikimedia Commons.

In 1908, Ada (Aida) Overton Walker, a versatile singer, dancer, and choreographer, did a Salome dance as part of the "Bandanna Land" musical revue at New York's Grand Opera House. She reprised the performance in 1912 on Broadway at the Victoria Theatre.

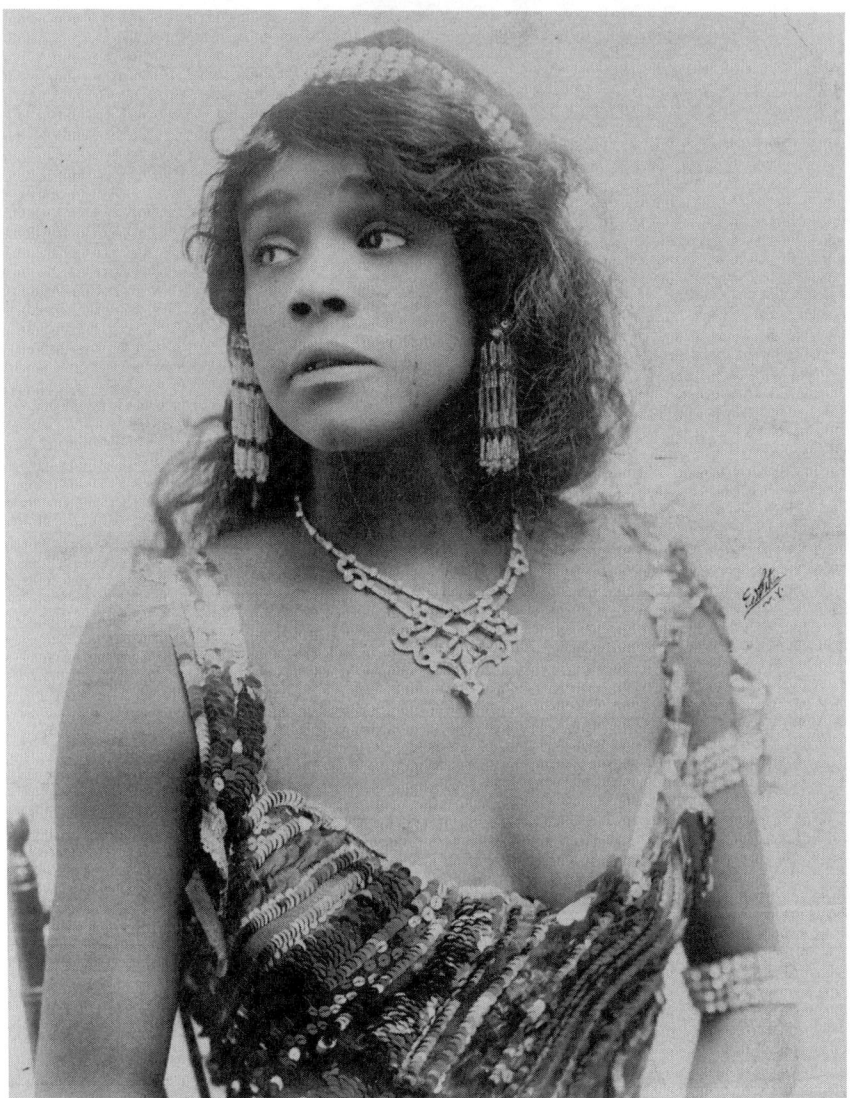

Image 96: *Ada (Aida) Overton Walker*, 1912, *New York World-Telegram* and the *Sun Newspaper* Photograph Collection, Library of Congress.

As Susan Glenn writes, "Rather than hype the sexual prurience of the dance, [Walker] characterized her black Salome as more artistic than erotic, more spiritual than sensational."

Reviewers concurred, with one observing that Walker "was clothed more than several of the other local Salomes" and "relied on the grace of her dancing for effectiveness."

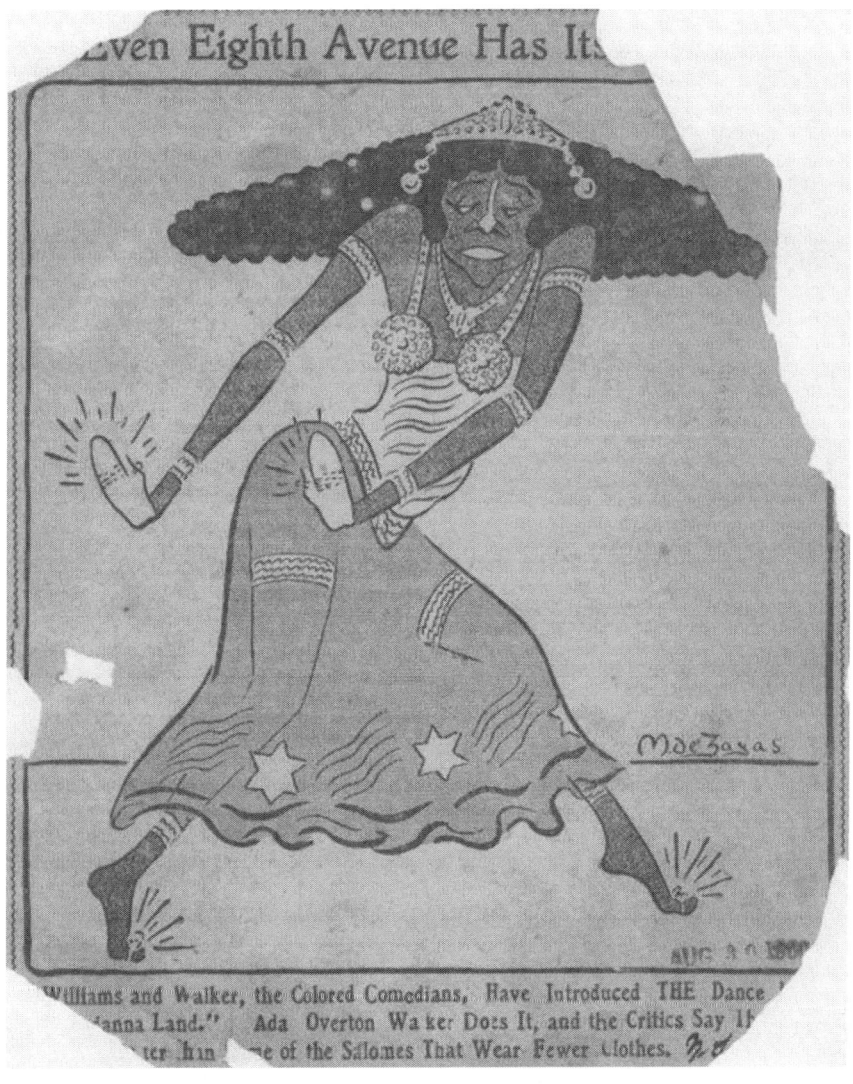

Image 97: *Ada (Aida) Overton Walker*, 1912, Billy Rose Theatre Division, New York Public Library.

Mademoiselle Dazie (Daisy Ann Peterson) danced as Salome in Florence Ziegfeld's "Follies of 1907" before Maud Allan conquered London. The

Salome interpretation was one part of her act, which also included "The Jiu-jitsu Waltz" and "The Living Doll Dance."

According to Glenn, Dazie's biggest contribution to Salomania was opening a "school for Salome" that, by the summer of 1908, launched "an estimated 150 newly minted Salomes . . . upon the vaudeville circuit every month."

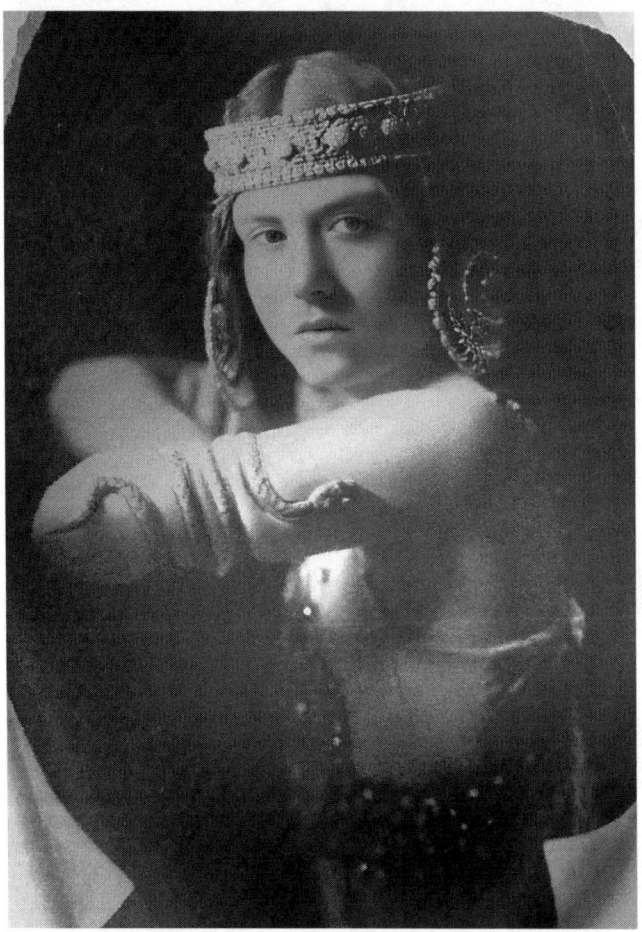

Image 98: *Mlle. Dazie,* 1908, *Cosmopolitan,* HathiTrust.

Dutchwoman Margarethe Zelle achieved huge success in 1905 Paris billing herself as a Javanese princess named Mata Hari. She wore a revealing costume while claiming to perform "sacred Hindu dances."

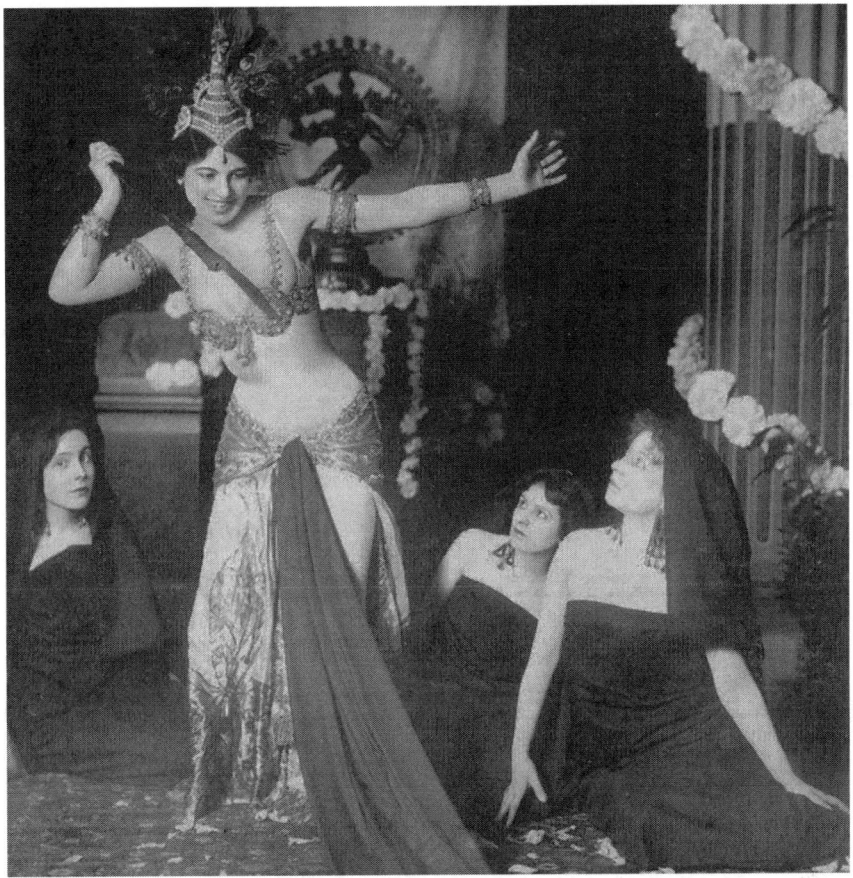

Image 99: *[Margarethe Zelle] Mata Hari Dancing in the Musée Guimet*, 1905, Wikimedia Commons.

Mata Hari was commonly associated with the Jewish princess, so much so that she felt entitled to dance in a production of the Strauss opera, claiming "Only I will be able to interpret the real thoughts of Salome."

Unsuccessful in convincing Strauss (by most accounts, she was not an especially talented dancer), Mata Hari's fame soared as she performed with fewer and fewer clothes. She originally began wearing a flesh-colored body stocking under her costume but soon discarded it in favor of her own skin.

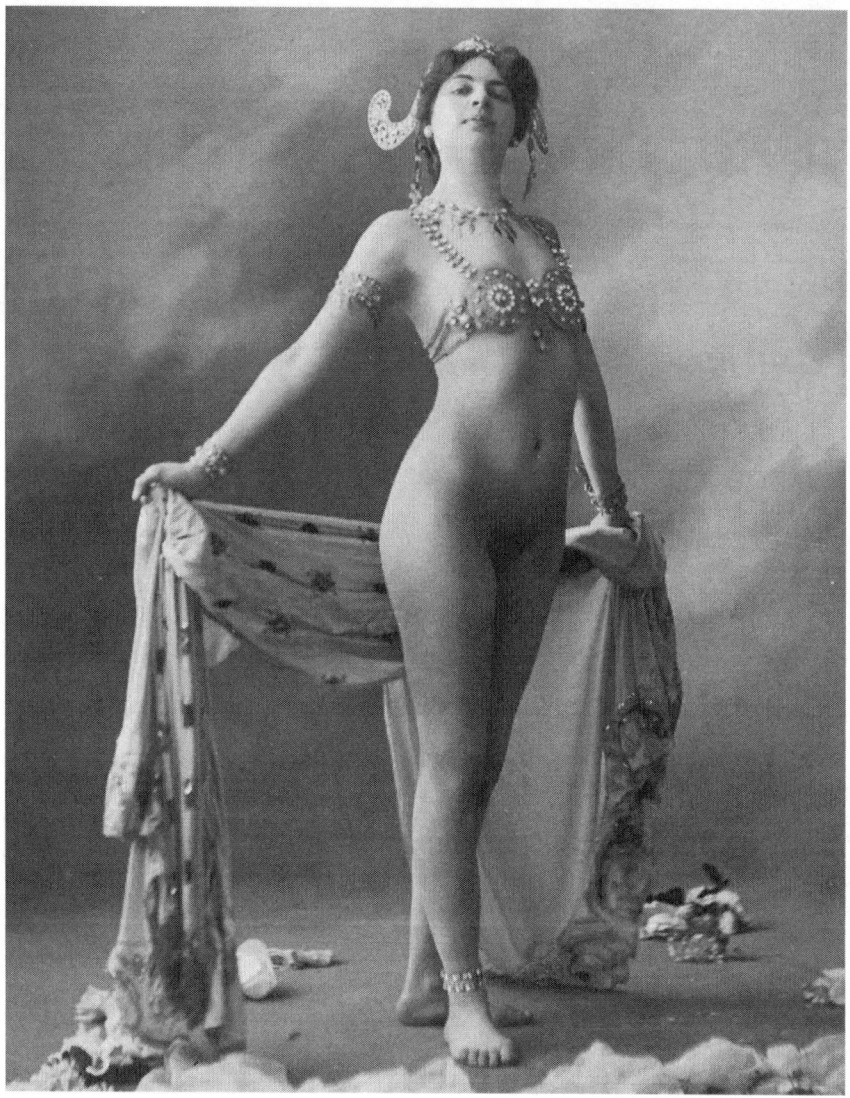

Image 100: *Margaretha Zelle Alias Mata Hari,* ca. 1908, Wikimedia Commons.

With her star fading during World War I, Mata Hari became entangled in an absurd espionage plot, and was arrested. A French firing squad executed her in 1917 based on the flimsiest of evidence. Tragic though her death was, it ensured her enduring fame as the personification of the seductive femme fatale.

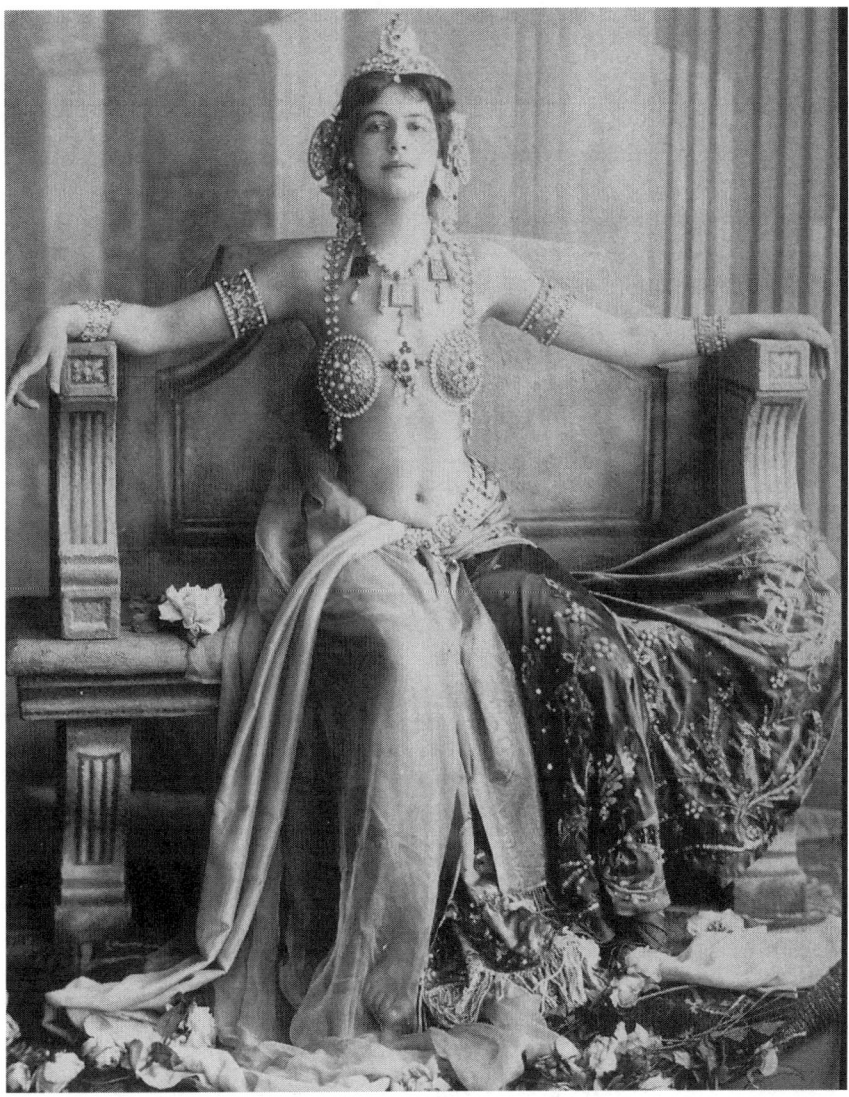

Image 101: *[Mata Hari]*, ca. 1908, Gallica, Bibliothèque nationale de France.

The success of Maud Allan and Mata Hari led to a profusion of "Salome dancers," a generic term that lumped together women who performed in vaguely Eastern headdresses, jewel-encrusted bras, bare midriffs, and flowing skirts and scarves.

The Baltimore-based Zallah, formerly known for her "Bathing Suit Dance," quickly jumped on the Salome bandwagon in 1908.

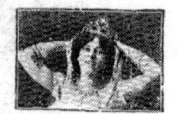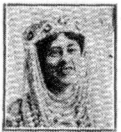

OPEN FOR ENGAGEMENTS

ZALLAH

PERMANENT ADDRESS
11 No. HIGH STREET
BALTIMORE, MD.

Image 102: *Zallah Business Card*, ca. 1910, collection of the author.

That year, she was "Queen of All Dancers," performing "Invasion of Salome" in Detroit. As time passed, she variously offered a "sensational version of Salome" and a Salome dance "within the bounds of propriety."

AVENUE Matinee Daily.
Home of Burlesque
THE COLONIAL BELLES
And the Queen of All Dancers
ZALLAH INVASION OF SALOME
60—PEOPLE, MOSTLY GIRLS—60
Next Week—The Strolling Players.

Image 103: Advertisement, *Detroit Free Press*, Sept. 1908, Newspapers.com.

One of the most photographed exotic dancers in Europe around 1910 was known as "Mlle. Hero" (or sometimes simply as "Herito").

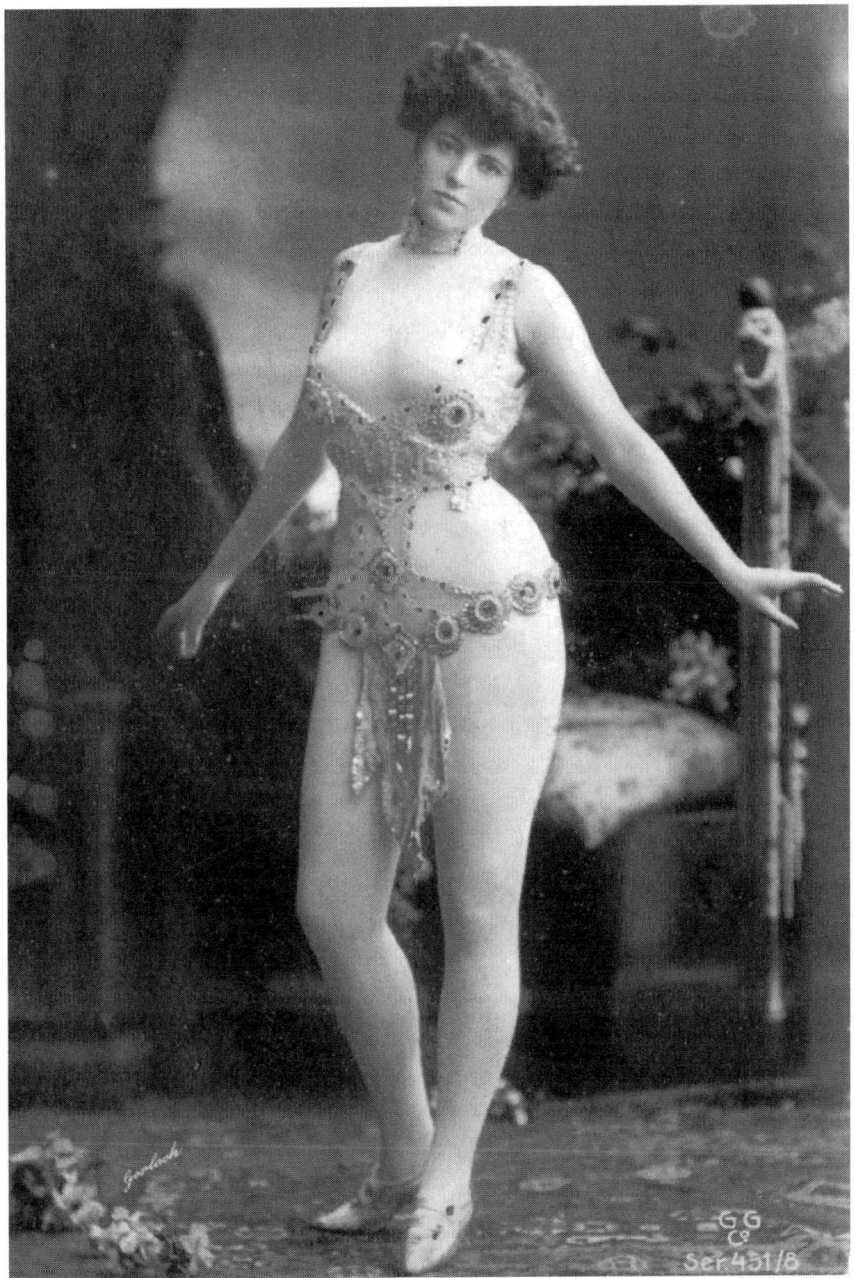

Image 104: *Mlle. Hero*, ca. 1909, collection of the Author.

The Bystander magazine described her in 1909 as "A dancer before various Herods who has outstripped many in the race for kingly favour," noting that she had performed "before the Kaiser, the Emperor of Austria, and the Kings of Spain and Belgium."

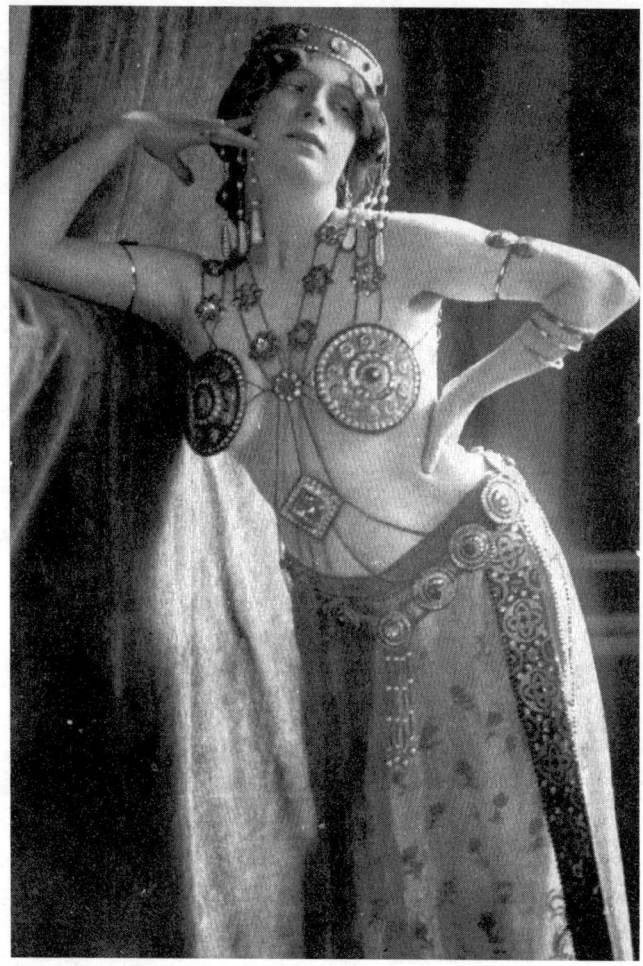

Image 105: *Mlle. Hero*, ca. 1910, collection of the author.

Odette Valery danced at the Folies Bergère, where she specialized in barefoot "Greek dancing," including roles as Salome and Cleopatra. She performed across Europe and shocked audiences in 1908 New York with a dance that included a live snake.

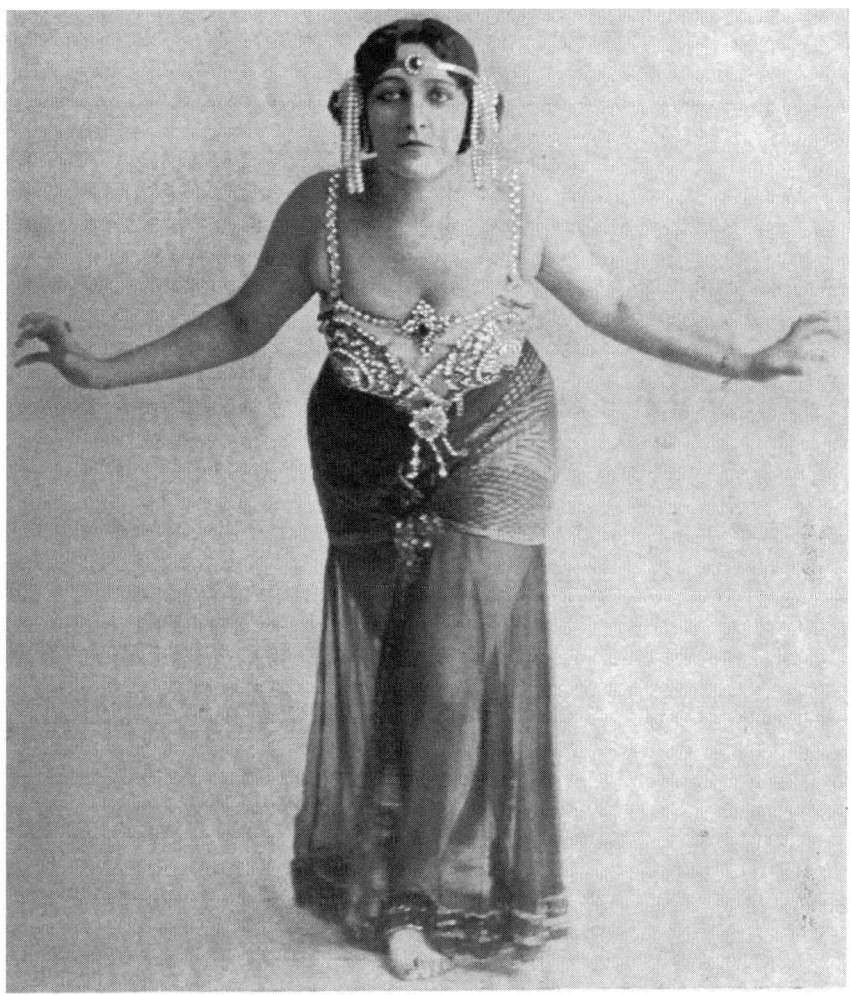

Image 106: *The Salome Cult - Mlle. Odette Valery, The Bystander,* 1908, HathiTrust.

Nicknamed "the bogey-woman of Paris wives," Valery lived in high style. The *Oakland Tribune* reported in 1909 that she danced "the Salome houchee-kouchee" at a New York party with playboy playwright Wilson Mizner. The fun ended for Valery in 1912 when she was found ill and penniless in a cheap London rooming house, cared for by her seven-year-old son.

Henrietta Sahary-Djeli "The Mysterious" was a Paris dance-hall favorite known for her extreme flexibility.

In 1912 Sahary-Djeli performed as Salome in "La Danse Prohibée." A critic said her act had elements of "the mysterious Orient . . . [and] the age-old grandeur of biblical visions." Her arms drew special praise for mimicking "a series of waves from the shoulder to die along the fingers . . . They give the impression of those 'charmed serpents' of which Baudelaire speaks."

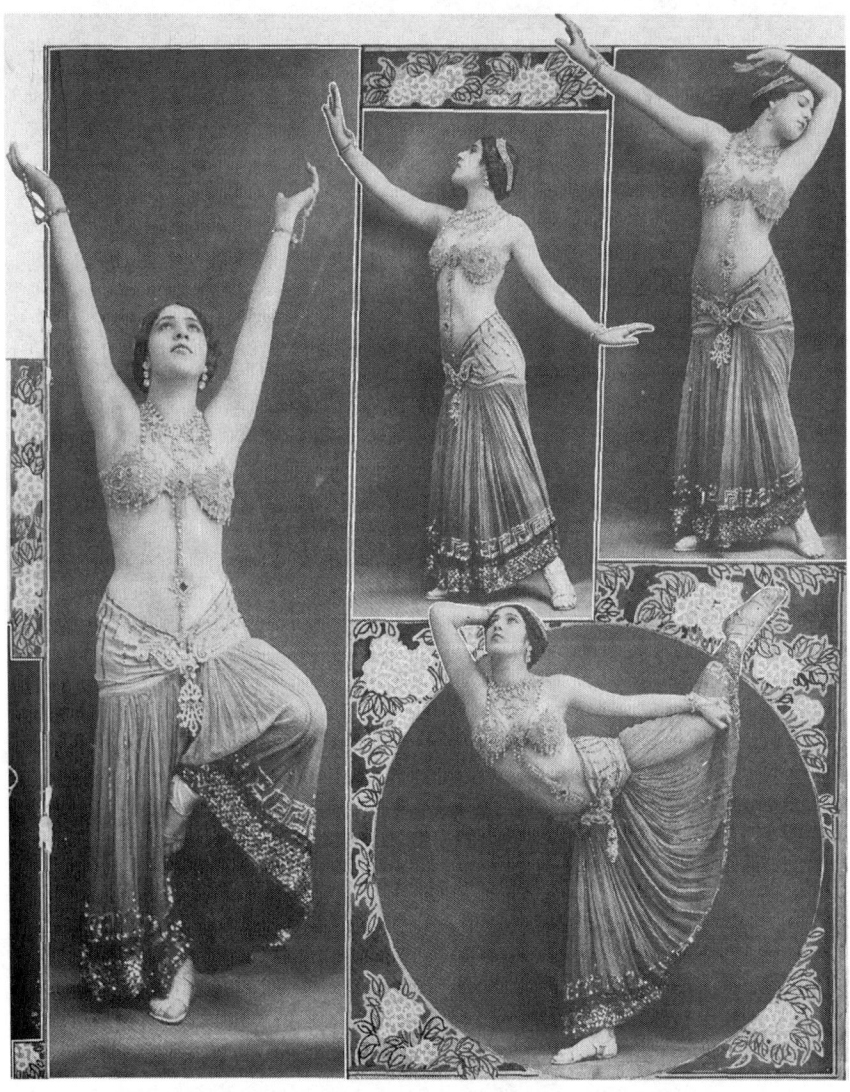

Image 107: *Henrietta Sahary-Djeli*, 1912, *Comœdia Illustré*, collection of the author.

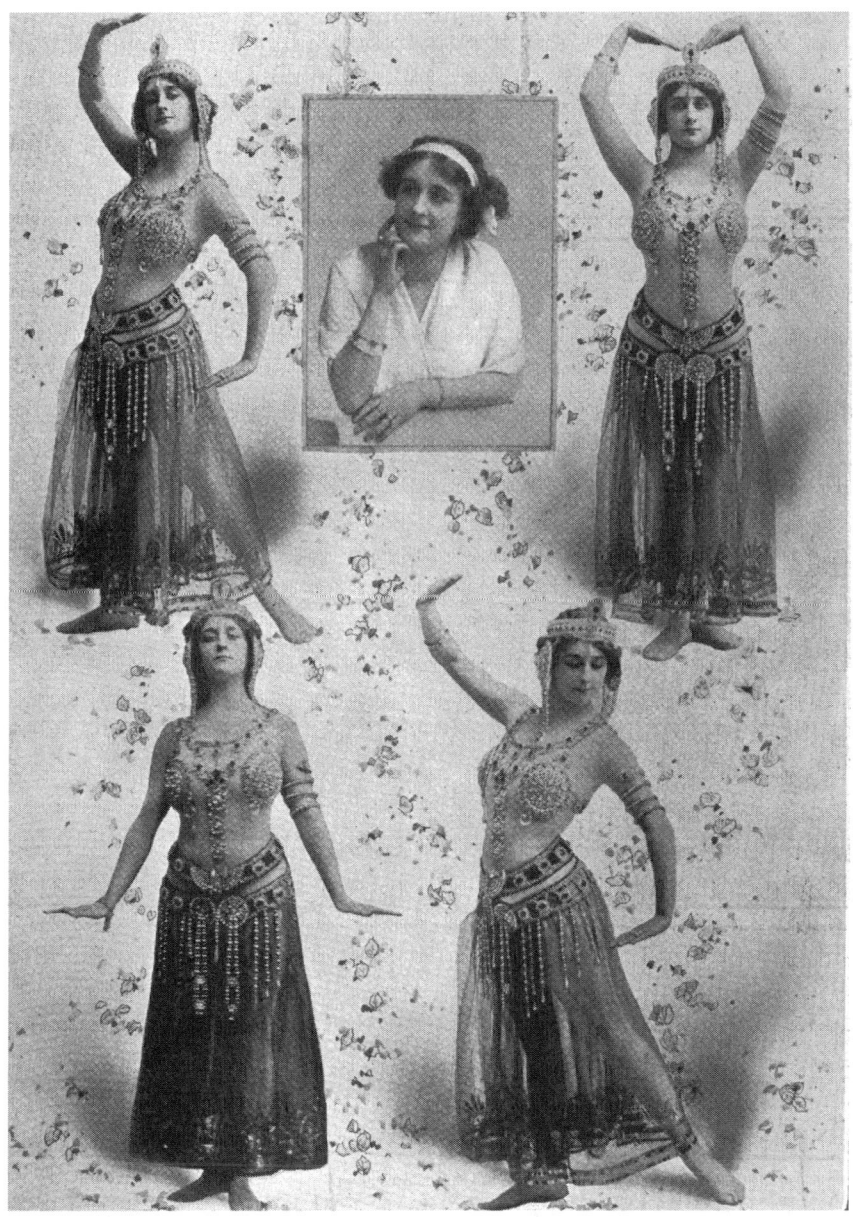

Image 108: *La Belle Leonora "Nautchy Sal, the High Priestess of Pure Art Mysteries,"* 1908,
The Sketch, HathiTrust.

Salomania inspired many parodies. La Belle Leonora, for example,
presented "Sal-Oh-My" in 1908 London. Another London show offered
"tiny 'Maud Allans' in . . . a child chorus parody."

95

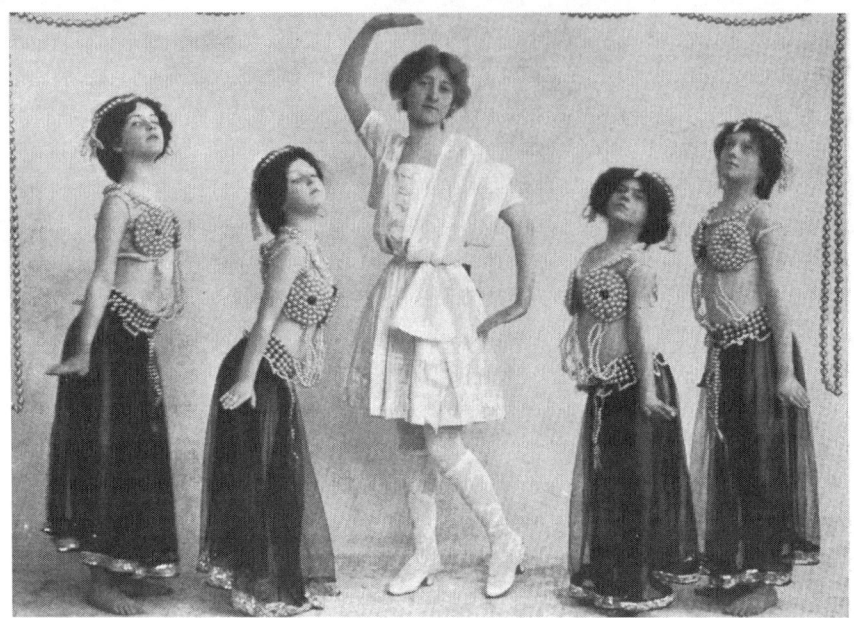

Image 109: *"Dressed in a Chic Ventilation" - Miniature Salomes*, 1908, *The Sketch*, HathiTrust.

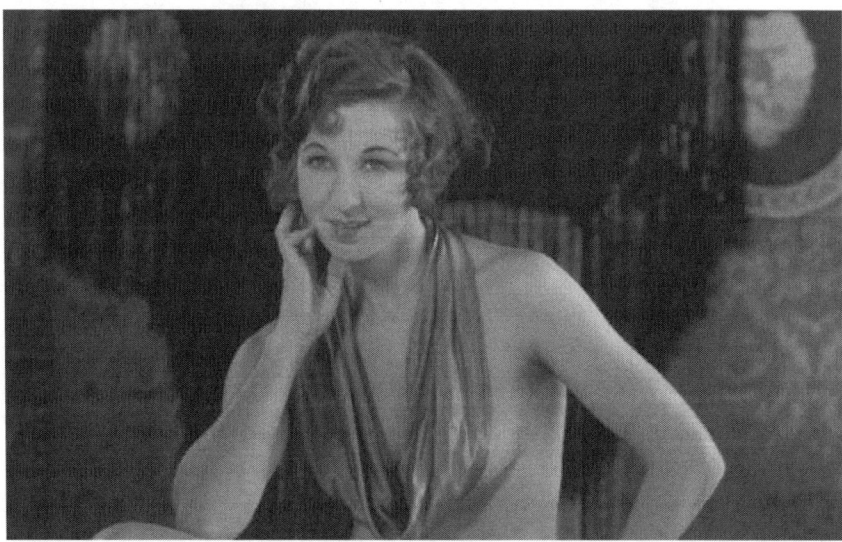

Image 110: *Fanny Brice*, ca. 1915, Wikimedia Commons.

Fanny Brice scored her first big hit with the 1909 Ziegfeld follies doing a Salome dance parody while singing Edgar Leslie's and Irving Berlin's "Sadie Salome, Go Home." The lyrics include:

Don't do that dance, I tell you Sadie
That's not a bus'ness for a lady!
'Most ev'rybody knows . . .
Where is your clothes?
Oy! such a sad disgrace
No one looks in your face

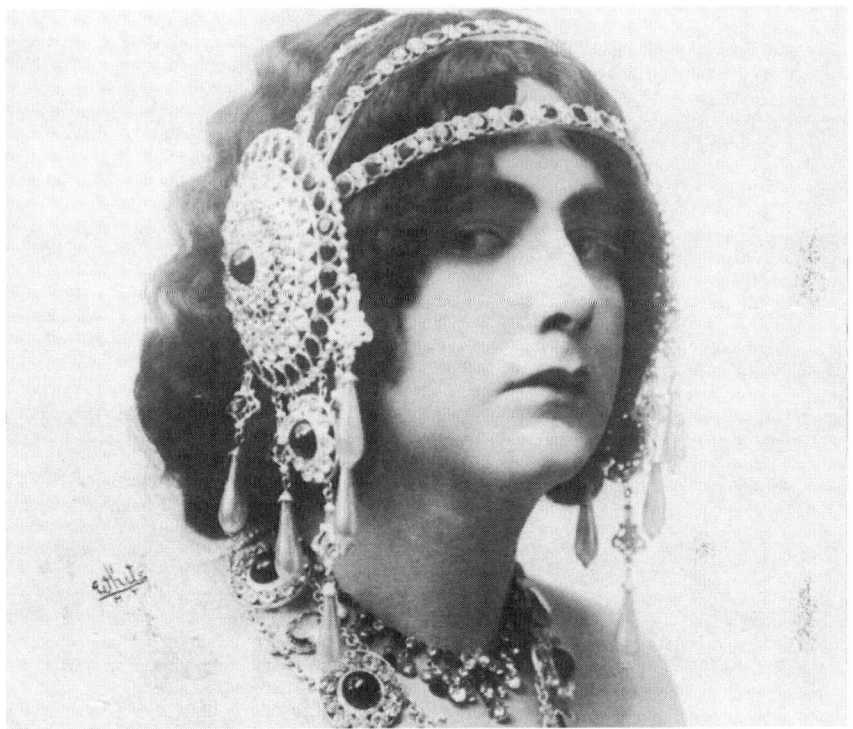

Image 111: *Julian Eltinge as Salome*, 1908, Billy Rose Theatre Division, New York Public Library.

Vaudeville star Julian Eltinge (William Julian Dalton), a female impersonator, put on a Salome parody in 1908. One critic declared that Eltinge "gives a more photographic interpretation of femininity than the average woman" and delivers "a better 'Dance of the Seven Veils' than any woman has yet presented on Broadway."

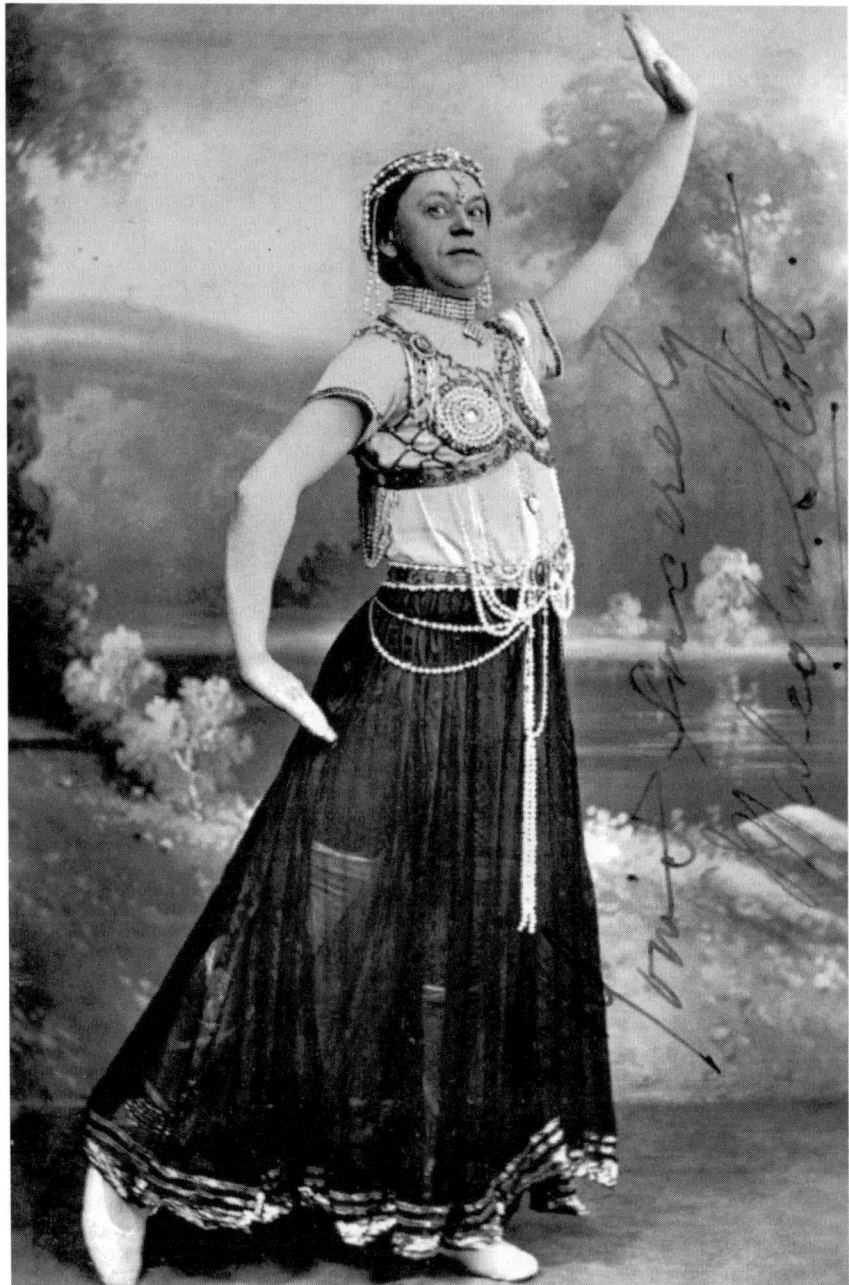

Image 112: *Malcolm Scott as Salome*, ca. 1908, collection of the author.

The Englishman Malcolm Scott won great reviews on both sides of the Atlantic for his portrayal of the Jewish Princess.

In 1909, *The New York Dramatic Mirror* raved about Scott's act, which substituted a bottle of whiskey for the severed head:

> Creeping upon it as stealthily as the usual Salome approaches the head of John the Baptist, Scott . . . breaks forth into a mad, whirling dance of joy, throwing himself upon the object of his affection and hopping ecstatically about. Nothing funnier than this moment has been seen in a New York vaudeville theatre.

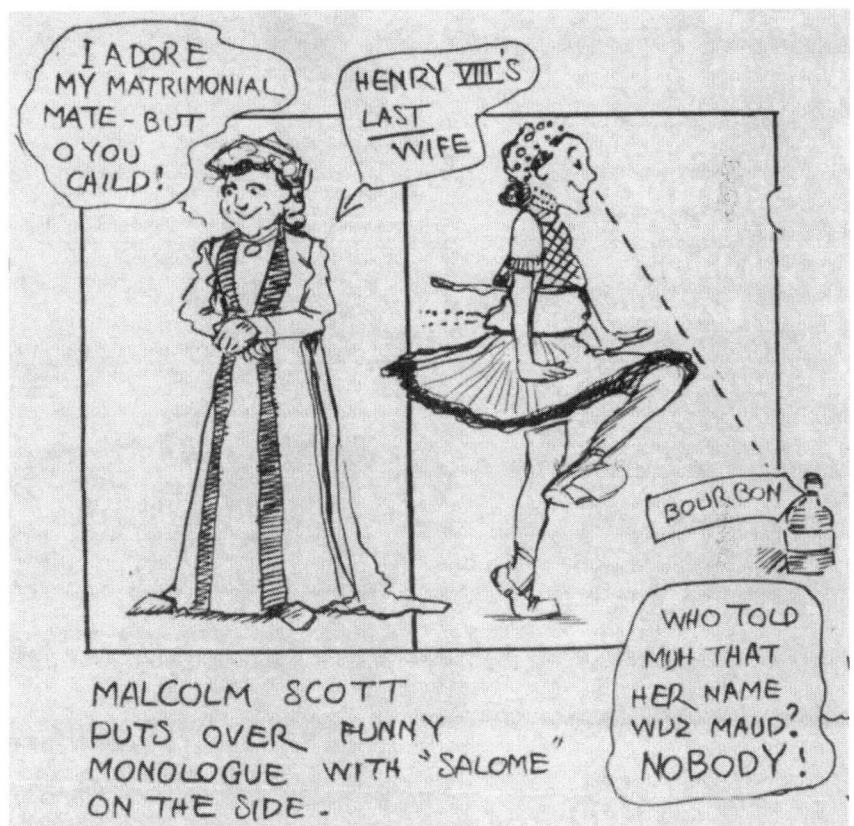

Image 113: *[Malcolm Scott]*, 1909, *The Show World*, Internet Archive.

Nikolai Fedorovich Barabanov (stage name Ikar) was one of the more obscure men to have staged a Salome dance. An Isadora Duncan performance impressed Barabanov to the point where he obsessively copied her dance moves for many weeks.

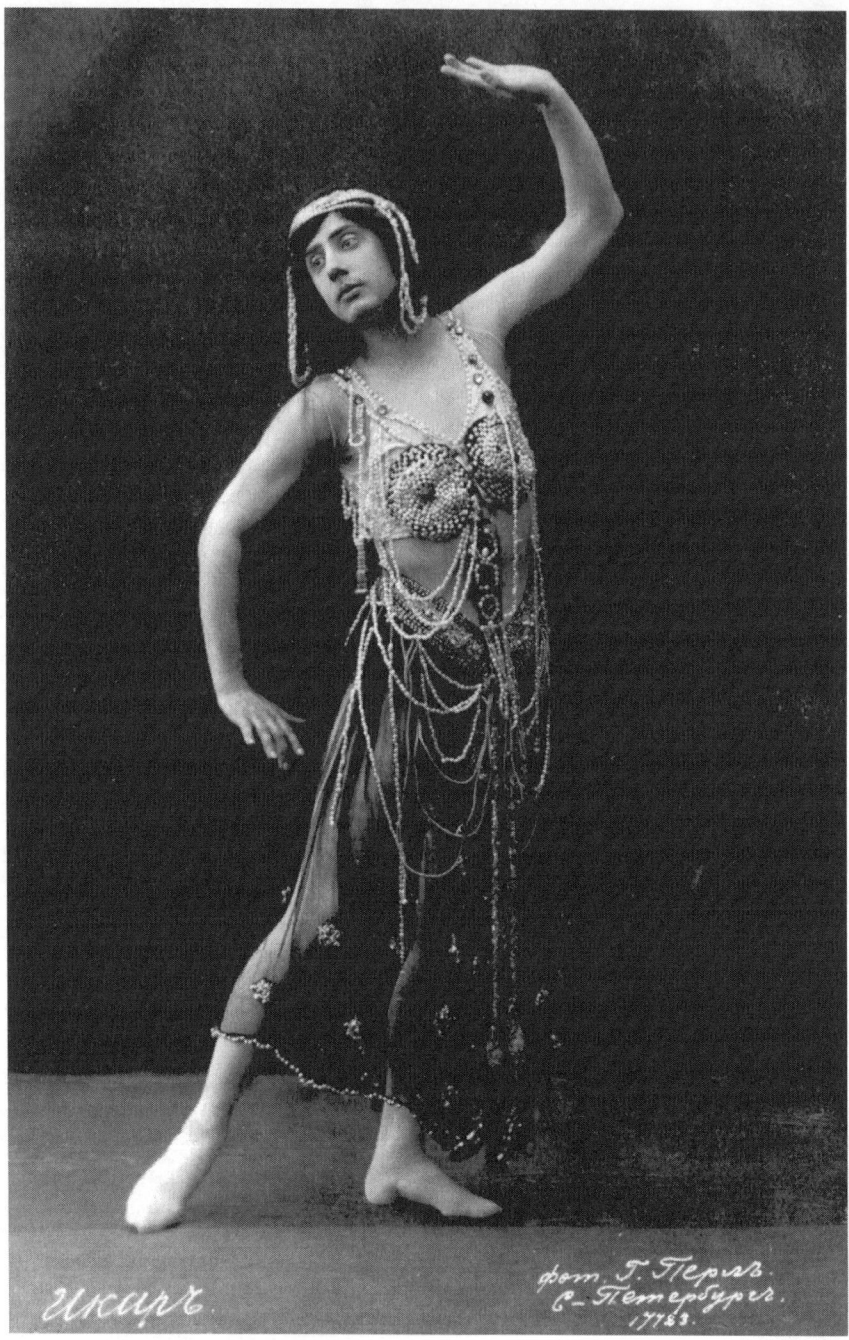

Image 114: *Nikolai Fedorovich Barabanov (Ikar) as Salome*, ca. 1909, collection of the author.

Barabanov did this work in private until about 1908 when he began performing in a Saint Petersburg cabaret known as the Crooked Mirror. The cabaret was a hotspot of the avant-garde in pre-revolutionary Russia and counted members of the Ballets Russes among its audience.

Barabanov did parodies of the leading art dancers, including Maud Alan's Salome. He became "the in-house ballerina," and his act was a sensation. As Mark Konecny writes:

> His parody was as much homage as imitation . . . Ikar carefully choreographed his dance with comedic elements; his keen eye for absurdity was vital to the success of his dance—for instance—mixing a dancer's jumps with a ballerina's flourish, giving both an air of sentimentality and the right note of parody to undercut his completely serious rendition.

CHAPTER 6 - FILM: THEDA BARA AND THE SILENT STARS

Salomania coincided with emergence of the motion picture industry, and the Jewish princess quickly made her way to the silver screen.

In 1901, Béla Zsitkovszky directed the first staged Hungarian film, *A táncz*. Early in the film, Emilia Márkus performs a "Salome dance" as part of the film's review of world dance history.

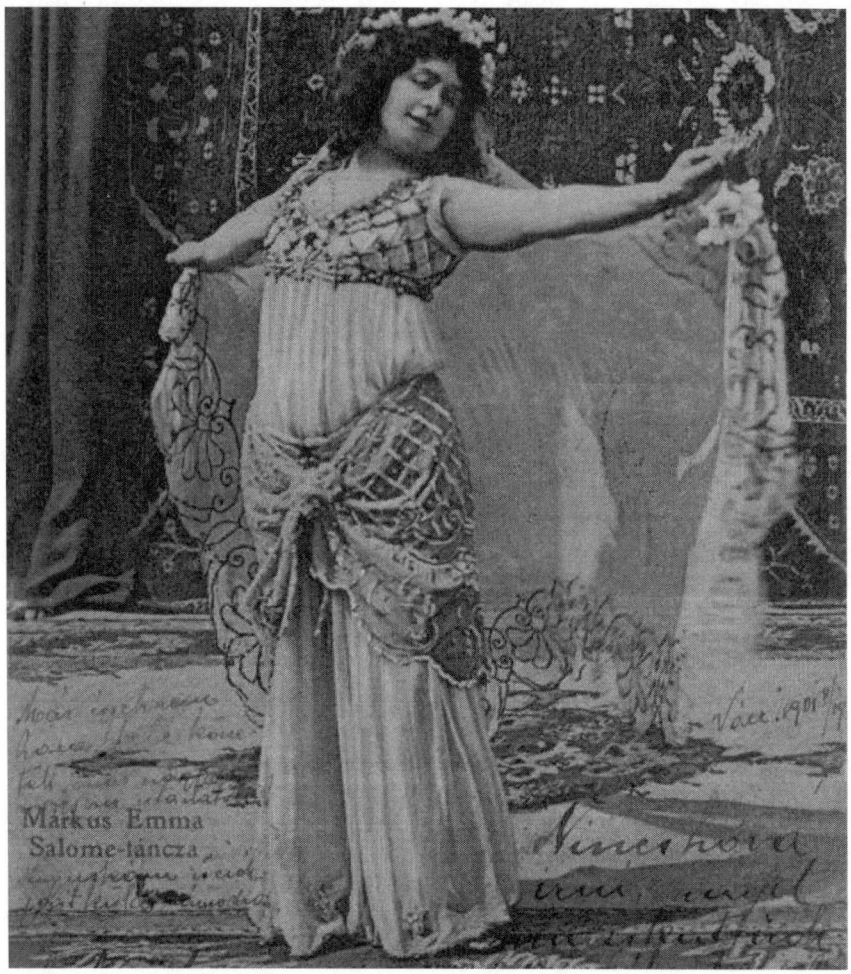

Image 115: *Márkus Emma Salome Táncza, 1901*, Ervin Szabó Metropolitan Library, Budapest, Budapest Collection (used with permission).

Márkus, known as "the blonde wonder," was one of the most famous Hungarian actresses. The film is lost, and the critic Pekár Gyula wondered what her dance might have been like. "Only the poetic imagination can help us here: the creative imagination of one of our greatest and most beautiful artists, who could better reproduce the dangerous, unconscious charm of Salome."

German director Oskar Messter made the short film *Tanz der Salome* in 1906, starring Adorée Villany. An art dancer already notorious for performing the Dance of the Seven Veils in an extreme state of undress, Villany removed most of her clothing in the film.

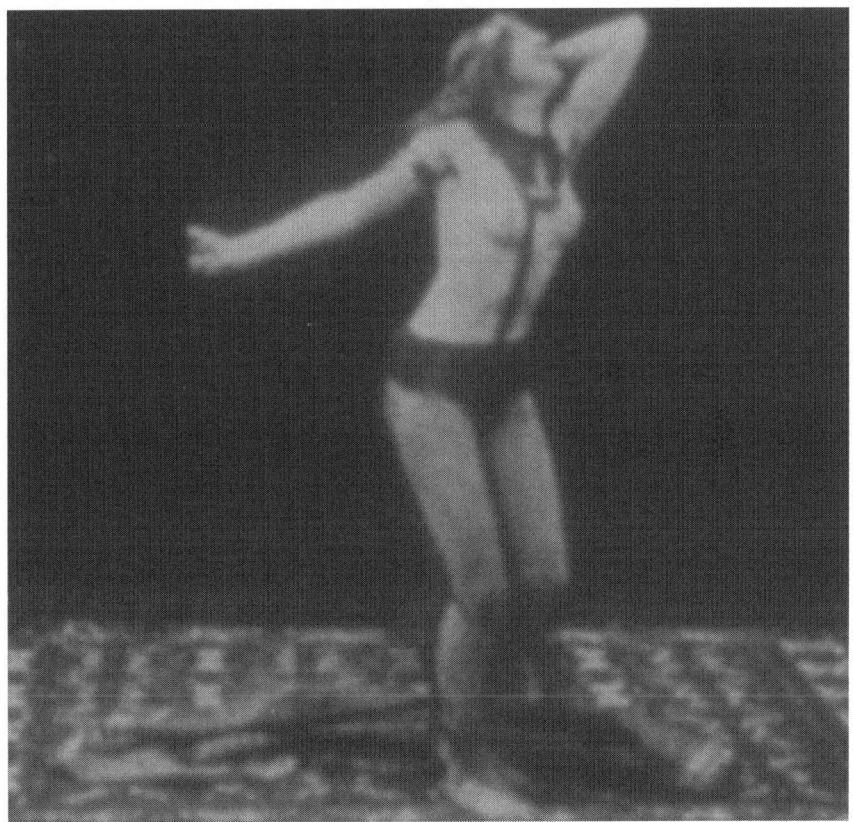

Image 116: *[Adorée Villany in] Tanz der Salome*, ca. 1906, Wikimedia Commons.

Villany also appeared in director Rino Lupo's 1915 Danish silent film *Slør-Danserinden* (*The Veil Dancer*), which has a Salome-like theme. The program noted that Villany was "popularly called 'the bare dancer'" and that the film features "art-reform-dance."

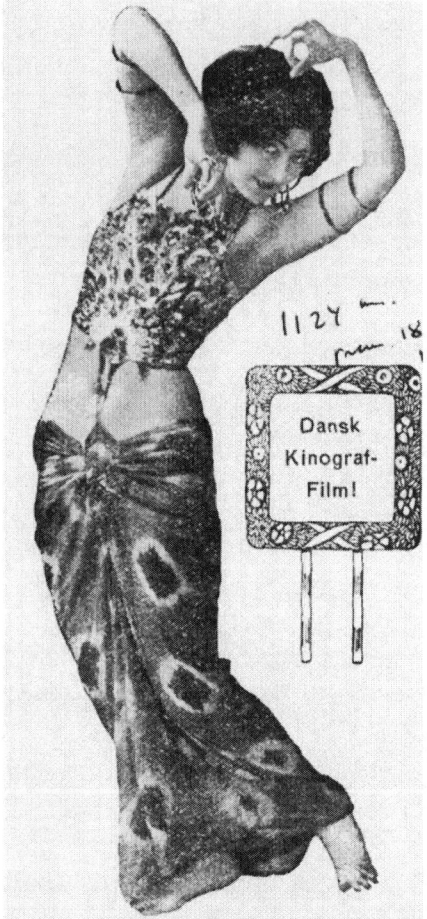

Image 117: [*Adorée Villany, Cover of Slør-Danserinden program*], 1915, Danish Film Institute.

Also in 1908, Vitagraph released *Salome* or *Dance of the Seven Veils*. This film is notable for casting Florence Lawrence—one of the first "movie stars"—in the title role.

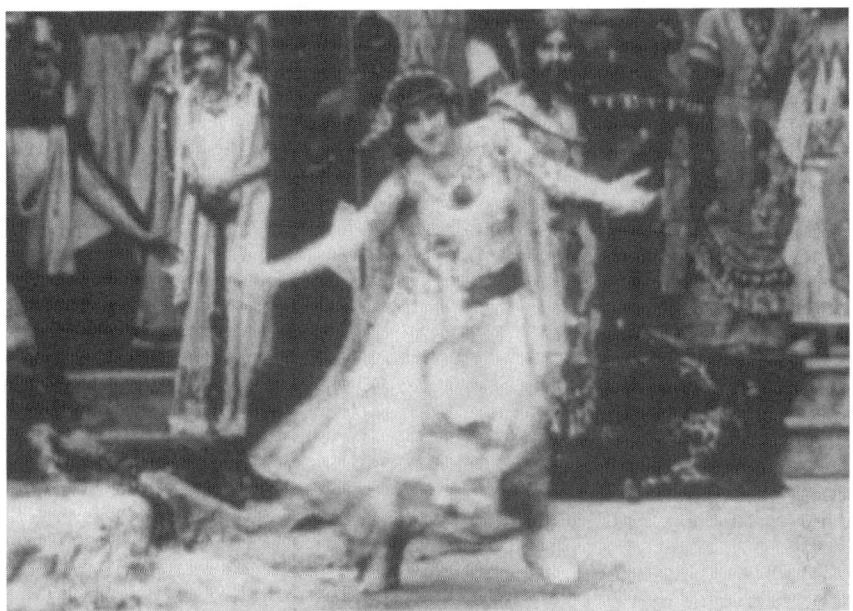

Image 118: *[Florence Lawrence in Salome, or Dance of the Seven Veils]*, 1908, *Library of Congress.*

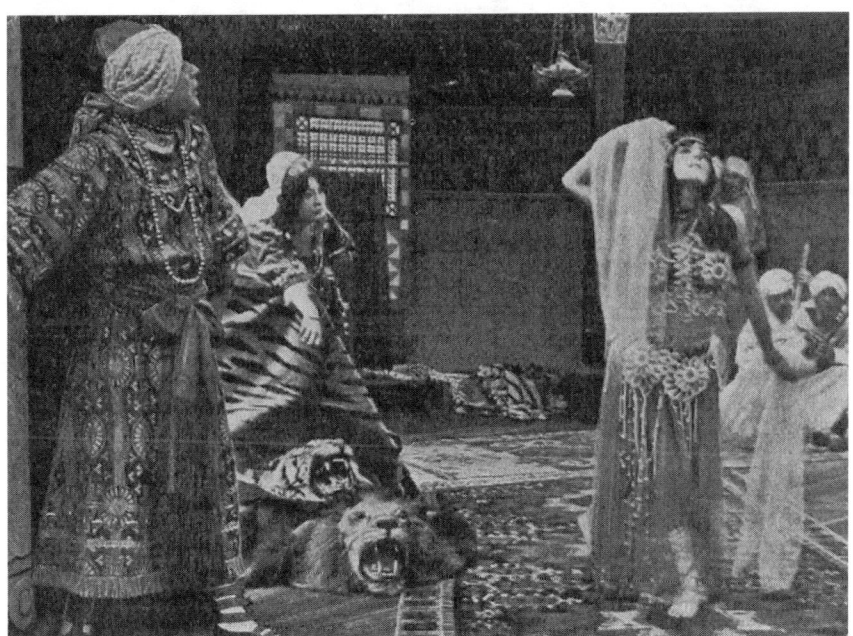

Image 119: *[Adriana Costamanga in La Salome]*, *Moving Picture World*, 1913, Internet Archive.

Oreste Mentasti directed *Erodiade* (also known as *La Salome)* in 1912, featuring Adriana Costamagna as the wayward princess.

Fox Film Company released *Salome* in 1918, featuring Theda Bara, a proven box-office draw. Big-budget for the era, the film featured elaborate sets and costumes.

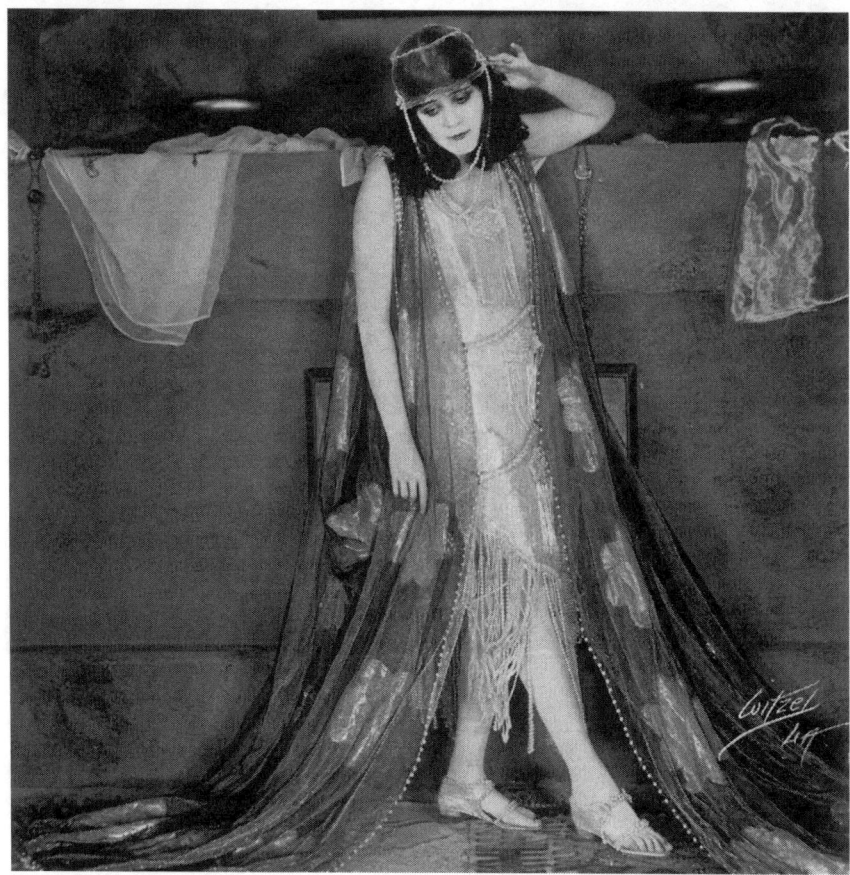

Image 120: *Theda Bara 1918 Salome*, Albert Witzel photographer, 1918, Wikimedia Commons.

Bara was one of the first Hollywood sex symbols and played femme fatale or "vampire" roles. A "vamp" sought to seduce innocent men, drain their wallets, and destroy their morals; Bara was so closely associated with the type that it was known as "Bara-esque." She played up the image, claiming her father was an Arab sheik (he wasn't) and that she was the reincarnated spirit of Lucretia Borgia, "the world's most picturesquely wicked woman" (she compared her face to Borgia's portrait as proof).

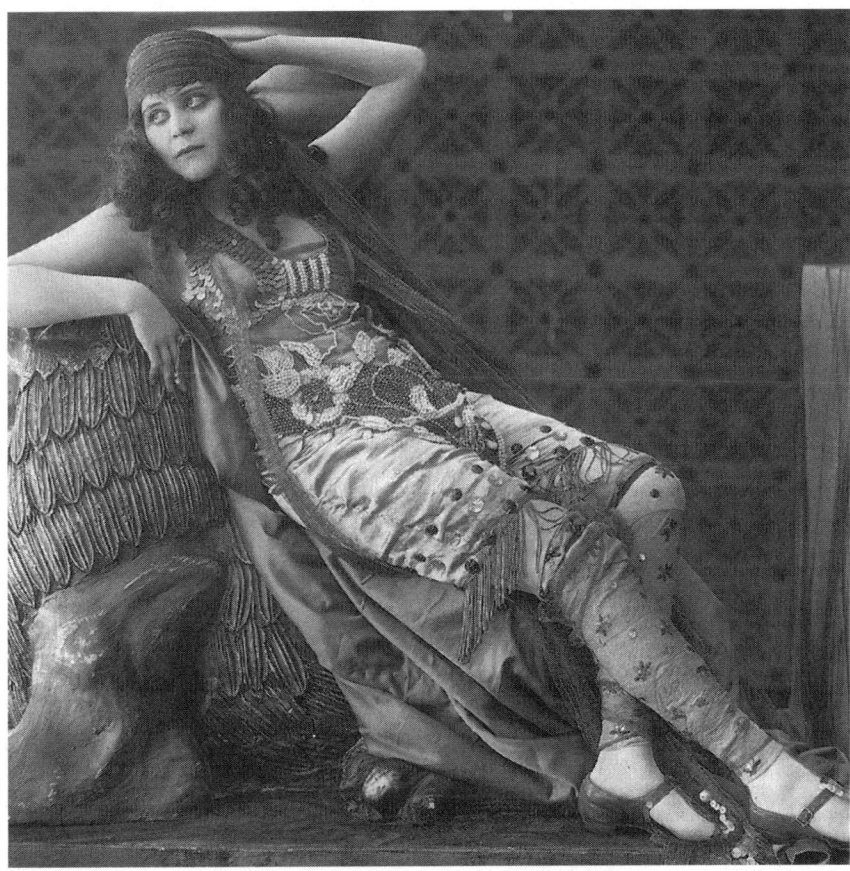

Image 121: *Theda Bara Promotional Photo*, 1918, FLÁ * PESSOA, Wikimedia Commons.

Bara's *Salome*, perhaps by design, caused an uproar. Bara herself was denounced as immoral, as well as "overbold and underclad." The film was a hit, however, with one theater charging an unheard-of 75 cents per ticket and still packing the house.

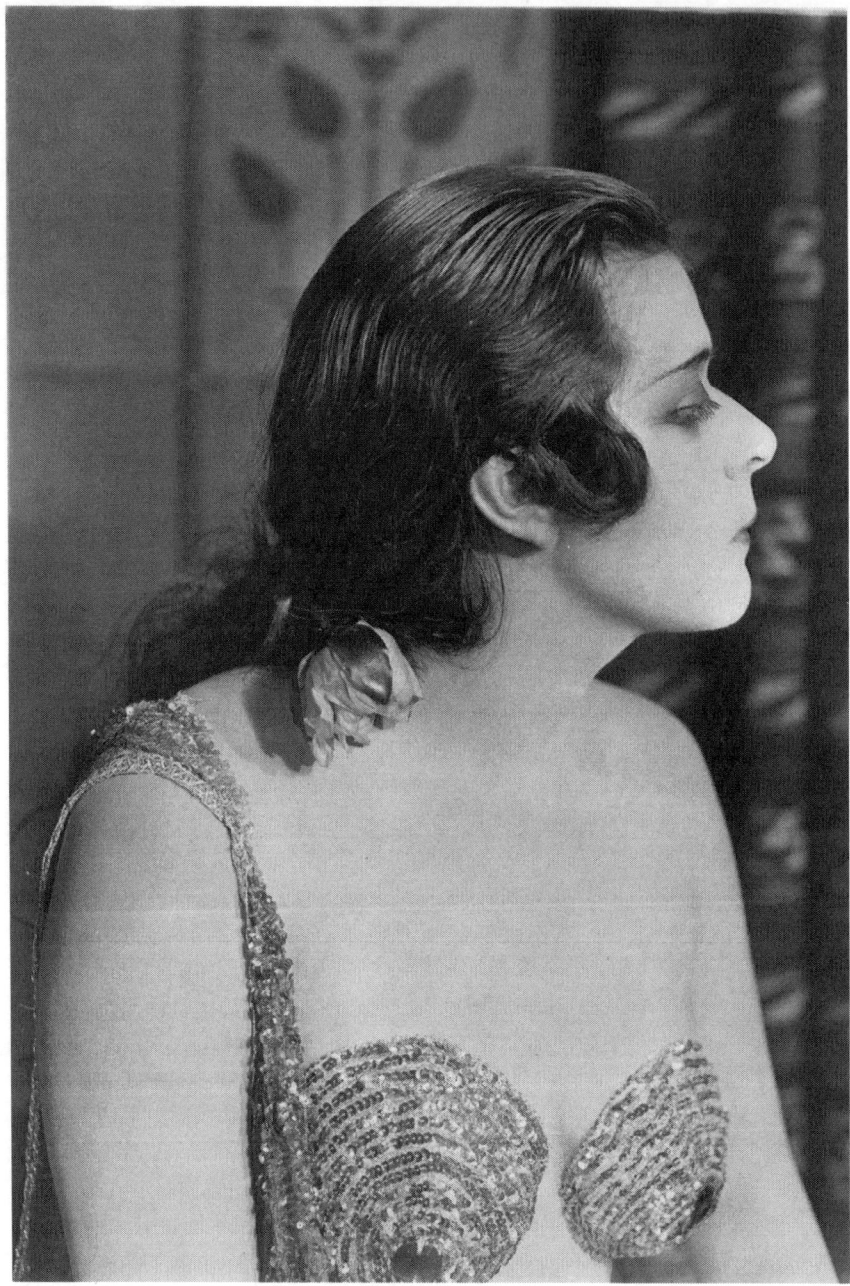

Image 122: *Theda Bara as Salome*, 1918, University of Washington Libraries, Special Collections, JWS18101 (used with permission).

In 1919, Mack Sennet offered *Salome vs. Shenandoah* starring Phyllis Haver. The film was a comedic mashup of two popular dramas, played for laughs: Wilde's *Salome* and Bronson Howard's Civil War show, *Shenandoah*.

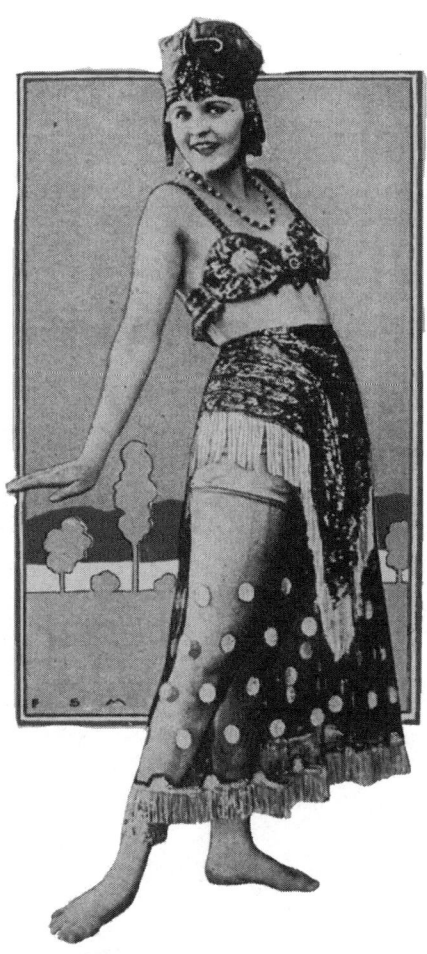

Image 123: *Phyllis Haver as Salome, 1919, Salome vs. Shenandoah*, Wikimedia Commons.

1923 saw Alla Nazimova starring in an art-house movie version of the Salome story. The production avoided recreating ancient Judaea in favor of a lush art-nouveau setting. Nazimova appears in various costumes, including remarkable headdresses.

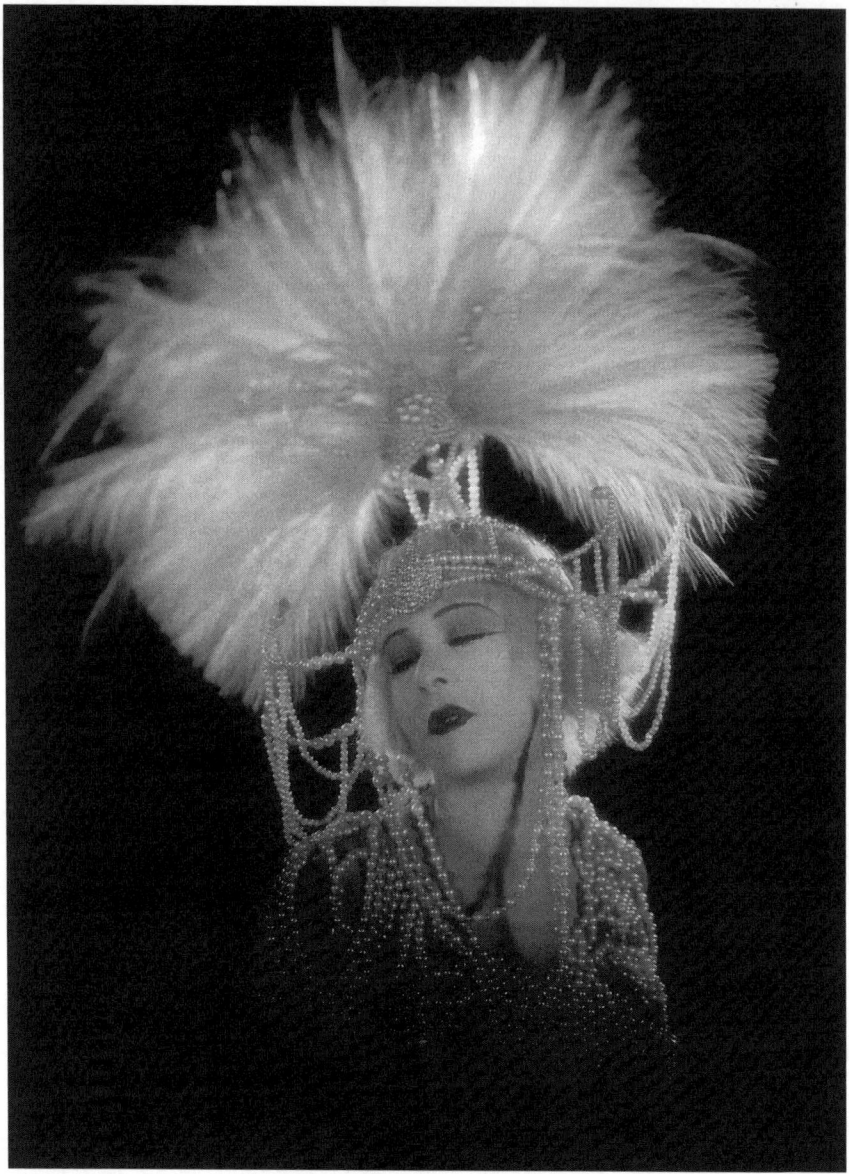

Image 124: *Nazimova Salomé*, 1923, Wikimedia Commons.

Many did not know quite what to make of the film. While *Photoplay* called Wilde's original story "a hot-house orchid of decadent passion," the review was skeptical of the film adaptation:

We are not sure whether we like Madame Nazimova's idea of Salome as a petulant little princess with a Freudian complex and a headdress of glass bubbles. We rather believe such a Salome would not have stirred men so in those good old pagan days. You have our warning: this is bizarre stuff.

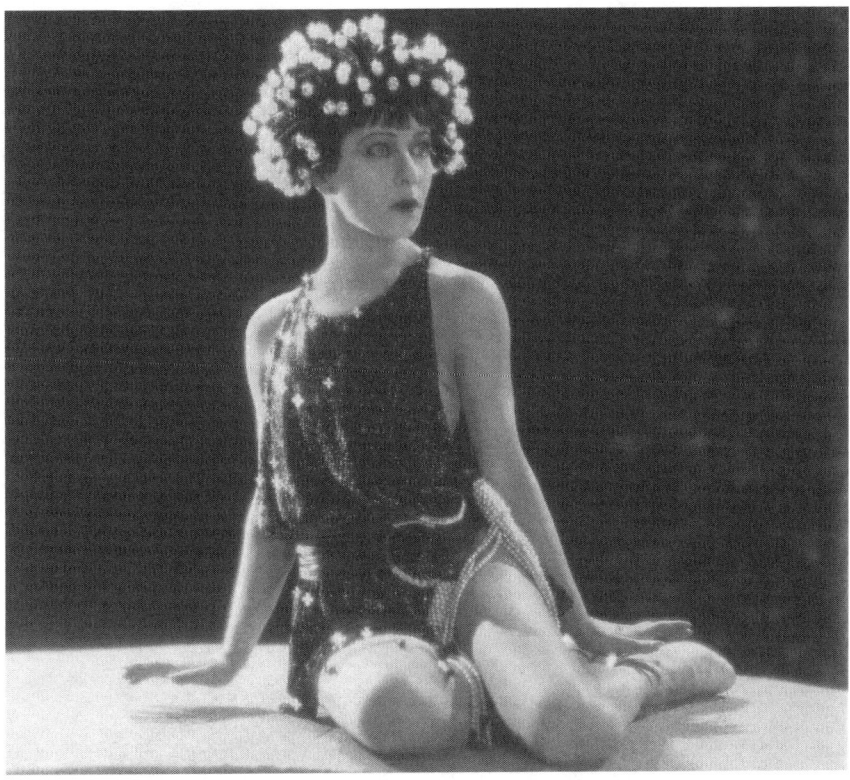

Image 125: *Nazimova in Salomé*, 1923, University of Washington Libraries, Special Collections, JWS12120 (used with permission).

The film was a critical and box-office flop, and Nazimova never recovered financially from the money she invested in the production. Her *Salomé* has since, however, won praise for its artistic ambition and daring.

Gloria Swanson took a turn as Salome in the 1925 film *Stage Struck*, playing a waitress who fantasizes about becoming the world's most famous actress. In a dream sequence, she declares to an astonished multitude, "Look! I am Salome!" She proceeds to collect John's severed head on a platter—only to have it transform into a customer's order on a tray in real life.

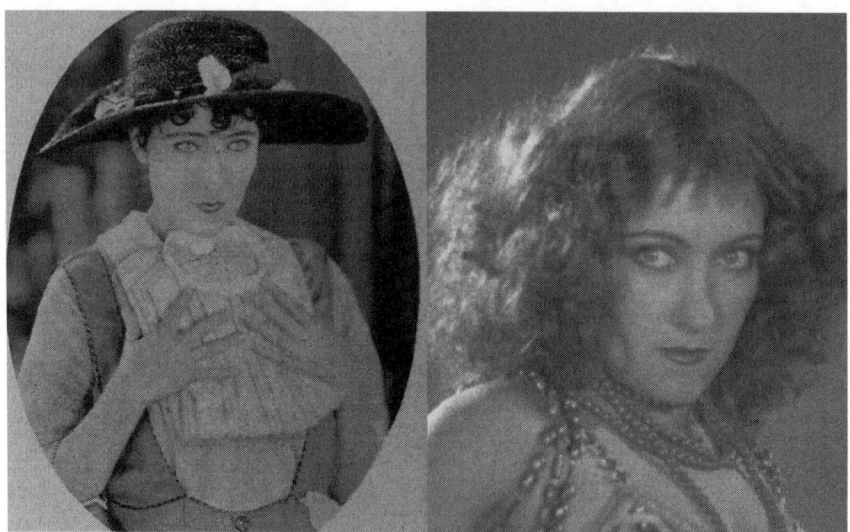

Image 126: [Left - *Gloria Swanson in "Stage Struck" as a waitress*], *Picture-Play Magazine*, 1925, Internet Archive; [right - *Gloria Swanson as Salome*], Wikimedia Commons.

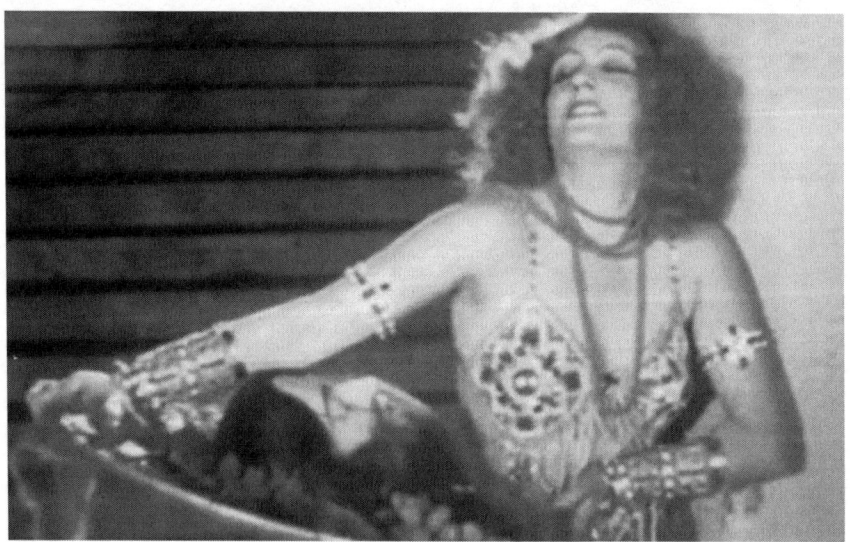

Image 127: [*Gloria Swanson as Salome in "Stage Struck"*], 1925, Wikimedia Commons.

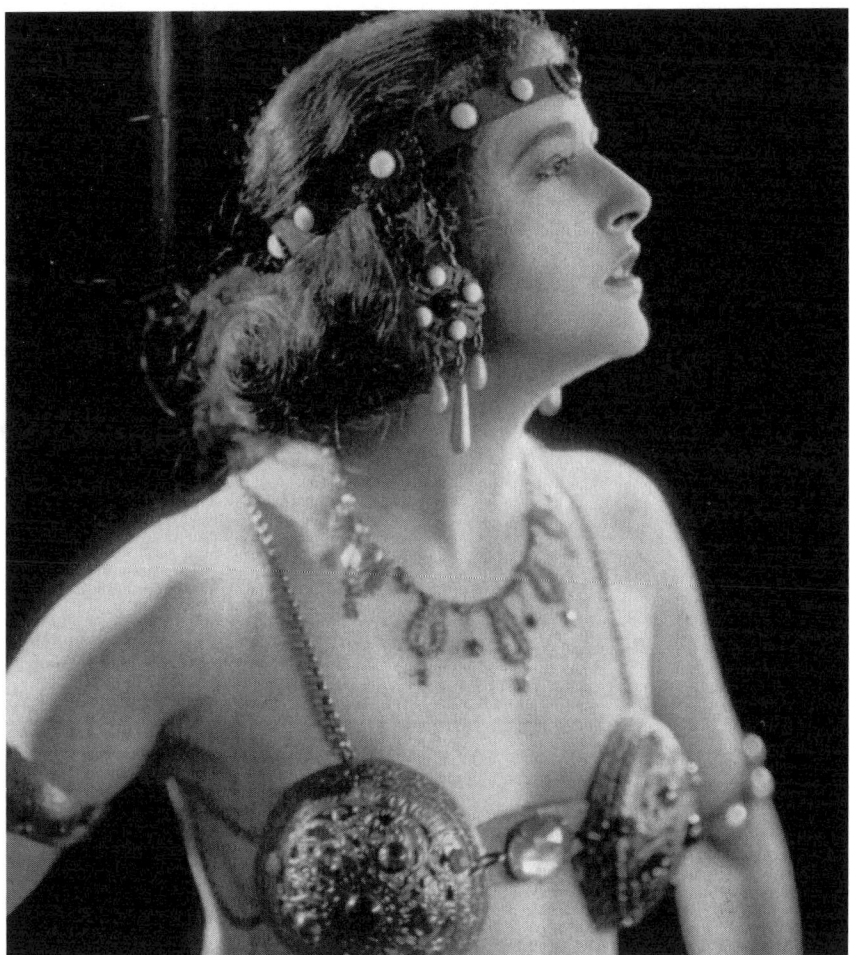

Image 128: *Marcella Albani*, ca. 1926, collection of the author.

Marcella Albani was a star of European silent cinema. She was photographed in a Salome-like costume to promote the 1926 German movie *Die Flucht in den Zirkus* (advertised in English as *Circus of Life*). In the film, Albani joins a circus as a scantily clad "snake dancer" to escape a Siberian prison.

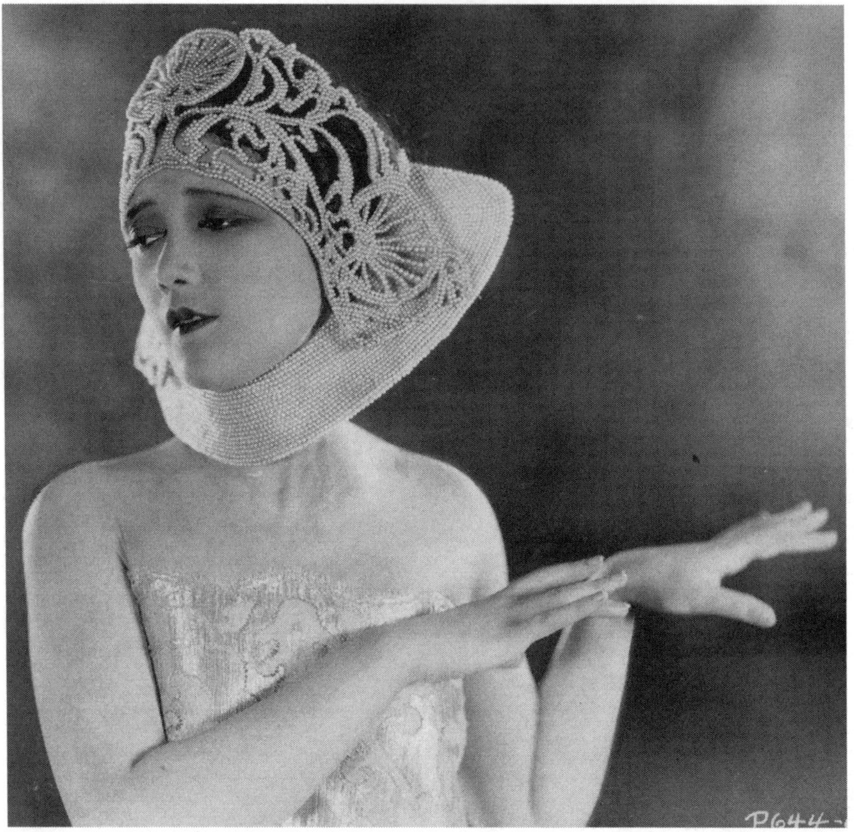

Image 129: *Film Actress Jetta Goudal* [in *Salome of the Tenements*], 1925, Wikimedia Commons.

The 1925 American film *Salome of the Tenements* was about a young Jewish woman from the impoverished Lower East Side of New York City who schemes and "vamps" to get her man, the rich John Manning. Jetta Goudal played the title role.

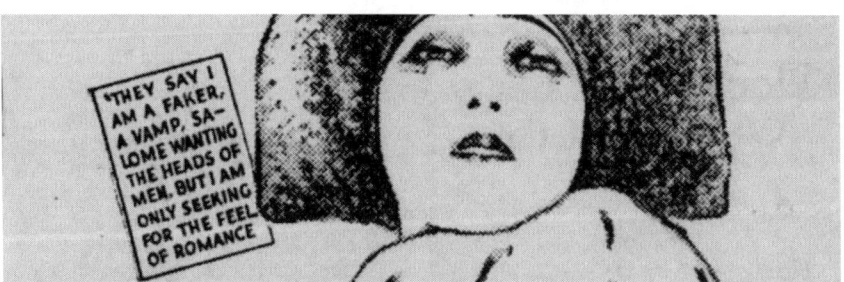

Image 130: Advertisement,*The Sedalia Democrat*, 29 April 1925, Newspapers.com.

Stacia Napierkowska was an actress and dancer who specialized in exotic, seductive roles. She had the distinction of playing Salome in three films. She first appeared in *Salomé,* a 1908 French film directed by Albert Capellani.

Napierkowska reprised the Jewish princess in the 1916 Italian film *La figlia di Erodiade (The Daughter of Herodias).*

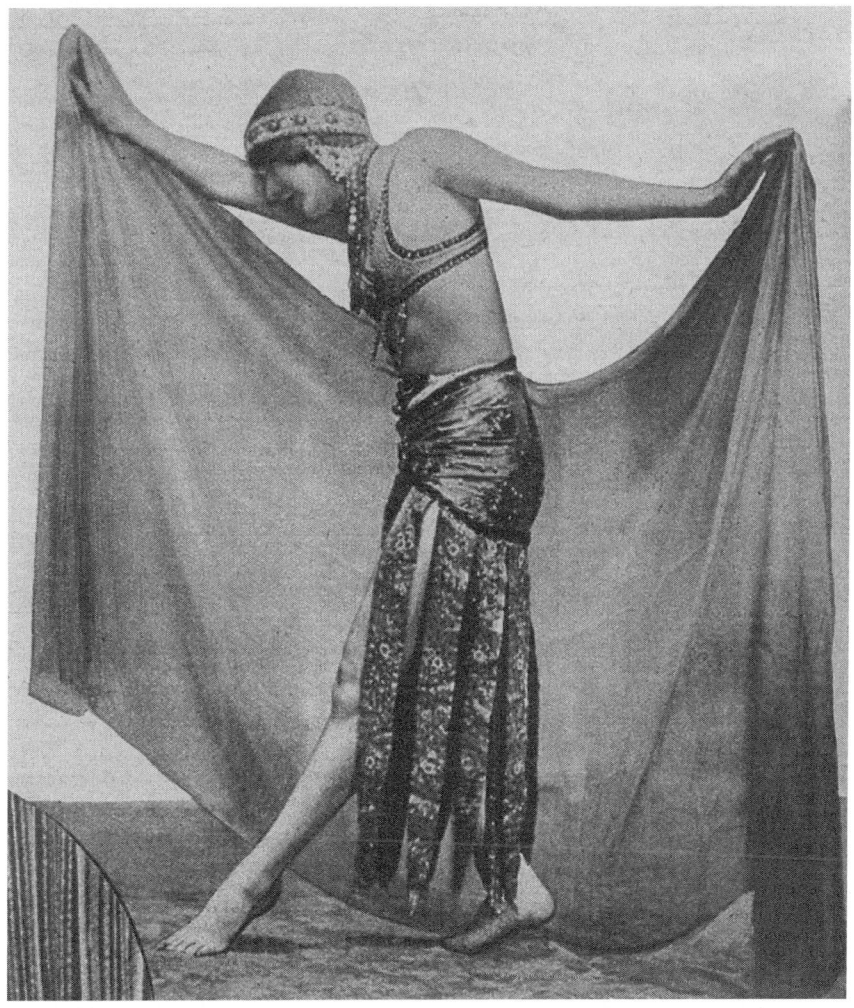

Image 131: *Stacia Napierkowska, "Daughter of Herodias,"* 1916, Wikimedia Commons.

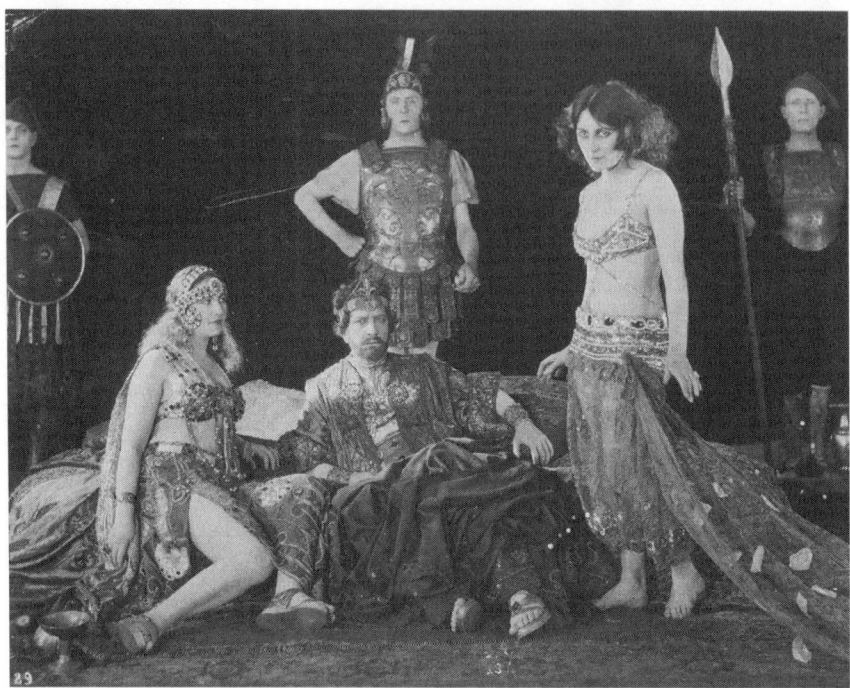

Image 132: *[Le Berceau de Dieu with Stacia Napierkowska as Salome (far right, foreground)*, ca. 1926, Wikimedia Commons.

In 1926, Napierkowska played Salome in the French production *Le Berceau de Dieu (Cradle of God)*, the last of her more than eighty films.

CONCLUSION

Oscar Wilde gave Salome competing, and in some cases contradicting, narratives. She is simultaneously tragic and monstrous, virginal and lewd, an overwhelmed teenager and a cruel adult. Salome is powerful to the point of castration (John's head is symbolic) while also doomed for execution at her stepfather's whim.

Wilde gave Salome so much complexity that the story lent itself to ongoing reuse and reinterpretation. The character initially shocked staid Victorian rectitude during the 1890s and early 1900s. During the early years of the twentieth century, Salome found herself at the forefront of avant-garde theater and opera. After about 1908, Salome conquered music halls and motion picture theaters worldwide.

Salome's thematic malleability allowed her to serve as a vehicle for challenging traditional ideas about sex. Openly displayed female sexual desire is undeniably at the center of the Salome story. After seeing this desire played out countless times on stage and screen, audiences had little choice but to rethink what went on in the bedroom—and perhaps what could and should go on there.

The performances also forced attention upon changing gender roles and promoted the idea of women as individuals equal to men. As a practical matter, many Salome performers took charge of their acts and earned an independent living.

As the preceding images show, Salomania centered on seeing women in a dramatic new way. This heightened stereotypes and sexual objectification but also contributed to disruption of the status quo. "Incarnating as Salome," writes Toni Bentley, "women gained a very particular forum for liberation . . . by appearing to act in accordance with a misogynistic point of view. In accepting the premise, they subverted it."

The subversion was in plain sight. As Edward Ross Dickinson puts it: "Modern dance didn't argue that women should be autonomous participants in the public sphere; it was autonomous women in the public sphere—demonstratively, even outrageously."

Salome performers played a key role in directing cultural attention toward modernity and the shock of the new. The women (and men) portraying Salome also led the way for embrace of performance as a transgressive spectacle, with artists breaking the rules of expected behavior as a calculated part of the act. Audiences were given a vicarious sense of excitement, liberation, and even a bit of danger. Salome performers pushed the limit on societal and moral standards, audiences loved it, and the culture changed.

In that sense, there is a direct line from Salome to more recent performers such as Beyoncé, Lady Gaga, Madonna, and David Bowie.

The artistry of early twentieth-century Salome performers—coupled with the irresistible lure of bare flesh and sexual suggestion—helped shape the rules, expectations, and shared meanings that make up modern culture.

APPENDIX: SELECT SALOME INTERPRETATIONS AFTER 1926

My pictorial account stops in 1926, a rough approximation of when Salomania waned. While the public appetite for Salome lessened, she remained firmly lodged in cultural memory and continues to inspire artistry up to the current day. Selective examples of post-1926 Salome productions are listed below.

- After the 1907 debacle, the New York Metropolitan Opera restaged Salome in 1934. The Met has since regularly performed the work, as have opera houses worldwide.

- In 1934, the American dancer and choreographer Lester Horton developed a ballet based on Wilde's play. Dancers and choreographers continued to evolve the work after Horton's death.

- Yvonne De Carlo starred in *Salome, Where She Danced*, a 1946 Hollywood western with an improbable plot. The promo tagline: "She made guns grow cold . . . and hearts burn hot—as she set the west afire!"

- In 1953, Rita Hayworth played the title role in the lavish film *Salome*, which *The New York Times* called "a flamboyant, Technicolored romance."

- Lindsay Kemp offered an all-male stage version of the play during the mid-1970s. Kemp played the title role in drag. *The Guardian* stated, "Whatever your aesthetic response you cannot deny the rare sensationalism and sensuality of this theatre in which the elements of music, lighting, costumes . . . often fuse and occasionally fail."

- Ken Russell directed *Salome's Last Dance* in 1988. The movie-within-a-movie is set in a brothel where prostitutes and their clients stage the play. The eccentric production received mixed reviews, with *The Spectator* declaring that "The line between eccentricity and buffoonery has been crossed."

- The 1993 film (and 2003 musical) *A Man of No Importance* is about a closeted gay bus conductor obsessed with staging Wilde's *Salome*. Through the course of dealing with opposition to "that dirty play," the conductor comes to terms with his nature.

- *Fatale: Exploring Salome* is a 2009 video game (actually, an "interactive vignette") based on the biblical story. It, of course, features the famous dance, choreographed by contemporary dancer Éléonore Valère-Lachky.

- The television series *True Blood* included a 2012 story arc involving Valentina Cervi as the vampire Salome Agrippa. Described as seductive and smart—as well as two-thousand years old—this Salome added a twenty-first-century pop culture spin to the story.

- Jessica Chastain starred with Al Pacino in the 2013 film *Salomé*. The *Los Angeles Times* praised the production as "a chilling and watchable look at lust, power, reprisal and decadence that . . . validates Pacino's obsessive interest in Wilde's still-resonant play."

- In 2017, the San Francisco Ballet offered contemporary *Salome* by choreographer Arthur Pita. The San Francisco Chronicle called the work "erotic, repellent and fascinating" and noted the performance's no-children-under-12 advisory.

- Also in 2017, the London National Theatre presented "theater maker" Yaël Farber's version of the play *Salomé*. *Switch* described the work as "a powerful feminist revision" that redefines the Jewish princess "as a symbol of feminine power and revolution."

- And again in 2017, the Royal Shakespeare Company staged Wilde's *Salomé*. *The Guardian* observed a Salome as a "gender-fluid heroine" who explores "the complex issue of what it means to be gay today," but ends up merely italicizing "what is already evident from Wilde's transgressive, bejewelled text."

SELECT BIBLIOGRAPHY

Bentley, Toni. *Sisters of Salome*. Yale University Press, 2002.

Brandstetter, Gabriele. *Poetics of Dance: Body, Image, and Space in the Historical Avant-Gardes*. Translated by Elena Polzer, Oxford University Press, 2015.

Cherniavsky, Felix. "Maud Allan, Part III: Two Years of Triumph 1908–1909." *Dance Chronicle*, vol. 7, no. 2, Jan. 1983, pp. 119–58.

---. "Maud Allan, Part V: The Years of Decline, 1915–1956." *Dance Chronicle*, vol. 9, no. 2, Jan. 1985, pp. 177–236.

Cucullu, Lois. "Wilde and Wilder Salomés: Modernizing the Nubile Princess from Sarah Bernhardt to Norma Desmond." *Modernism/Modernity*, vol. 18, no. 3, Sept. 2011, pp. 495–524.

Davis, W. Eugene. "Oscar Wilde, Salome, and the German Press 1902-1905." *English Literature in Transition, 1880-1920*, vol. 44, no. 2, 2001, pp. 149–80.

Dickinson, Edward Ross. *Dancing in the Blood: Modern Dance and European Culture on the Eve of the First World War*. Cambridge University Press, 2017.

Dijkstra, Bram. *Idols of Perversity: Fantasies of Feminine Evil in Fin-de-Siècle Culture*. Oxford University Press, 1986.

Evangelista, Stefano. *The Reception of Oscar Wilde in Europe*. Bloomsbury, 2015.

Glenn, Susan A. *Female Spectacle: The Theatrical Roots of Modern Feminism*. Harvard University Press, 2021.

Gordon, Mel. *The Seven Addictions and Five Professions of Anita Berber: Weimar Berlin's Priestess of Depravity*. Feral House, 2006.

Hamberlin, Larry. "Visions of Salome: The Femme Fatale in American Popular Songs before 1920." *Journal of the American Musicological Society*, vol. 59, no. 3, Dec. 2006, pp. 631–96.

Holland, Merlin. "Then and Now, 1994 [We look back to a piece by Merlin Holland about photographs of "Wilde in costume as Salomé", from July 22, 1994]." *The Times Literary Supplement (TLS)*.

Hutcheon, Linda, and Michael Hutcheon. "'Here's Lookin' at You, Kid': The Empowering Gaze in 'Salome.'" *MLA Profession*, 1998, p. 13.

Huysmans, Joris-Karl. *À Rebours (Translated as Against the Grain or Against Nature or Wrong Way)*. Charpentier, 1884.

Kendall, Elizabeth. *Where She Danced: The Birth of American Art-Dance*. Univ. of California Press, 1984.

Konecny, Mark. "Flying Too Close to the Sun: Impersonations of Duncan in Russia." *The Poetics of the Avant-Garde in Literature, Arts, and Philosophy*. Lexington Books, 2020.

Koritz, Amy. "Dancing the Orient for England: Maud Allan's 'The Vision of Salome.'" *Theatre Journal*, vol. 46, no. 1, Mar. 1994, p. 63.

Kultermann, Udo. "The 'Dance of the Seven Veils'. Salome and Erotic Culture around 1900." *Artibus et Historiae*, vol. 27, no. 53, Jan. 2006, p. 187.

Marcus, Sharon. "Salomé!! Sarah Bernhardt, Oscar Wilde, and the Drama of Celebrity." *PMLA*, vol. 126, no. 4, 2011.

Mora, Kiko. "La Representación Contra-Hegemónica de La Negritud: La Perla Negra, Entre La Rumba y La Danza Moderna (1913-1928)." *Sinfonia Virtual: Revista de Musica Clasica y Reflexion Musical*, vol. 32, 2017.

Neginsky, Rosina. *Salome: The Image of a Woman Who Never Was*. Cambridge Scholars Publishing, 2013.

Rachamimov, Alon. "The Disruptive Comforts of Drag: (Trans)Gender Performances among Prisoners of War in Russia, 1914–1920." *The American Historical Review*, vol. 111, no. 2, Apr. 2006, pp. 362–82.

Robbins, Ruth. "Always Leave Them Wanting More Oscar Wilde's Salome and the Failed Circulations of Desire." *Economies of Desire at the*

Victorian Fin de Sicle Libidinal Lives. Routledge/Taylor & Francis Group, 2016.

Ross, Alex. "The Endless, Grisly Fascination of Richard Strauss's 'Salome.'" *The New Yorker*, 21 Aug. 2019.

Rowden, Clair. *Performing Salome, Revealing Stories*. Routledge, 2016.

Santini, Daria. "'That Invisible Dance'. Reflections on the 'Dance of the Seven Veils' in Richard Strauss's *Salome*." *Dance Research*, vol. 29, no. 2, Nov. 2011, pp. 233–45.

Simonson, Mary. *Body Knowledge: Performance, Intermediality, and American Entertainment at the Turn of the Twentieth Century*. Oxford University Press, 2013.

Sine, Nadine. "Cases of Mistaken Identity: Salome and Judith at the Turn of the Century." *German Studies Review*, vol. 11, no. 1, Feb. 1988, p. 9.

Stein, Richard L. "A Strange Magic: Gustave Moreau's Salome." *Victorian Literature and Culture*, vol. 42, no. 1, 2014, pp. 148–52.

Streete, Gail Corrington. *The Salome Project: Salome and Her Afterlives*. Cascade Books, 2018.

Thoms, Victoria. *The Shock of the Risky (Qué) Female: Femininity and the Trauma of the Great War Era in the Dancing of Maud Allan*. Coventry University, 2018.

Toepfer, Karl. *Empire of Ecstasy: Nudity and Movement in German Body Culture 1910-1935*. University of California Press, 1997.

Tydeman, William, and Steven Price. *Wilde--Salome*. Cambridge University Press, 1996.

Villany, Adoree-Via. *Tanz-Reform Und Pseudo-Moral: Kritisch - Satyrische Gedanken Aus Meinem Bühnen - Und Privatleben*. [No publisher], 1912.

Visconti, Will. *The Queerness of Salomé - Putting the Spotlight on Oscar Wilde's Controversial One-Act Play*. 27 Mar. 2018.

Walkowitz, Judith R. "The 'Vision of Salome': Cosmopolitanism and Erotic Dancing in Central London, 1908-1918." *The American Historical Review*, vol. 108, no. 2, Apr. 2003, pp. 337–76.

Walton, Chris. "Beneath the Seventh Veil: Richard Strauss's 'Salome' and Kaiser Wilhelm II." *The Musical Times*, vol. 146, no. 1893, Dec. 2005, p. 5.

Yohalem, John. "The Salome Scandals of 1907." *Opera News*, 68, no. 9 2004: 34-36.

About the Author

Bill LeFurgy is a professional historian and archivist. He has studied the seamy underbelly of urban life, including drugs, crime, and prostitution, as well as more workaday matters such as streets, buildings, wires, and wharves. He has put his many years of research experience into writing gritty historical fiction about Baltimore, where he lived for over a decade. It remains his favorite city.

Bill has graduate degrees from the University of Maryland and has worked at the Maryland Historical Society, Baltimore City Archives, National Archives and Records Administration, and the Library of Congress. He has learned much from his family, including patience, emotional connection, and the need to appreciate different perspectives from those on the autism spectrum and with other personality traits that are undiagnosed, misdiagnosed, or unexplained.

Subscribe to my email newsletter: http://eepurl.com/gUf6CD

BillLeFurgy.com

Made in the USA
Monee, IL
07 July 2026

56550195R00081